How to Conquer Negative Emotions

BY ROY MASTERS

Edited by Melrose H. Tappan III

Published by The Foundation of Human Understanding
Printed in the United States of America

For information, please direct your inquiry to:
The Foundation of Human Understanding
P.O. Box 1009
Grants Pass, Oregon 97526
1-800-877-3227

Cover Design: David Masters

Library of Congress Catalog Card No. 88-80163
ISBN 0-933900-01-5

Contents

About the Author

Roy Masters is well known not only for his books (HOW YOUR MIND CAN KEEP YOU WELL; THE SECRET OF LIFE; UNDERSTANDING SEXUALITY) and lectures, but also for his nationally syndicated radio program, "How Your Mind Can Keep You Well and A Moment of Truth," which originates daily from Los Angeles.

A frequent guest on radio and television talk programs, Mr. Masters' incisive, no-nonsense approach to complex problems of the human mind and spirit have made his personal counseling sought after by thousands of people each year.

HOW TO CONQUER NEGATIVE EMOTIONS is Roy Masters' most important book. In it he details the simple instructions, taught privately for twenty-seven years, by which anyone may learn how to eliminate guilt, anxiety, pain and all forms of suffering from his life forever, completely without effort. He also points out the hidden dangers inherent in any of the currently popular forms of meditation, hypnosis and mind control.

What This Book Is All About

Cruel people have power; they get their energy from you through the way you respond to them. Hypocrites have the same wickedness operating through a deceptive shield of phony innocence. It, too, gets inside you by the way you react to it.

Your life is in danger from people, some of whom could even be members of your own family, who chip away, harp, nag and aggravate the life out of you until you feel like killing them or yourself. YOU CANNOT FIGHT THEM WITH RESENTMENT, because they use your resentment to drive you crazy, to make you conform, to bring out the worst in you and terrify you into not facing them and their kind.

Take heart. There is not one single problem in the world that you cannot solve if you will learn to stop being resentful toward people.

You are indeed the sum total of your experiences, but another way of saying this is that you are burdened by your past. Unless you learn how to respond properly in the present, you will continue to let the ugly world get inside you and build on that past. And without self-control, that is the only kind of future you have.

Respond wrongly to pressure just one time—and what aggravates you has got you. Your mind and body must go on responding slavishly until you find the Truth that makes you free.

You are not alone in your dilemma. The wrong emotional response to all sorts of pressure is currently making everyone sick and depressed and driving all of us into conflict with ourselves. To solve the pressure-caused conflicts, people turn to drink, tobacco and drugs, legal or illegal.

Look at it this way: Your reactions, being compulsive, have become a subtle form of obedience, and emotional obedience is really a form of slavery. Behind the cruel and relentless pressures that zealous people apply to you (sometimes in the name of good) is a selfish motive that compels you to be like it and to go along with it—to sin, in other words. Because it has upset you, you are out of control and not living your own life. No wonder you feel guilty and depressed.

Because no one has cared enough to teach you how not to respond, and because you have not yet discovered this vital secret, life now seems meaningless, hopeless, and depressing. You have worried, but worrying has made matters worse.

All your sexual, family, and business problems arise directly from your failing to respond in a right way to what is wrong and, I might add, making everyone respond wrongly to you when you have been upset. Conflict with yourself becomes conflict with others as you take it out on them.

Most of the things that are wrong with your life, your marriage, your health, your children, can be straightened out very easily by discovering how to conquer your negative emotions.

Your emotional upsets have made you feel guilty. Even though you might have been technically correct in what you said or did, if you did it resentfully, your emotions confused you, and when you began to doubt yourself, you experienced conflict, depression and fear.

Resentment destroyed your objectivity, and, failing to see clearly, you made terrible errors of judgment. These, in turn, led to a fear of making decisions, so that perhaps you began to lean too much on others for guidance, and you know how upsetting it can be if those others happen to be wrong or to take advantage of you.

You must learn how to be patient with cruel and thoughtless people. You must learn to be poised and calm; otherwise, what is wrong in them shows up in you and makes you look like the bad guy. Everyone then becomes so fascinated with what *went* wrong with you that they fail to see what they *did* wrong to you, and that experience is upsetting, frustrating and scary.

Cruel, unthinking people feed off the way you respond to their needling; they walk away self-righteous and satisfied, leaving you frustrated, confused, revengeful and depressed. They get their power from your reaction, while your resentment often makes you feel like the guilty one. "Successful," domineering unprincipled people lord it over you, drain you and make your life wretched; BUT THEY ARE ALWAYS SURE OF GETTING TO YOU THROUGH YOUR REACTIONS.

The dehumanizing pressure to achieve and to study is changing people into animals, animals out of control, in mortal conflict with other animals.

Of course, we all respond to pressure, but that response is what is wrong with us.

Upsetting you is the key to motivating you; it is the hidden reason behind all of your suffering.

Manipulating and winning through intimidation is a common practice among all corrupters: tyrants, high-pressure salesmen, successful businessmen, and the like. No doubt you have your own private dictator currently aggravating the life out of you.

Only through the shock of emotional upset can a compelling or morbid suggestion be planted in your mind, and this is especially true when you are resentful. If it doesn't cause wild and senseless rebellion, you find yourself obliged to give in, to ease the pain that the pressure of wrong resistance causes.

Giving in to tyrants and zealots who make the pain of your upsets unbearable is a common but unhealthy form of love, loyalty, and closeness between husband and wife, mother and child, and between churches and their believers. (It is also the way you lose your identity.) It is hard to say "no" to pushy, irritating people. You tend to favor people who apply pressure: your boss, your wife, and your kids. Then the breaking point is reached; there is rebellion against work and study; debilitating disease and nervous breakdown take their deadly toll.

Being upset is your weakness—your Achilles heel. All heartless, cruel, power-hungry, unprincipled people inherit the know-how to make your slavish emotional responses work for them, and they have no qualms about casting you aside after you are spent and broken.

The world is dominated by tyrants, tempters, and psychopaths. Some of them get to you through cruelty, while other types manipulate you with a holier-than-thou, irritating "kindness." They might use both methods to confuse you, upsetting you one moment and being "kind" to you the next. Their bold, unprincipled manner upsets you and makes you feel guilty; then, by suddenly changing roles and becoming "nice," they intensify your guilt feelings and make you doubt yourself. In that manner you are made to believe that they were right all along and that you were wrong. And so you learn to go along with their wishes; you find yourself doing things you would never have done in your right mind, and that upsets you all over again. This vicious cycle, with a built-in upset, repeats itself endlessly, until you feel like killing them or yourself.

Irritating people are really victims themselves; they tempt you in order to retrieve something they have lost to those who aggravated the life out of them. By needling you they drain you of your vital energy, and with this power they torment you again and again. As you become a parent, you find their identity welling up inside you, yelling and screaming at your own kids, unwittingly destroying them with the same projection techniques of aggravation that your parents and other pushy people once used against you.

We may be legally free, but emotionally and morally we are still in the Dark Ages. We all live under an emotional feudal system of slaves and tyrants. It is a devilish, military chain of command, where everyone who responds and becomes a slave also lords it over a slave.

Cruelty rules the roost. A subtle, god-eat-dog emotional pecking order of pressure is everywhere: at home, school, and at work. Everyone feels the meaninglessness, the futility of it all. THIS IS THE MAIN REASON FOR ALCOHOLISM, DRUG ADDICTION, CRIME, DEPRESSION, NERVOUS BREAKDOWN AND A MULTITUDE OF DISEASES.

One of two things always happens to you under pressure: You become upset and blow up—but rarely at the person who upsets you, because you don't have the guts—or you will give in. You might even "fall in love" with someone you resent, or champion the cause of your corrupter, especially if the pressure is religious or political. All manipulators know that your capitulation is simply a means of relieving pressure as well as a way of making up for guilt you feel for being upset with them. But from your point of view, it might seem as though your changed behavior has somehow affected that cruel person's attitude for the good, compelling him to reward you with approval and appreciation and love. For a while it could seem as though you have a marvelous power to control and redeem evil people. If that is your delusion, you find yourself addicted to selling yourself down the river to keep peace and control various situations. All manipulators carefully cultivate this behavior. This is how wicked people use you and get ahead, because in reality all they are doing is rewarding you for being unreasonable and for serving their bizarre purposes.

Once you have been conditioned to give in to pressure, you could begin seeing that way of life as evidence of your divine goodness. And if you don't become a tempter yourself, you develop a knack for spoiling people, compelling them to make the kind of demands that become the pressure you need to give in, to be reminded of, and be rewarded for what you have come to think of as goodness, and for your imagined power to make naughty people right and happy. So when you don't have a motivator, you create one—your child perhaps?

Creating your own tyrants in the form of spoiling your children is the cause of juvenile delinquency and crime. It is why you parents become frightened of and submissive to your violent brats. The worse they get the better you look compared with them, and the more you are compelled to be good to them, believing that your only error is not being good enough to them. That is why bad children come from what appear to be good homes. It is also why we often see nice, gentle, kindly people living under the tyranny of a dictator. Their natural goodness is merely weakness, born out of a need to be submissive to realize their goodness.

As soon as everyone's demands grow so great that you become drained of energy, and when you discover that you have nothing left to give, to be "loved" for, you start blaming and being secretly resentful, and that leads to nervous breakdown and mental illness.

Man was never designed to be externally motivated, as animals, but because of a little understood weakness, we are. This is the main reason why we all have paralyzing conflicts, anxieties, and fears; that is the basis of all our problems, right there. UNTIL YOU DISCOVER THE SECRET OF TURNING YOURSELF ON FROM WHAT YOU REALIZE IS RIGHT DEEP DOWN IN YOUR HEART, YOU WILL ALWAYS BE AN EXTERNALIZED ZOMBIE, COMPELLED TO ACT AGAINST YOUR OWN BETTER JUDGMENT, HURTING PEOPLE YOU LOVE AND DOING THINGS YOU ARE SORRY FOR.

Being upset is a conditioned reflex; it is an inferior way of reacting to pressure. That is why you feel inferior, helpless, angry; and it is also why you are so compulsive in the way you are forced to relieve the pain of tension built up by those pressures; it is another reason why you hurt the ones you love. But what if you could learn to look injustice straight in the eye without flinching, without being upset, calmly and with endless patience? Surely you would not have the problems that arise from repressing or expressing resentment. This then, is the aim of the book, HOW TO CONQUER NEGATIVE EMOTIONS, to show you the secret principle of patience and self-control.

I know what you want. You want relief from your nervous tension and guilt feelings. You want solutions to your sex problems and family problems. You want to stop smoking, drinking and overeating; you want happiness. But you will never find what you are seeking until you discover the hidden cause, AND THAT CAUSE IS ALLOWING PEOPLE TO UPSET YOU TOO EASILY.

Emotional self-control is the key you are seeking. Without it, you will always be in conflict with yourself. If you are ever to be free of guilt and fear, you must learn the secret of responding in a right way to what is wrong with people and the world.

Your main line of defense (and attack) is to stay calm and patient. So, seeing you unmoved, the motivator himself becomes upset and panics. Learn how to put up an impenetrable, invisible force shield of patience that lets the good come through and prevents the ugly world from gettng in and growing up inside you.

Roy Masters writes about one simple principle that will KEEP YOU SAFE UNDER ALL CONDITIONS OF STRESS AND PERSECUTIONS. You will marvel at how easy it is to say "no," to over-power and to disarm pushy individuals. Surely, Roy Masters has nothing less to offer you than the secret of life itself.

What You Should Know About Being Upset

If you are subject to fear, anxiety, guilt or depression, if you smoke, drink, take tranquilizers or drugs—you are out of control. And it is your reaction to the people and conditions around you that is causing all of your problems, making you sick and moving you closer, moment by moment, to death. It is your own negative emotional responses that are causing the subtle changes in metabolism and body chemistry that are eating away at your health and well-being even as you read these lines.

The very experiences of everyday life exert a hypnotic influence upon you, causing you to react emotionally and to lose awareness—and that is the basis of your dilemma. Too much emotion or emotion of the wrong kind, such as anger, may elevate your blood pressure, give you ulcers, or strike you down with a heart attack or stroke. This kind of wrong reaction to the stresses of life may even be the hidden cause of cancer, which is, after all, only a mass of body cells out of control.

Your emotions make you act blindly, irrationally; they are the underlying cause of guilt, for under the spell of emotion you get into arguments, fights and family feuds. You cause great damage both to yourself and to others, which you may later come to regret. In a fit of temper you may even maim or murder; and thus, the same emotion, which has already taken control of you, claims other victims by means of their angry response to your hostility.

And when you are filled with rage, what does that excess of emotion do to your body—to your blood pressure, your body chemistry, to delicate internal organs, to the tissues themselves? Living on the verge of being continually upset like a frightened or vicious animal can cause a change in your blood clotting so that you may have a stroke. And what about those unbearable tensions that squeeze your veins shut and restrict your circulation—those tension headaches that make you climb the walls? Migraine, ulcers, hypertension, colitis, asthma are only a few of the long list of illnesses that can be caused by your emotions.

What really happens when someone succeeds in getting under your skin? Doesn't your angry response upset him into upsetting you still more, until you are caught up in an endless cycle without hope of solution? Even when the experience of anger is over, there is more unpleasantness to come, because whenever you react incorrectly to any experience in life—whenever you respond with resentment and without patience—you will experience fear, anxiety and guilt: the pain of hindsight.

You must realize that if you are experiencing fear, anxiety or guilt, there is something seriously wrong with you; and you must also understand that these symptoms are invariably caused by your wrong reaction to your environment. Like most symptoms, anxiety is a warning that something is wrong, but instead of heeding that warning and realizing the true cause of your problems, you attempt to escape—"to relax"—you smoke, take alcohol or drugs, pursue senseless hobbies, or simply retreat into the ceaseless images in your mind. You lose yourself in thought and feeling all over again; you wallow in the future and the past, and by doing so you repeat the mistake that brought you to this sorry state in the first place: You meet each moment without the proper poise of awareness.

Whenever you are involved with your feelings and lost in your own thoughts, you are not sufficiently aware to deal properly with the present moment, and it is of many such moments that life is composed. There is really no such thing as a big problem; instead, there is a complex of many little ones you did not know how to meet because you were too preoccupied to respond correctly.

Anger, resentment, or any kind of excitement submerges the conscious mind into the subconscious thought stream so that you lose awareness of the mistake you are poised to make. Later, when you cool off, you experience anxiety and conflict; but since your ego is afraid to admit that it is not in control of its own action, it manufactures an excuse. And this excuse is the incontrovertible evidence that hypnosis has taken place.

The mere presence of an excuse in your mind is certain proof that your actions are not your own. Excuses are a smoke screen that your ego produces so that it cannot realize its error. You see, whenever you behave improperly—whenever your actions are not truly your own—you are aware of that fact to some degree, and if your mind were not distracted or involved with making excuses, you would realize that you are not in control of yourself. After all, if you were really doing as you wished, why would you need an excuse, and to whom would you make it?

Look at your excuses carefully. See how they shield your ego from realizing the truth. Many people become so adept at making excuses that whenever they do something foolish, they excuse it so smoothly and quickly that they become completely incapable of recognizing that they are being manipulated—much less, *who* their manipulator is. They are painfully conscious of their problems, but they cannot see what, or rather *who*, has caused them.

Under this spell of emotion we can be made to act irrationally: to commit crimes, accept religions, take drugs, marry the wrong person, be unfaithful and "swing." We become the puppets of those who either cater to us or upset us and pull us further from innate common sense and reason. Illness festers in the guilt of emotional conflict. The body continues to react emotionally and hypnotically. We continue to rationalize our mistakes until our minds boggle under the strain, and finally we break down—mentally, physically and emotionally.

So long as you continue to excuse the things you do, the hypnotic influence of life becomes stronger. You will remain prey to those who continue to control your destiny by nagging, exciting and upsetting you so that you do their will, believing it to be your own. You see only symptoms, and you cannot understand why your life is in such a mess. You are afraid to make decisions, for since they are not your own, they are always wrong, and this is why you will remain unhappy, sick and frustrated.

If only you would face the reality of your emotionally hypnotized state and then learn the technique of staying calm and aware under pressure, you would be less emotional, less suggestible and, therefore, more in control of yourself, healthier and happier. *Control your emotions and you can begin to solve every problem you have.*

But once you have learned to be upset in order to function, you become addicted to being upset; you *need* to be upset in order to be motivated. You can't move a muscle when you wake in the morning unless someone burns the toast and makes you mad. You are motivated then, all right, but you are motivated in the wrong way.

When you discover that guilt and fear arise from your own impatience, you become terrified of the very emotion you thought proper and natural. Because of emotion you become a monster, but without it you cease to exist, for you need its ability to blind you in order to continue to see yourself as the fine person you have always believed yourself to be.

There seems to be no way out of this dilemma of building emotion and experiencing its consequences. And the sheer agony of these internal pressures, the fear of becoming like those they hate, drives a million people to suicide each year. Others escape from the knowledge of their failings through resentment, a more subtle form of anger, through which you can project your own faults into others and become challenged by their short-comings into a state of judgmental ecstasy and omnipotent self-righteousness. Seeking out and hating the wrong in others makes you feel clean and good. Energized by this egotistical point of view, you set out to destroy evil, thinking that to do so makes you the Great Good.

We are even challenged by the very problems we create, and from those challenges we derive the energy to become self-righteously angry again. We fail to grow toward the realization of our potential as human beings; instead, we become like monsters, hating the other monsters and becoming greater monsters in the process. We see a great deal of wickedness, but it is always in others. At some point in this process we either become a bigger beast by becoming worse than they are, or else we yield and serve the beast.

You can see this process at work in your own family. Instead of acting as a correction to your children, your anger either causes senseless rebellion or else it destroys their true character and identity by causing them to conform to what is wrong in you. If you are weak, your anger weakens you even more so that you may wind up knuckling under to your children and excusing their outrageous behavior.

Misguided doctors do immeasurable harm by telling us that it is normal to be angry and encouraging us to express our anger. Think for a moment. Does it seem fair to you to upset some poor soul out of his wits in order to relieve the pressures in your tormented brain? Think back for a moment and you will probably realize that you inherited most of your own problems as a result of someone else taking his hostility out on you. While it is true that if you repress your anger it will cause you great harm both physically and mentally, it is equally true that if you unload your feelings upon someone else, that person will be similarly hurt and forced to pass it on.

In effect, we are a chain gang of miserable people, constantly being upset and passing our misery down the line. One moment we are the victim and the next we are the mad bully, continually repeating the cycle until we all go out of our minds or die from degenerative diseases. The boss upsets dad, dad upsets mom, she upsets the children, who, in turn, are mean to the dog; and the dog remains the only healthy member of the chain because it is normal for dogs to be angry, excited, motivated and conditioned by their environment. For us, however, such conditioning means deterioration, for we are no longer free to meet the present in the only proper way— spontaneously and intuitively—guided by the grace the

Creator has given to mankind: awareness. Whatever diminishes that awareness from moment to moment—excessive emotion, impatience, resentment or drugs—takes us away from our true senses and causes the conflict, guilt, fear and sickness to which we fall prey. We become less like the image of our Creator and more like beasts, increasingly conditioned to the rule of a panoply of tyrants.

Anger is a conditioning emotion, and it gives power to our enemies. Often we will do anything for them to avoid becoming upset and feeling guilty. We may even come to believe that we love our oppressors because we see the great lengths to which we shall go in order to please them. But we also need those people who taught us to hate because they reinforce the kind of hate-filled person we have become. By liking us as we are, they make us feel comfortable with what we have become.

Anger is the basis of every guilt you have ever had. Not only do you hurt others and make errors of judgment when you are blinded by rage—there is more to it than that. In an absolute sense the emotion of anger is in itself wrong. Further, anger causes fear because suppressed resentment makes us feel like running, yet if we fight instead of run, we are doing something we know will upset us later.

The whole sick world gets the energy to sustain itself from anger. People war against one another because of aggressive suggestions planted in their minds while they are upset. Anger is the emotion of conditioning and the basis of all negative suggestions, suspicions and doubts that enter our minds. Your children rebel; everyone fights with you. Those who agree with you do so only to justify themselves; and, supported by such "friends," you make an even greater mess of your life. Then—when you discover what has been done to you— more anger, more rage. But what is really happening is that being upset causes a new identity to grow up inside you, a counterfeit identity that obeys the tormenting world that spawned it—and it displaces the real you, preventing your development in the image of your Creator. The "Mr. Hyde" thrives on the chaotic environment of hostility, resentment and intrigue, to which it responds hypnotically. Everything that excites you emotionally and causes you to lose awareness contributes to its growth and to the ultimate death of the real you.

If you could learn the secret of how to control your responses, how to find that God-given switch in your mind that would allow you to energize and motivate yourself at will, you would never again feel conflict, guilt, fear or depression. The alien identity would find no source of nourishment for his kind of existence, and he would die; but you would live, growing from within to become the truly human person you were meant to be, discovering purpose in your life, and joy.

Observe carefully your reaction to reading these lines. Who is it that is disturbed? Who is afraid to discover more about this way of life? Is it the real you, or is it "Mr. Hyde" who does not want to listen?

To recover from your affliction and become truly human, you must learn to live and move from what you now know as your conscience, instead of from animal emotion. You must learn to observe vain, rage-laden people around you with the calm composure that will serve as the compassion, patience, love and correction they need and may even come to respect.

Surely it is not difficult to see that if wrong emotional response can cause so much misery and unhappiness, then right response can restore us to happiness, health poise and better relations with one another. Unimpeded by error, the body tends toward health, the mind toward happiness and the soul toward the acceptance of grace, which is the basis of human well-being.

If you are willing to be shown how you can become the person you were created to be, the following chapters will introduce you to a simple procedure that will prove to you, through your own experience, that control over yourself *without unbearable suppression* is not only possible but vital to your health, your present and future happiness—to your very existence.

1 Caution: Be Careful How You Meditate

The very experience of life itself exerts a hypnotic influence upon you, and that is why you are confused: You are simply out of control. The meditation exercise that follows, should you elect to practice it, will give you back the conscious control you need in order to be a poised, calm, healthy, happy, self-motivated person. A new energy must emanate from the center of your being, and this life force, directed by an infallible reason, will project a new order upon your entire life, including your family and your business affairs.

The key to this new order is objectivity. It is essential that you discover how to become objective, in order that you may be free from the prejudice and confusion inherent in your thinking, so that you can perceive clearly, with patient, unmoving, immovable certainty, things and people as they really are. Here, in this objective state, is where self-control and the mastery of life begin for you.

The unique method of meditation that assists in

leading you to this enlightened state of consciousness is compatible, however, only with a very special attitude— a spirit of humble inquiry coupled with a burning desire to realize the truth. Without this pure longing to know, that highly desirable blessed state will be denied to you.

If you learn to meditate with the proper attitude, you may spontaneously experience a falling away of nagging personal problems, release from habits and compulsions, freedom from neurotic fears, and a renewal of good health, but it is a perversion of the meditation to attempt to use it for achieving such ends or any other goals you may set for yourself. Meditation is not a way of getting what you want; it is a way of knowing what is right.

There are two possible approaches to meditation— the right way and the wrong way—although there seem to be many more, since the wrong way takes many forms, and these are by far the most popular. Just why anyone in his right mind would reach for something alien and far-out is an interesting question. In fact, an expose is an interesting place to begin a discussion of meditation; the contrast will make true meditation easier to grasp.

There are really two factors to be considered here, and the first has to do with the "powers that be" wanting to remain the "powers that be." Over the centuries the true technique of meditation was either lost or supressed, and even though it has been revealed again and again to some of our greatest mystics, the church itself has made no concerted effort to nurture and teach this fundamental approach to wisdom to its members.

Governments and ruling classes generally find little advantage in a populace that is self-controlled, healthy and truly happy. Who would follow mere mortals, having once been led by an indwelling Spirit? Who would need such a profusion of problem solvers if there were no problems to be solved? A majority of political leaders, doctors, lawyers, ministers, generals and locksmiths, as well as others I'm sure you could name, would be dead set against the idea of not being needed. People whose egos aspire to glory and greatness need to be needed. The entire idea of promoting needs and answering to those needs becomes a source of life to the leader; it makes him feel like God. But victims must be sacrificed to satisfy this growing need to be needed; people must be debilitated, crippled, reduced to the status of whimpering animals for the glory of the leader.

Consider the principle: If your ego is dependent on being needed, then it must surely follow that your beloved has to be weakened in order to provide the security you require. Once it begins, this entire system of answering to needs is self-perpetuating and self-promoting. While pretending to promote the good of the people, the power and glory of the leader is built at the expense of the people.

Whenever a relationship with external authority replaces the proper bond between a human being and the indwelling self, then all answers and all actions, humanly speaking, are always wrong, even if they are technically, technologically or moralistically correct.

So long as man remains separated from his true identity, corruption will take its toll, causing the mass mind to cry out for a champion. Recognizing this need, the aspiring leader sees that simply by keeping people from the truth he can become that champion of what appears to be the public good. And so the leech who profits and revels in the glory of leading is going to do his damnedest to keep light from coming into the world, whereas the true leader leads all men back to themselves.

Man is a religious creature; the very nature of his separation from reality—his guilt, in other words—demands religion; and here again we have leaders rising to the occasion of man's need for righteousness. The fact is, man cannot exist without some form of relationship either to the indwelling Spirit or else to the external environment. And true life *is* the proper relationship; it is not a system of beliefs or a series of actions, however correct. No belief, no thought, no deed has any value unless it is motivated by being in a true relationship with the indwelling Spirit.

This realization leads us to the second part of our discussion, which has to do with the proclivity of the egocentric human mind to shy away from seeing the truth about itself. It is the nature of pride to demand to *seem* right even when it is not. Out of such a need, on a widespread basis, come the mental giants, the geniuses of an age—and they seem to come out of the bosom of God to recognize the god of their creation and to say what God wants to hear, but it is our egocentric need that creates these giants who appear to serve us.

4

It is a curious yet discernible fact that the hypnotized person always escapes into his hypnotic state to avoid seeing the embarrassing truth that concerns it. The same is true of the hypnotic influence that life has on us. No matter how low a man sinks as a result of life's hypnotic pressures, he always identifies with his failing in order to avoid facing it. If a man is a pervert, he will excuse perversion; indeed, he will even seek to evangelize it. Drug addicts, alcoholics, murderers, thieves will all rationalize their conditions in order to make everything seem quite normal to themselves. Such forms of behavior are the evidence of debilitating and degrading influences; but in order to save face, the victim always escapes into the condition itself. He becomes more of a pervert to escape from the knowledge that there is something wrong with perversion—and the process repeats itself endlessly.

There are, in reality, only two factors that cause all of your problems: One is the weakness that allows hypnotic pressures to get under your skin, and the other is the compulsion to rationalize everything that happens to you. This second error arises from the first weakness and leads back to it, leaving you exposed to yet another round of pressure, so that in the end you will not be living your own life at all, but rather a miserable excuse for a life, which has been imposed upon you from outside. You will not be your real self, the self that you were created to be. You will suffer guilt, anxiety and fear, but you will not understand why, because you have always escaped from awareness into the problem itself, and then you have excused everything you ever did. Now, if what I am saying is true—and it is—you need only reverse this process: Stop responding and stop excusing your responses. Let us now consider how you can stop this process of dying.

Have you ever made an excuse? Of course you have. But just what is an excuse? Surely it must be some kind of shield to protect your ego against being made aware, for through the mechanism of the excuse you can avoid seeing that you have failed. You can remain unaware that somehow you have been hypnotized into working against your own best interests. At each point along the way you tend to see the truth, but should your ego desire to avoid that guilt experience, it will employ the excuse and related devices to preserve the ego face. This very need of yours brings into existence certain types of people who cater to your ego need for concocting answers at various levels of pain and suffering. The mere presence of an excuse in your mind is the certain evidence that something is wrong with you.

Dishonest politicians, doctors, lawyers, preachers, lovers and friends have a lot going for them. In the first place, the more they comfort, soothe and justify you, the more deeply involved in error you are likely to become, and the more you will be in need of their gratifying services; furthermore, there is little chance that you will see what they are up to, simply because the way in which they help you reduces your awareness, so that by losing sight of your failings you also lose sight of what is wrong with them and their methods. Once they fasten their vampire teeth into you, their entire existence is related to needing you, so they will not let you go. Drugs, marijuana, alcohol and cigarettes afford the ego some relief by reducing the soul's awareness of its guilt. The byproduct of this process is a kind of false innocence that gives rise to a false peace and even a false salvation, and these all make for a false type of happiness. The kind of mind that permits the ego to aim at preserving its own emotional security will always prefer the false meditation to the true one; therefore, we can see that the question we posed earlier, having to do with why anyone would choose the false meditation, relates to the proclivity of the ego itself.

To the ambitious, self-justifying ego, false meditation is the ultimate high. It is a means of seeking peace apart from God—a way of following the selfish course to its ultimate conclusion without regret, remorse, conflict or guilt. But peace apart from God is not peace at all; rather, it is a state of no awareness, which comes from avoiding the knowledge of what is wrong with us. False meditation is simply a spiritual analgesic; it merely anesthetizes the pain instead of curing what is wrong. Stilling disturbing thoughts is a far cry from having a still soul that stands apart from thought. Peace apart from God is really a movement away from reality and toward illusion and death. If you can block or sever enough nerves that carry the message of pain from the cancer that is killing you, you will have a kind of peace, but you will not preserve your life.

Perhaps an example might drive this point home.

One might compare a love of mathematics with the passion for the true life, for it is easy to see the value of objectivity in mathematics. The mathematician is glad to see where he went wrong because only then will he be able to solve his problem. You cannot possibly teach mathematics to the student who wants to excuse his failures and never admit his errors. He will fight your admonition and even denounce you with vehement and elaborate arguments proving that it is wrong to see his wrong. Such people are so well skilled at this game they play all of their lives that you might very well be persuaded to their point of view unless you are well grounded.

It would be wise to follow the road map outlined in this book; your aim should be diametrically opposed to glory-bound meditators and their power-happy gurus. To the degree that you shrink from all image-building processes, to that degree will you discover the prize of objectivity. THE AWARENESS THAT COMES FROM OBJECTIVITY IS THE KEY TO EVERYTHING THAT YOU SHOULD BE SEEKING. Objectivity is true understanding and innocence, and through it comes love, patience, self-control, true identity, education, development of sound judgment, success, prosperity, happiness, health—and even eternal life.

Since objective awareness is a progressive experience, you must be content to let it unfold in gradual stages. If, in an instant, you could be as objective as it is ultimately possible to become, you would vaporize like a snowflake in a furnace. It would be impossible for you to cope with what you saw. Be grateful, then, for the opportunity to thread your way slowly out of the environment of your world of imagination. It will not always be easy to hold to your objective state. The spirit that inhabits the imaginative life now has a claim on you, and it will endeavor to hold you. Each time you wrench free from its grasping, however, you will gain a little more perspective and a little more freedom from compulsive thoughts, words and deeds.

Until now, what you have been doing all of your life is simply running away from the fact that you have had no choice. When you begin to practice meditation properly, you will, for the first time, taste true freedom: You will be aware that you have been provided with an alternative course of action. Your journey will be in two directions at once—inward and onward. To the degree that you come closer to reality, to that same degree you will see what to aim toward in the tangible world. This onward movement will always reflect externally your inward journey toward the Light.

The only real peace you will ever find has to do with awareness itself being still, separate from the dream-like stream of illusion and fantasy. False tranquility arising from improper techniques of meditation, on the other hand, involves blocking or stopping thoughts and finding a euphoric quiet by dulling the mind and the mental processes. When you are in this state, there is no error to observe, nothing embarrassing to realize, because the soul will have become oblivious to its failing.

One of the most effective ways to this kind of oblivious peace, joy and happiness is the use of the mantra. The mantra is a meaningless word or phrase, which may be shouted, spoken or merely repeated silently in the mind in such a way that it blocks awareness. The use of the mantra is a master technology, which, in brief, reduces the screaming, writhing hell inside your head to a meaningless, harmless sound. It must be meaningless to be meaningful, since it is designed to dull the thinking process. In the mind of the meditator who uses this technique, any unintelligible nonsense appears to be the Word coming directly from the mouth of God. At first glance it seems harmless to go along with this perfectly distracting sound; it hardly seems to be a movement away from God. Instead, in the mind of the meditator it becomes like a movement from the stillness of the Logos, and it seems glorious and creative. In fact, we are witnessing a counterfeit motion and rest, which duplicates, in pride's way, the purposeful motion that emanates from the stillness of God. The vibrating mantra outshouts and stills the Word of God. In this silence the sound then appears to come from the only remaining source of relative stillness, and you move out of yourself as if moving out of the stillness of God. There can be no awareness of guilt here, only a false peace and the dubious joy of being the only awareness left in the universe with a creative word pulsating out to fill the cosmos with your own glory. There is indeed a surrogate peace that follows such activity, and there is never a trace of shame. The mental blocks of conscience vanish, and in their place you will discover the perfect "freedom" for "God" to do whatever pleases him.

When meditation is used as a means of gaining such ego assurance, it is the most dangerous of all human practices; it is worse than any drug because it seems so holy and innocent. The practitioners of such meditation chatter like a gaggle of geese about peace, brotherly love, oneness and joy, but these empty noises cannot fool you if you are sincere in your search for reality; you are equipped with an awareness to detect deception. It will be just as difficult for you to practice fantasy as it is for the self-deceived to practice reality. When a fool speaks of discovering himself and God, what he is really saying is that he has discovered that he *is* God, and he will tempt you to follow, somehow sensing that once you are caught in this trap you too will be obligated out of guilt to go on being "God" just as he does, and then he will have support and justification for continuing his own way of being. When such people speak of living forever, it is because they have finally found the way to recognize themselves as deities. If you believe that you are God, it follows that you cannot die. People who get high on drugs often similarly identify themselves as ultimate beings, and they believe themselves to be so invulnerable that they attempt to perform dangerous feats to prove that they cannot be harmed. Almost any daily newspaper reports the results of these tragic delusions. When they speak of being one with nature and the universe, they have merely projected their puny egos into the enormous mass of creation and, neatly slipping away from the humiliating awareness of their actual nothingness, they aspire to the greatness of creation itself. Like God, they are identified with the infinite vastness of creation, but all that actually has happened is that they have left behind the awareness that they are nothing. Just at this point, at the farthest remove from reality, the ego discovers yet another reality—the father of all deception. Here there is either the shock of horror or a mad whoop of delight as the identification with the demon god is completed, for he is the only god with whom the ego can identify without repentance.

Another reason why escape meditations are so extremely dangerous is that they are so easily confused with a true meditation, just as "churchianity" has often been confused with Christianity. The true Christian mystic has ever been persecuted for heresy by that that stood unholy in the place of the Holy—the false Christian church in the place of the true Christ. The human perception of reality is often a very delicate thing, so that when "churchianity" is confused with Christianity, the true seeker may rebel against religion entirely and become afraid of the very thing that could save him. I do not want you to become confused about the true key to Christianity, which is found only through the true meditation.

It is the nature of obstinate pride to avoid the experience of repentance and to perpetuate a sense of its own eternal innocence. It is the nature of the evil one to lead his unconscious quarry away from the seeming hell of true self-knowing. The truth, as it applies to us, is very simple: If you want to find reality, you need only give up struggling; the writhing within your soul is symbolic of running away. Objectivity is quite a natural thing, but once you have become involved in the process that leads to unawareness, you become bogged down through your efforts to extricate yourself: This preoccupation with the losing battle—the struggle itself—becomes another subtle form of distraction. You need special guidance, precise knowledge to lead you from the prison of your mind up to the threshold of the Light. You need the vital clues contained in this book. You need to meditate.

The conscious can only begin to exert an effective influence over the unconscious when it ceases to be a part of the thinking-feeling process. When the real you becomes separate from the unconscious processes, the perceiving you becomes free and clear of distortion and the cause of your problems is seen to be as it really is. Understanding, then, exerts an influence upon the thinking process that is expressed as meaningful direction and self-control. The calmness of detachment becomes patience; the harmony with reason, true peace and joy, and the foundation of all of these is the certainty of the outcome, which is faith and confidence.

Let us consider just one facet—awareness—and see how it becomes patience. Look carefully at patience and see how it is also love. Patience is self-control and, therefore, happiness. Since patience is calm, unresponsive and disobedient to evil pressure, it is also peace and joy. Patience is waiting without anxiety; therefore, patience is timeless. The list of joys is endless.

Can you see how simple it all is? Only find that magical viewpoint of objective awareness, and you have everything.

Pride is only willing to be made aware in the subjective sense, that is to say it becomes involved with glorifying illusion stuff. You see, there are two kinds of awareness, and each of them arises from a different attitude; and these two attitudes are diametrically opposed to each other, moving as they do in opposite directions toward different realms of self-knowing. The movement of the proud mind away from the awareness of guilt adds even more guilt to what was there originally, because of its movement away from the truth; whereas the movement toward awareness of guilt adds innocence to innocence by means of the sorrow that we experience on seeing the truth about ourselves. The quality of life that each soul receives in its searching has to do with the type of hunger it has. Do you reach for the glorious illusion or for the humble reality? To reach for illusion awareness is to reject reality awareness. To reach for reality is to be able to reject illusion. For this reason, it is impossible to instruct the wrongly inclined soul properly.

If your motive is wrong, you are bound to be caught up and carried away by the very technique that is designed to bring you back to yourself. You will be "hung up" on the technique, in other words. You are afforded protection only through true intent, and it is an infallible safeguard. Your true desire carries you forward in a credible sequence of events so that you confront problems with perfect scrutiny, and so long as you move by the Light, strange experiences cease to be terrifying to you. Beyond them you will find new joys and fearless adventuring.

Do not set up a pattern of expectations when you meditate. Expect only the unexpected. There is really no way to predict in advance what the experience of any individual might be. Perhaps an old illness that you thought was cured will reappear. You may be confronted by something from you past; you might even encounter presences or see spirits. But don't worry; your true desire will see you safely through. There comes with this perfect attitude an accompanying rule of thumb that the sincere seeker can readily comprehend. Whenever you encounter anything at all that you don't understand, regardless of what it might be, just wonder and watch from the neutral zone just beyond thought until you do understand or until the problem ceases to exist for you. Certainly you may be concerned, but don't worry, and, above all, don't *decide* what to do. Just watch quietly from a meditative, neutral, observing, nonjudgmental state of awareness. Make no evaluation of the experience that is before you. Just observe it and wonder; that's all. Do nothing more or less, for nothing else is needed here. There is something magical that operates through the soul of one who wants to do good and yet suffers from the stark realization that he is incapable of determining exactly what that good is. The true desire within the soul is alone qualified to experience such a realization. Such a soul already knows the basic truth that will carry him through all threats: SOMETHING, not nothing, must cause a soul to realize, and the seeking soul recognizes this fact. There is a mystical abandon, an indefinable comfort in being shown the negative truth that you can do nothing, of yourself. Do you see the importance of such a revelation and why this basic knowing will carry you through otherwise dangerous experiences? There is nothing more terrifying to the enemy than a soul who truly knows that he knows nothing at all and who, when tested, is never tempted to decide what to do.

If your desire is not absolutely pure, however, you will not have this kind of confidence and protection, and when various forces make their approach—and they will, even in meditation—you will most certainly be panicked into the activity of decision, and you will be confounded. It will be your destiny to go from bad to worse until you are willing to realize that folly that is born of pride. Don't you see that if your aim is imperfect you will not be able even to see, let alone rely on what is greater than you are? That imperfect desire itself will block out the light of revelation so that the proud you will be forced to grapple alone with complicated things that will engulf, involve, torment and destroy you at the end of your lonely battle. If you are able to see this truth, you already have the quality of healthy abandon that allows you to know that you need not worry about not knowing.

This is an extremely important point and one that I think bears restatement: To realize that you do not know means that *something* has made you realize it and that it is the same as knowing the Truth greater than you are when you know *by* a Truth greater than you are, because you love or yearn to know the Truth that is greater than you.

In this state of consciousness one does not have a valid reason to fear anything at all. Fear will belong to the enemy and to the realm of the blind and faithless. There is nothing so terrifying to evil forces as a soul who does not judge, one who simply discerns what is before it. Simply defined, the stages of giving up judgment and struggling amount to humility in the making, and this is the state of consciousness that allows the Light to pass through. It is the Light, not the will, that acts on the problem before you, and at that point you either know what to do or the temptation simply melts before you and ceases to pose a problem or even a question.

For the faithless soul there is nothing greater than itself to rely on, and so the moment it encounters something mysterious beyond its comprehension, it is challenged to worry and to decide the issue for itself. Consequently, the problem invades such a soul, and as the problems become greater, so does the temptation to solve them. Simply stated, the soul being drawn away from the Light finds it more difficult to discern and easier to judge. Indeed, the tendency toward confounding judgment becomes a terrifying compulsion, and so the soul is damned if it judges and struggles and just as damned if it doesn't. For even if such a soul does give up judgment, it will do so only from guilt and fear and out of the stark terror of what another forced judgment will bring. Such resignation of the ego at this point is not the result of love for God; it is only capitulation to the tormenting hell that lurks in the hypnotic, dehumanizing pressure.

Fear not, beloved of God, for the chances are that you will not experience such complicated dilemmas as these; but if you should, realize why! Then out of the light of that realization will come the purging sadness that allows you to go on—to continue to observe and to wonder, fearless in the face of those things you do not yet understand.

It should be clear by now that you must learn to reverse your present subjective state of consciousness, and that means doing just the opposite of what the escape meditator does in his devotion. The technique discussed in the following chapters will show you how to become separate from dream stuff, how to pull out of that tendency to fantasize, to excuse and worry your way out of every problem and to come up into the light of reality.

Everyone except the true seeker can practice the false meditation. It is quite easy to do, and one does achieve the desired state of peace almost instantly. The reason for such rapid results, however, is that nothing new is required of you. You simply do in a more sophisticated way what you have always done before without having sufficient knowledge to carry it to its ultimate limit. Fantasy and illusion are attractive to the soul's need to escape reality, and as long as the soul's inclination is to escape, it is impossible to teach it the true meditation. So the technology you are about to learn is compatible only with your proper attitude.

The central question is this: Do you want to preserve and glorify an image of yourself, or do you want to find God? If your answer is the former, then you will encourage the involvement of your soul with the process of imagination. The path to reality will destroy the fantastic imagination that is the seat of the mad ego, and it will usher in an age of reason and peace on earth to men of good will.

The meditation technique described in the following pages is a more advanced version of the basic one that was presented in my first book, *How Your Mind Can Keep You Well*. I strongly recommend that beginners learn the original exercise first and then come gradually and with grace to this one. The first exercise is more elaborate in that it not only teaches you how to be objective, but also how to get in touch with your own feelings—and this is a most important factor. The meditation contained in this text proceeds from the assumption that you already know and have been practicing the basic exercise, and it is designed to build on that initial foundation. It will, however, do no harm for you to try the exercise in this book. If it works for you, go right ahead and practice it; if it doesn't, then tape the exercise from the first book in your own voice and play it back to yourself. Then, after a while, proceed with this advanced lesson.

You may have some difficulty relating to your own voice on tape. If you do, I have prepared both versions of the meditation on records and in tape form. I believe that you will learn to meditate more efficiently by relying on my recordings, since the delivery and timing on the records are the result of twenty years of teaching and practice.

Elsewhere in this book you will encounter descriptions of various phenomena that you will encounter along the way. They have not been presented at an early point in the book out of a concern that your anticipation might precipitate them artificially. I strongly urge that you read this book in the order that the chapters are presented and not skip about. One of the main problems that we all share is our suggestibility. If we were not suggestible, we would have no problems of fear, confusion or guilt. All of us are externalized to some degree, so until you learn the principles of turning yourself on from the inside, the fewer details the better. Learn to meditate before reading beyond the next chapter. After all, yearning to know is a part of the meditative process, and your attempt to answer questions for yourself tends to stifle that process, particularly in the beginning.

Your emotions stimulate an energy flow similar to the electric current in a telephone line, thereby causing the brain to respond to and to dramatize messages from the outside. But when you learn to get in touch with your feelings, incoming calls and demands are censored, and your body will respond only to what you know is right in your heart. At this point there is no longer conflict or nervousness; there is no more struggle against terrible desires and compulsions because they simply cease to exist for you. In other words, your body will begin to respond only to you; you will see, hear and feel with a difference; you will no longer be shocked, disturbed and upset by what you experience. Those reactions will leave you, and as they do, you will become progressively more in control of yourself as well as of the circumstances about you. The most notable factor of this change is that it focuses upon the instant of emotional response. Once you have learned the principle of self-motivation, it is yours permanently. Once your body learns to respond only to you, an inner conditioning process is set up among your understanding mind, your feelings, and your body, and you will begin to answer less to external pressure and suggestion and more to what you perceive with a clear mind. As your emotions diminish it will become easier and easier for you to perceive what is wise, and it will also become easier for your body to respond graciously from that seeing.

A diminishing response to people is the evidence of response and obedience to your inner self. On the other hand, an increasing response to people is the evidence of a failing: Your body does not obey you; it learns to obey the pressure, and it is there that the problems begin to grow up inside you. That Power that separates the soul and makes it still and quiet also gives it knowing. It is the same cogent force that will act upon the body internally to make it obey. Since inner response is obedience to what is good and disobedience to what is wrong, it follows that guilt and tension will simply disappear from your life. Learn the principle of patience, and you will be free.

Let me emphasize that the meditation set forth in this book is no plaything, so be consistent with your practice of meditation from the outset. It is very unwise to stop meditating once you begin, for this is not an entertainment to be toyed with in moments of leisure or boredom. Do not begin meditating until you are prepared to continue it, for it may be impossible to start meditating again after you have once stopped. Furthermore, a number of unpleasant complications may arise, and you would be well advised to avoid such experiences by having a sincere commitment in the very beginning.

It is best to learn meditation sitting upright in a straight-backed chair, preferably one without arms. You can meditate, however, lying on your back with your hands at your sides. You should start your practice in the chair in order to avoid falling asleep, but once you have mastered the technique, the prone position may be a more desirable and comfortable one for meditating over a longer period of time. Remember, you are *not* trying to lose consciousness; you are seeking a greater level of awareness.

Sleep is the enemy of meditation, and sleep is certainly not meditation. A fool who goes to sleep awakens just as he was—a fool—but the fool who "awakens" out of meditation is a wiser man. If you should find yourself nodding off to sleep, go ahead and get all the sleep you appear to need. When you are certain that you have had enough, again try meditating in earnest. Sleep is a common means of escaping from reality, and it is especially compelling during attempts to meditate, so sleep until it becomes obvious that your natural needs have been met. Then, if you find yourself dozing, you can be sure that the reason is that you are not yet ready to face yourself. Often the full realization of this lack of commitment is sufficient to change your next meditative experience.

Another fact you should take into consideration as a beginning meditator is that there are two basic types of physical dispositions: The one may be highly motivated all of his life and the other undermotivated. Perhaps the reason for the lethargic, undermotivated state is a fear of motivation itself. If this is the case, a defensive shell surrounds that individual. Usually the undermotivated person is more fortunate than the achiever, for he is not burned out and run down like his overstimulated, enervated, debilitated counterpart. The effect of meditation on this so-called "lazy" type is usually quite profound. Suddenly he or she becomes a beehive of activity, full of zest for life and prepared for action. The overmotivated, on the other hand, will go into reverse gear, as it were, experiencing a period of convalescence and recovery. The achiever must be prepared to experience long periods of lethargy and listlessness. His overworked mind and run-down body need time to rest and become restored. The kinds of diseases that often make sudden and dramatic appearances in the lives of such types are always preceded by unrecognized but devastating stresses. Meditation takes such a person out of high gear, so to speak, and lets him recover. If you happen to be one of these energetic, productive persons, you simply can't work as hard as is your custom. What of it? Perhaps you can't drive a shiny, big new car and live in a mansion. Does it really matter? Can't you drive a small, dull, rusty, old car, live in a hut and pull your belt tight for a year or so? Isn't that better than a wooden box or a living death in a wheelchair or charity hospital ward? Who will pay the exaggerated bills for your high standard of living when you are sick and disabled? How can you work when you are sick? Surely, prevention is better than cure. Sooner or later you will have to stop, and better sooner than late. You need a great deal of extra time to ponder and examine your errors. You need time to become acquainted with your family again. In fact, your family will very likely be grateful to see you slow down; if not, the chances are it is *you* who have conditioned *them* to expect such a great deal from you. If that is the case, it will be good for you to understand their compulsion to help you and to worry about you. In any event, remain calm; it will probably be good for them to feel a little insecurity about not being able to push you in order to get their own way.

Enough details. You are as ready as this book can make you. So find yourself a hard chair or a nice soft bed, depending on your state of proficiency, and begin to meditate.

2 Meditation Exercise

Sit in a straight-backed chair without arms. Let your right hand hang loosely at your side.

It is important that you remain awake and alert during this exercise, but you may, if you wish, lie down in a comfortable position with your hands beside you.

Close your eyes. Notice your right hand. Observe your hand until it begins to tingle just a little. Do not force your attention to your hand—simply notice your right hand *gently.*

If your mind wanders away with a thought, just be conscious that it has done so, and continue being aware of your hand until it begins to tingle again slightly. Once you learn how to become aware of your hand, there is no need to think of it in order to feel its presence.

To help you keep your attention focused on your hand, use this simple technique: Shift your attention from one finger to the other. First, become aware of your thumb . . . feel the awareness of your thumb until it begins to tingle. Now shift your attention to your first finger . . . feel the awareness of it until it tingles. Do the same with the second finger . . . shift your attention to the third finger . . . now the fourth finger. Start again . . . be aware of your thumb until it tingles.

While your attention if focused on your hand like this, become conscious also of a point in the middle of your forehead. Now, as if you were looking through the middle of your forehead, include the awareness of your hand until that hand tingles with gentle warmth. I don't want you to look up with your eyes; simply be conscious of a point near the middle of your forehead about an inch above the bridge of your nose.

Notice every thought that tries to steal your attention away from being aware of your hand. Become conscious of each thought *as if* you were looking right through the center of your forehead; and, at the same time, feel the awareness of your hand until it begins to tingle and feel warm, as though it were flushed with blood.

There is no need to look up with your physical eyes. Just be conscious of your head with your mind's eye—as if you were standing back inside yourself being aware of your own mind through the center of your forehead.

Become very conscious of passing thoughts that take your attention away from the awareness of your hand. Don't allow imagination to draw your attention. Don't follow your thoughts into the stream-of-dream stuff. Pull back. Merely become aware when your conciousness is captured by a thought. And, as if you were looking right through the middle of your forehead, extend your awareness of distracting thoughts down your right arm into your hand until it tingles—feel your hand glow warm, as though it were becoming flushed with blood.

Become conscious once again of your thumb until it tingles. Shift your awareness to the first finger . . . to your second finger . . . third . . . fourth. Become aware of your hand until it tingles and feels warm and flushed with blood.

This is important. Do not strain. Do not force your attention. REALIZE. No effort is required.

Observe gently. Become conscious of the thought that tends to pull you along with it. Watch the thought gently, which is to say, GIVE your attention. Be aware of the thought that pulls you away from being aware of your hand; now feel your hand tingle with the warmth of life feeling.

Don't struggle to free yourself from musical impressions, entertaining, distracting mental noise and chatter. As soon as you become conscious that you have become involved with thinking, become aware of thought itself—that's all there is to it.

While being conscious of the thought or thought sound that involves you, become also aware of your hand until it tingles warm and seems to fill with an energy that is really life flowing from within.

Repeat this exercise again and again on your own.

As if you were looking through the middle of your forehead, quietly watch that thought pulling your attention down toward it . . . and then include the awareness of your hand until it tingles.

Be aware in such a way that you feel your awareness extend and flow right down into your arm to make your hand glow warm, tingle and feel full of life. You can feel the ache of your body's need calling for this life feeling of fulfillment.

Don't meditate on anything in particular or hold onto any thought, no matter how lofty, noble or beautiful. Become aware of any thought drawing your attention toward these things. Observe that thought as if you were looking through your mind's eye and also include the awareness of your hand, so that your hand tingles and begins to glow warm with life feeling.

Practice becoming conscious of thoughts until you find yourself being less involved and fascinated by them, so that by merely observing layers of distracting thought, they gradually dissolve and lose their power to hold your attention captive.

Repeat this exercise again and again, listening to or reading what I am saying as a backdrop to what you are doing: Be aware of your hand . . . feel it tingle with gentle warmth.

Become conscious of thoughts arising and trying to pull your attention away from being aware of your hand. You must not allow thoughts to entertain or hold your attention captive. Simply be aware of that thought while becoming aware of your hand, until your hand tingles and glows warm, as though it were becoming flushed with life.

Become aware of daydreaming and so stay out of daydreams.

Become aware, and through that simple awareness of thought, you, the observer, are gradually being separated from the dream state.

Become objective; allow the thinker to separate from the thinking by being conscious of your thoughts as *thoughts*.

Become conscious of your thoughts, and, being aware of thought, be less involved with the thinking process.

Calmly observe the apparent strength and variety of your imagination, *without resenting what you see*, until your fantasy loses its kind of reality.

Be careful now. I don't want you to repress any memories or feelings. Be aware of whatever comes, and if nothing comes, wait for thoughts and feelings to surface and pass by the grandstand of your awareness. When they do appear, realize them out of their power to mislead you. CULTIVATE THE AWARENESS OF WHAT IS GOING ON INSIDE YOUR MIND. Do nothing about what you see. Continue to realize: Don't let thoughts pull you away from realizing that they are present. Become aware of your hand, so that your hand tingles warm and feels as though it were flushed with blood.

When you become aware of thoughts as thoughts, they lose their power to distract you. Weaken those distracting thoughts by becoming conscious of them; and don't be alarmed when you realize the real problem they previously concealed from view.

You must *give* your attention to a thought—quite a different thing from being fascinated and entertained by thinking. Become conscious of what you are thinking and feeling, and this will prevent your being pulled along in a daydream or fantasy. This awareness will slowly change the way you feel. But don't try to program yourself with a new set of concepts or feelings; let it be of itself. Your new thoughts will come through not being immersed in thought stuff.

Do nothing more than this: Be aware of thoughts . . . as though you are looking through the middle of your forehead; and, at the same time, become aware of your hand until it tingles and feels full of life. You may extend this exercise to include your other hand if you wish.

Never struggle with your thoughts. Never talk back to or enter into dialogue with what appears as your very own thinking. Be especially alert for the presence of excuses in your mind. Avoid planning the future—revenge, vacations, imaginary conversations with people— as well as resentment concerning past events.

Don't ask yourself a question and give yourself an answer. Don't look to your thinking for answers.

Don't try to figure things out.

Become conscious of the thought that pulls you away from being aware of now. Become aware every time you discover yourself daydreaming along with worry and planning. A mental world can be real and frightening when you are immersed in fantasy and involved with thinking, because, in that condition, you have lost consciousness of the Reality That makes you aware that thoughts are only thoughts and not real. Awaken Love and Truth; become aware of the emptiness, the vanity of your dreaming and planning. The light of Reality is where thoughts are not. You realize and experience the Truth when you are not involved with thoughts of past glories or failures or with plans for new triumphs. You can never find understanding in the resources of memory or in new experiences and feelings.

Your most important aim and desire must be objectivity: to be a clear channel through which you realize the Truth for each delicate present moment. Such a mind discerns error, but does not judge or condemn. As you begin to desire to do what is right, you realize your selfishness, and then resentment—at various levels—will also be recognized, and it will fall away, carrying with it those problems that grew out of resentment. All of these will resolve through realization.

Guilt, fear and jealousy all contain elements of resentment that sustains them. First realize the role of resentment in any problem, and later other more subtle feelings will yield to observation.

You can never overcome your frustrations or conquer your wrong reactions to life so long as you set any kind of goals for yourself, ahead of doing what is right in each given moment. No matter how small, insignificant, or apparently unselfish these goals may be, they constitute ambition, which is a part of pride; and every surge of pride creates a backlash to which you become defensive. That process leads to excuse making and the mistaken belief that your problems are *out there* somewhere, assaulting you from the outside.

Look carefully—see if there isn't some little thing that is much too important to you—something like a vow made in anger, a resolve to have a happy home life, never to be poor or lonely—some little thing of that sort that you feel is more important that anything else.

Realize the correct order: Desire, yearn, above all, realize what is right and see all other values added in due course—health, happiness, even financial security.

Be patient. Impatience and frustration are the evidence of goal setting—the signs that there is something that is more important to you than what is right and fair. Be patient. You have a lot of sorting out to do in your mind as well as in your external affairs. There is a lot of catching up for you to do.

Confusion originates through pride—ambition: from being locked into your thoughts. Down there in your dreaming, there is foolish hope for selfish advantage, as well as escape from being aware of the errors caused by pride.

The emphasis from now on should be not on getting out of your troubles, but out of your thoughts. When you are dishonest, you become less conscious of the Truth, and that is why you have been unable to understand your problems.

You will realize truth only when thoughts do not hold your attention, so don't let your thoughts pull you into them, and you won't have to experience their kind of reality. A dream is just a dream, and a thought is merely a thought, if they are observed. Yearn to know the purpose for which you were created, and you will become aware again—conscious of your thoughts and of the mistakes you have made.

Practice not being caught up in dreaming, planning, revenge, escape, and you will make no more errors of judgment.

Each moment when you become consciously aware of thought in order to know the Truth—*if only for a timeless second*—Truth slips through the armor of your infidelity and changes the quality of the reality you experience, giving you back control and self-respect.

Observe morbid thoughts and lying doubts. They cannot help you to resolve your problems—neither can they harm you, *so long as you remain objective* to them and recognize them for what they are: thoughts—empty, useless thoughts.

Be careful at this point. Do not be tempted to make resolutions or positive affirmations. You cannot choose to be right. No choice is within your power.

But you can *yearn*—desire with all your heart to be saved from the compulsion to sin that has come down to you from an original wrong choice. Through this yearning comes realization, and through realization sorrow—repentance for what you have become, and through repentance, salvation.

Abandon pride and self-image by becoming objective—self-aware. Realize the folly of wanting things and building your ego instead of doing what is right. Ambition blinds you and makes you forget the Truth so you can't see the traps you fall into: Therefore, you are full of rage and frustration and fear of making mistakes.

Becoming better is not a matter of arranging things in the mind or in the world. Rather, it is realizing the Truth into existence. Stay in the present long enough to realize what is wrong and to do what is fair.

The new direction you need lies just beyond shrinking from every folly. Not going in the wrong direction leads to the right path.

Never set goals to forget the futility of setting goals, as people drink to forget the guilt of drinking . . . as people eat to forget the guilt of eating . . . to forget the frustrations arising from ambitions that failed or failed to satisfy.

Do not seek to possess.

Do not encourage pride or let anything or anyone serve you a sense of pride.

You become possessed by what you seek to possess, even in the losing of it.

Remember, frustration comes out of pride's attaining or failing to attain, so yearn to know what is right . . . practice it. Acquire things without guilt; lose things without a sense of loss; watch frustration disappear; see patience appear . . . and through patience, more understanding with patience.

You cannot control your emotions and be self-seeking and ambitious at the same time.

Be industrious: that is, move with or toward opportunities you have realized unselfishly, instead of those you have created for yourself. Work at your own pace at what is meaningful *for you* without puffing up with pride. Even under pressure, realize away the resentment toward the pressure source. Don't let your response to outer authority get between you and your true inner Authority. Don't let the grace robber change your reasons for or your feelings about learning or doing things.

Instead of following thoughts that rise from anger and feeling, let your realization hold sway and set the pace through calmness. DO WHAT IS RIGHT BECAUSE YOU ALONE SEE IT OR BECAUSE YOU *ALSO* SEE IT. ABSTAIN FROM WRONGDOING BECAUSE YOU ALONE SEE IT OR BECAUSE YOU ALSO REALIZE IT.

No more confusion now—no more senseless rebellion—no more agonizing conformity. Do everything with a clear mind—one that is never lured by selfish advantage or concerned with outcome. Do all things for the pure joy of doing what is right because you want what is right more than anything else in your life. Do everything that you do because you want to, not because you have to.

At times you may need to be strong and use force. If it is necessary, you may, provided that you act without resentment.

What you fear is violence—force from others motivated by resentment and hatred toward you. And you fear it only because you have resented it; therefore, you may fear to use force because you have become resentful. Fear not! Don't feel resentful toward the frightening force of others, and you need not be that terrifying force to others.

Be careful that you don't preach to others and forget to look at your own wrong. Let what you are speak for itself. Love is a chastening and corrective force, but you must find it before you can give it. Be good natured in your correction of others.

Your new self will be composed of millions of little realizations flooding into your mind, even as your faulty existence was made up of many temptations, lies and excuses.

Realize, therefore, the basic theme that points the way to life. Abandon pride and ambition; be objective to the knowledge of good and evil in your mind. Discern, rather than judge, what is good or evil by removing the one factor—resentment—which changes innocent discernment into the guilt of judgment. Now observe what appears to be wrong or unjust without feeling bad about it; observe what appears right and good without feeling good about it. Realize faults in people without resenting them. Realize the virtue in a person without liking him unduly. Then, if there is no condemning or condoning, no hasty conclusions to cloud and puff up your judgment, you will find yourself innocently discerning the truth of the matter before you. Then you may never again fall into the trap of feeling guilty for seeing evil as evil and then forcing yourself to like evil in order to ease the guilt of resenting and judging it. Guilt and confusion stem from emotionally sustained judgment of pride—never from reserving judgment in the Light: discernment.

Realize the folly of judging; wait till you can discern clearly in the Light. For the same reason, do not seek praise or look for reasons to be judgmental. Abandon rash judgments that are rooted in resentment. To the degree that you do not seek approval or praise, to that same degree you will not feel judgment or condemnation.

Don't be so quick to form judgments. Wait and see. You will be glad you did. Even then when you know, discern, rather than judge. Know without resenting. You have no more need to make agonizing decisions. Stand back, gently observe with a clear mind; wait and see. Don't be ambitious; let things fall into place on their own. Be patient and have faith.

Timing is important too. Just go on being aware of your need for answers. Don't be impatient. The answer will arrive in its own time. It is all so simple, really.

It is enough to become aware that you are resentful—emotionally locked into past memories with blame and to the future with vengeful premeditation.

It is sufficient to become aware that you have been losing awareness of what is wrong with you. Preoccupied with thoughts and angry feelings, you could not see the folly of resentment itself.

Awaken then. Become aware that you are not as aware as you can be. See how emotion always pulls you into daydreaming and prevents you from being sorry through realizing what is wrong in the light of the present moment.

Whenever you find yourself involved with thought, realize that you are; this is the same as being in the right place again, observing imagination as imagination and not as reality. Then watch the stream of thought passing by in the present moment. Feel your awareness cause your hand to feel warm, as though it were becoming flushed with life fulfillment.

Through being aware of your hands, commune with your feelings and your body, and let your soul search out the way. Feel the state of awareness so you can now do what you realize is right, without conscious effort.

Be still only with your awareness. Be careful that you don't still, suppress, or dull your thinking. Allow thoughts to pass by the grandstand of your awareness, which, being still, observes, because it is not moving along with the thought stream.

Watch your errors as they appear. Realize them objectively, and they will disappear. Now your mistakes can come to mind without your soul being affected or being stained by them. Even if you should hear profanities uttered in your subconscious, you will realize that you are not the one who utters them or sins against the good.

See things as they really are, not as you thought them to be when you were escaping into emotional thinking, making excuses, defending error against the Light of Reality.

Be objective. Don't cling to the image you have of yourself, whether it be a good one or a bad one. Nor should you reinforce the image of yourself through fantasy or comfort; don't escape from seeing the corruption by identifying with the identity that has gone wrong in you.

Don't be afraid to face what you were running away from in yourself—things will be different now; you'll see.

Allow the light of understanding to shine through your conscious awareness until your hand tingles warm with life.

Fear not; you will be able to cope now. Just learn to be objective to your feelings in the Light of Reality.

In the past, when you reacted to temptation, your mind became filled with a flurry of meaningless trivia: musical chatter, excuses, reasons, commercials—all kinds of nonsense, as if to shield your ego from seeing what you did wrong. Your ego found refuge in that mental world.

Until this moment, it was impossible for you to realize what was going on, because you were defensively caught up—away from the Light That lets you realize anything at all.

Now you can realize.

Stand back. Begin to understand yourself. As the chatter peels away, begin to see the errors of your way.

Be conscious of the present and live in the present moment.

BE CONSCIOUS OF THE NOW.

When you discover yourself thinking in the past or

future, just become conscious that this is so, and you will be living in the now moment again, allowing Truth to slip through that moment of awareness.

Some of your problems are caused by your ego's failure to respond correctly to the cruel challenges and temptations of life. You have worried and tried vainly to work things out, and by worry you escaped from being aware in the present, where shame is—where repentance is.

The world of error slips through the soul that is involved in its thinking. In a similar way, the world of good comes through the objective soul.

Be concerned, that is to say, realize problems in the light of the present, but resist the temptation to worry or deal with them in any way.

Simply become conscious of worry until it ceases. Let the pain of the problem become an inquiry to God. Wait until the question answers itself.

Worry is not only a thing of pride; it is also an escape through which you have always added guilt to sin and problems to problems. Observe worry until you are no longer part of the scheming-planning-analyzing-worrying process. Become aware of your hand tingling till your hand becomes warm and flushed with life.

Again, whatever problem you have, don't think it through—leave it as a question; be patient until it answers itself. Wait patiently until you perceive the way to go.

You can't BE your thinking any more. *You* are not your thinking.

Don't just think about what I say, or else you cannot truly realize it. Look, if I ask you not to worry and you remember not to worry, all you are doing is worrying about not worrying. You are still worrying by recalling those thoughts that activate negative feelings. Again, if you stop worrying by not thinking at all, then there is no inquiry and no answer. Just be aware of worry objectively. Observe the folly of worry. Be patient for an answer. Impatience means you have too much faith in your own self. Realize this fact— that's all.

Every time you become aware that thoughts have carried you away from the present moment, from the Presence of the revealing inner Light, become aware of it, that's all. And, as if you were looking through the middle of your forehead:

give your attention

become aware of that captivating thought, and

feel your hand tingle warm and flushed with blood.

Practice this exercise again and again till thoughts let go of your attention, and you slowly become free to realize and do what is right in your heart without trying to understand.

A new discovering and thinking process is developing in and through you as you become less and less in volved with thinking.

Discover how to wonder about things without words, and let this kind of inquiry into life's purpose and meaning slowly and surely realize the way for you.

Careful. Don't force changes or make things happen. Realizing is power enough. Relax by realizing that of yourself you can do nothing.

Realizing the Truth as it is revealed each moment becomes faith. And out of this knowing in the Light comes patience, understanding, self-control; and a new kind of love that you can't *feel* is there within you.

Don't be afraid to look at your ugly side. The first truth you see is always something negative about you. So don't cringe or shrink back from seeing faults that must eventually come to light.

Don't overreact to what you see. Don't panic!

You must see your faults or else you can't be truly sorry, and if you don't repent, there can be no change—no salvation. STOP.

Take it easy; there is far more resentment in you than you realize. Your faulty ego life is built on it. Don't fight against what you see surfacing in its own time. Learn to watch without being part of what you are observing.

Neither accept nor reject what you see. Don't believe that there is something wrong with what reveals your errors to you.

Realize wrong as wrong. Stand your ground. DON'T RUN. Dare to observe. Realize whatever might be there. Be mindful that the reason why you can realize is because the Light of Truth is there to expose all things to your searching soul, to the end that you might repent and shrink from your involvement with evil and incline toward the revealing, purging light.

Careful that you don't resent being shown and don't resent what you see. Don't block the redeeming Light. It is foolish to resent what you see; it is also dangerous to resent your conscience for showing up your ego for what it is.

The Light of Truth reveals the lie, so that you know the lie is the lie.

Don't be defensive. The Truth That causes the chastening pain is not really hurting you—unless you resist and resent.

The Light Who makes you realize—He is a friend, not an enemy.

Anxiety is not a bad thing. Don't try to cope with anxiety. Wait; let it phase back into guilt—but don't try to do anything about guilt either. Bear it without resentment till it phases back into an understanding of what you have done wrong or what you have failed to do right.

Wait to be repented. Humility is the lesson you need to learn. Even if it is somehow tormenting and frightening, stay where you are.

To experience genuine sorrow, you must realize this course of action. Even if you feel no remorse at the time, become aware of the pleasure you have derived from the harm you have done or that you are poised to do or to speak to others. Suffer the pain that appears when you deny your faulty self the satisfaction of hurting others by word or deed.

Afterwards, you can then turn around and cope patiently with the harm people have done to you and the troubling images and impressions they still try to put into you. Forbear to use others, and you will never again be used by others. Be patient with their faults, and you will find a healing patience with your own shortcomings.

Resenting, and so remembering another's wrong, is how you forgot how wrong you are. Resenting wrong has made you feel right, but through patience you will begin to feel your old wrong again.

Wait to be repented of it.

The exercise you are doing reverses a lifetime of escape from the Light into the world of imagination. It brings your awareness back to see things as they are. You will become conscious of faults that have grown up in the absence of the Light.

Wait, therefore, to experience genuine sorrow, not the phony, manufactured sorrow or the kind of pernicious, worldly sadness that comes out of misery and depression, frustration, or grieving after things you have lost or failed to gain.

You can be truly sorry only to the degree that you come up out of your imagination to be aware and objective in the presence of the Light.

To experience God's forgiveness, remain aware; stay out of either positive or negative thinking. Don't try to save yourself.

Don't try to make yourself feel guilty or sorry.

Don't put on a show for God or anyone else for approval.

Don't feel sorry for yourself.

There is no need to make up for past mistakes.

It is enough to live on as you realize.

Slowly but surely you will see how, by escaping into

your thinking, you escaped from the Light Who wanted to make you conscious of His correcting Presence. The Light pursuing you in your headlong flight became conscience and then anxiety. Only when it is not welcome is conscience painful, and only then does it appear to be an enemy hounding you. If you would accept its admonitions, it would give you peace.

Wait patiently to experience the true sadness that will refine into joy. Repentance is good and acceptable to God; it brings to you His divine pleasure. His unmerited grace, which is life, motivates you to move and have your being without fear or guilt, resolving your need for resentment and unhealthy pleasure.

The true sorrow that saves is impossible without His Presence to cause you to realize the full extent of the folly of pride, and this Presence is impossible to recognize unless you are objective to your thoughts.

You must not force yourself to repent or make yourself feel guilty for not feeling guilty.

Wait to be repented.

Emerge from your dream state to realize the truth about yourself.

Realize the Truth, and the Truth will set you free from sorrow and sadness.

And if you should find tears flowing down your cheeks without knowing why, it is because your aware, stilled, quieted self is experiencing the soul's repentance: a spiritual purging of sin in the Light.

After this time, your soul, less tainted by the sin of being wrongfully involved with thoughts, will be able to

45

approach psychological complications and compulsions and understand them out of existence.

Through understanding, you will become more settled in your thoughts. Understanding the past errors in the present Light takes the fear out of the future. Things are not as hopeless as you thought they were. Only in your thoughts are things hopeless.

It is the Light from God That makes you conscious of what is wrong. Do not affirm a wrong as a wrong as if you were God. Don't give yourself positive commands such as, "be patient, be better."

Realize error.

Realize the need for improvement and patience.

Do not seek comfort and sympathy from anyone or any thing. Your mistakes will then become clearer to you.

Be sorry. Wait to feel true comfort beyond the sadness for what you have done wrong.

Abandon any image you may have of how a wife, husband, son or daughter should be.

Abandon also what you expect to receive from playing your role.

Watch resentment leave and real concern enter—concern for the well-being of others instead of yourself.

Don't idolize the author of these words or take on these words or the image of his goodness or his knowledge.

You must not commune with or find comfort from him or any other person imagined in your mind.

What you hear now is not to be stored word for

word in your memory. It is meant to spark a recognition.

Recognize principles, but don't commit them to memory; otherwise your heart will remain unchanged, justifying evil, selfish motives with lofty principles.

Catch yourself in stubborn mental habits until they break down.

Simply be *aware* of what it is that should *not* be thought or done, as it begins to occur to you.

Become very aware and alert.

Now open your eyes.

A meditation exercise like that described in the chapter you have just read is available through the Foundation of Human Understanding on records or cassette tapes.

3 Practicing the Presence

Words are only symbols representing reality. The trouble with most learning is that the ambitious student often mistakes words *about* something for the actual thing or experience. So when he learns, he learns words, not meanings, and he ends up with a gaggle of noises in his head but little practical understanding, which can only come from true intimacy with the subject.

Because religion is intangible and elusive to the senses, it can be *realized* only by one's soul. For that reason, most people mistake words *about* religion for the religious experience itself.

The most important thing any true religion can offer is a set of instructions leading one to the threshold of intuitive understanding or self-knowing. But instead of being led to the Truth through the medium of words, most students become entangled in rituals, techniques and philosophies. The Christian who thinks he knows Jesus may be confusing familiarity with the name (word symbol) with a true understanding of Who He is.

When the pseudo-Christian thinks he is experiencing the touch of God, he is, in reality, drowning in a sea of holy noises that makes him lose sight of his transgressions; he is experiencing a delusion that he mistakenly calls salvation.

The main reason people can't find the Truth is that far too much "truth" has been written telling them what they will discover or what will happen if they don't discover it. What they need instead is practical instruction on how to find the awareness—in the Light.

Life is really so very simple—the only difficult thing is *realizing* just how simple it is. When people have lost their natural understanding of life, they fall into a desperate longing for and a clinging to symbolic words, rituals and rules.

I realize that this book contains many words, but instead of entangling and absorbing yourself in them, I want you to scan them until they spark some recognition in you. Don't be in a hurry to devour these pages.

The more you *learn* in the sense of merely acquiring knowledge, the harder it will be for you to *realize*, because conventional *learning* tends to defeat the process of *realizing*. You are not *more* because you *know more*, but you are *more* because you *realize more*. Knowledge is fulfilled only when it becomes understanding. As you *realize*, knowledge will assume a new dimension, for it will develop into understanding.

Knowledge can lead you to discover for yourself. Intellectual knowledge can bring you to the brink of understanding about that knowledge. And sometimes what you *realize* and what you have already learned in a formalized way will be identical. When this happening occurs, your rote knowledge will take on a real vitality, validity, dimension and an endless flow of meaning.

Once you have reached the threshold of discovering for yourself, *learning* becomes an awakening process—a journey—a way of growing toward and in the Light, a far cry from learning in the old way by cramming facts into your head.

You should be relieved to know that I don't want to be a source of information to you. Instead, I desire to be a means of awakening you to that Source of Truth within you, which even now bears silent witness to your need for It and to these words about Truth.

Everything you read here is intended to bring your mind more completely to the viewpoint of objectivity.

You have not been objective—self-aware, separate from your thoughts. You have been subjective, unable to separate yourself from your intellect. As you have fallen into its endless stream of thoughts, you have also left behind the understanding of your first mistake. You will continue to blunder, caught in the dream world of the intellect, unless you discover the secret that will make you objective to your problems.

Now if you find it difficult to concentrate on the following instruction, don't throw in the towel. Persist!

Since childhood, your mind has been lost in your imagination, just as Alice lost herself in Wonderland. You have probably confused fixation and fascination with true concentration and meditation. You have been so involved with fascinating things that you could not be aware enought to realize the vital difference between fascination and concentration.

Concentration is the voluntary giving of your entire attention, whereas fascination is the state in which your attention has been captured or stolen without your voluntary consent.

Until you become objective, you cannot concentrate, and this lack of concentration—the giving of your complete attention—is the basis of every problem you have in the world.

Every human dilemma evolves from a simple beginning—from subjective consciousness, that is, the state in which the mind is compulsively attentive to things, to people, and to thoughts. Free your conscious mind from its slavish involvements and you will *realize* a far superior way of observing life, for you will be viewing it in an objective manner.

This experience is like nothing you have ever known: You will enjoy a higher state of consciousness; you will stand at the threshhold of the problem-solving process, near the very source of life. So be persistent! Don't throw up your hands in despair if you should find it difficult to be objective.

The sick ego always seeks what is comforting. Concentration and meditation are difficult because they do not begin with comfort. Instead, they bring you back to the pain of reality, to anxieties you must face.

Whenever you feel that you would rather be somewhere else, don't give in to the feeling. Concentrate and meditate until you find the comfort that lies beyond the chastising pain.

The good life is waiting for you after you are freed

from the prison of your own thoughts. If you fail to concentrate as it is being taught here, there is no hope whatsoever that any of your problems will be resolved. Futility, misery and suffering will follow you all the days of your life. You will be out of control, wallowing and, ultimately, drowning in your thoughts.

I would like to recommend that you use the instructions found in these pages and get the recordings or tape cassettes of the concentration exercises. Alternatively, you can tape-record the written exercises for your daily use, but if you do this, be sure to pace your words slowly and place the proper emphasis on key phrases.

If you just read the concentration-meditation exercises in the book, you will tend to make an intellectual effort to understand what you are reading, and that will block the purpose of the exercises: to bring you to the *realization* that understanding is a process that results not from trying, but simply from yearning to know the Truth. Study usually stimulates ego involvement with the intellect, making it more difficult to grasp the reality beyond the words. Once you have learned to concentrate, however, you may read these words without any danger of becoming hung up on them.

The exercises lead you out of involvement with the intellect into a state of objective awareness. You *realize* in a way totally different from the way most of you were taught in school.

Everything written and said here is intended to sever your conscious attention from its fascination with thought-knowing. I want to make you progressively aware of the areas in which your conscious mind fixates and thinks it knows answers because it thinks and worries.

As you become conscious of each layer of fixation, you will discover the power of *realization*. By the simple act of *realizing*, you become free—unlocked—more aware than you were moments before . . . progressively aware of other subtle relationships that have locked your attention in to them.

Because of your seeking, you will make a simple discovery when you do the concentration-meditation exercises: You will find, to your surprise, that you can't concentrate. Prior to doing the exercise, you were so fascinated with thought that you believed you were concentrating. And because fascination is a subjective experience, you could not see otherwise.

Your first discovery, then, is usually that you have poor concentration. And as you slowly separate your attention from your thought stream, you will *realize* that this subjective, nonobjective state has been the reason for all your problems.

At times, it will be more difficult to concentrate than at others. You will always wrestle to unlock yourself from flurries of thought. And as you do, you will awaken and bring a new inner force to bear on the problems you face.

Startling as it may seem, becoming aware of your poor concentration—if it is done in the right spirit—can be the beginning of a new way of seeing and dealing with life, one that will bring you true peace and happiness.

If you are like most people, you are afraid of being truly conscious—aware—because you do not want to face the ego-shattering discovery that you are not in control of your life *You* are not really living your own life. Because you are afraid to face this disturbing truth about yourself, you have been living in an animal way, seeing in the animal way. Animals are limited to seeing with their eyes and hearing with their ears, but man has been given the gift of perception. He can observe in his mind what he sees and hears, be aware that he is doing so and understand the meaning of what he is hearing and seeing.

When ordinary seeing or hearing shows your ego that it is failing, you can deny your gift of perception and limit yourself to seeing and hearing in the one-dimensional, animal way. Because you *realize* guilt and inferiority when you are in the objective, aware state, you can only avoid perceiving what is wrong with you by refusing to be objective, seeing only people and objects and not perceiving your inferior position to them.

You can create the illusion of being above everything and beneath nothing by allowing some form of emotional excitement to fuse your conscious mind to your thinking-feeling, animal self. To reinforce this state you need more and more excitement.

Even if you do not wish to live in this egocentric, hypnotized state of deception, you will remain an unwilling prisoner of your subconscious, animal self—as long as you are emotionally excitable.

For this reason, it is vital that you learn how to be

calm under pressure and not to seek excitement. Massive doses of excitement will drown your wavering consciousness in your gross animal self.

When your conscious awareness is reduced by emotionality, you lose your ability to perceive, and you forget to *realize*. You may be conscious of what you have done, but you are not aware of what is wrong with it . . . and for a very short while, you can sweep your guilt, feelings of inferiority and fears under the carpet.

You could get away with this practice indefinitely were it not for one thing: The means you employ to escape from Reality cause such terrible degeneration in your being that eventually the very thing you were running away from overwhelms you.

Your attempts to find false innocence only make you more guilty, for Truth cannot be denied. We were created for the sole purpose of acknowledging Our Maker and His Truth.

When we leave behind the higher way of looking at life, we can accept and believe every self-justifying excuse or self-glorifying concept our ego finds. Until they are proved false, they are the only reality to us.

Reassured by these false realities, which are grounded in emotion, we blunder through life, controlled by clever manipulators who keep us blind while making us serve their devilish purposes. We dramatize the evil purpose that moves up through them.

You cannot *realize* that your dreams of glory and gain never originate within your because, for a season, you are not able to *realize*. In order to avoid guilt, to maintain the illusion that you are above everything and beneath nothing, it is imperative to your ego that you should *not realize,* that you suspend the humble but Godly way of perceiving life by His Light. So you are left alone with a false sense of innocence derived from the one-dimensional, animal way of seeing and not understanding.

In this state of mind you are left to grab everything you can out of life, to make life serve whatever your prideful ego needs in order to survive. You do not *realize* that you are sinking lower and lower, that you are becoming worse rather than better, for the reality of what you are is intolerable to your pride.

As long as you remain on an ego trip, the Truth will never dawn on you, for you are preserving the false idea that you are on top of everything.

You are seeing life in the limited, animal way. Unlike man, the animal has no soul or consciousness through which he can perceive and, therefore, no ability to control his life; he is meant to be controlled by his environment. But when you see in the animal way, and allow yourself to be controlled, you are not fulfilling your destiny. What is proper for the animal is wrong for man.

Perhaps you are beginning to see why objectivity is so important, why it is imperative that you reclaim your God-given gift of perception. For when you are objective, you are only subject to God, and nature, in turn, becomes subject to you; deceit loses its power over you, and you cease being its pawn.

Your separation from illusion—the one-dimensional, animal way of seeing—can be quite frightening, but for goodness's sake, resist the temptation to be drawn back into your thinking-feeling self.

Stand your ground. Remain objective. Wait for the dawn of a new way to meet life and let it work through you.

* * * * *

As you read or listen to these words, become conscious that you are reading/listening . . . that your eyes/ears are following these words.

Are you losing yourself in the images they stir up in your mind? Are you struggling to understand? Or are you separating from what you are seeing? allowing the words to trigger a natural process of understanding?

You should feel as if there were two of you: one observing what the other is seeing or hearing. You must have the distinct impression that your body is not you.

First observe with your eyes . . . and then through your eyes. Let it be as though you were observing your surroundings from a distance within yourself. Instead of feeling that you are close to the objects you are seeing, feel a slight distance between yourself and things.

Close your eyes for a moment. Become conscious of a lingering image. Being conscious of the image is not the same as being involved with it; you are merely the observer of the image in your mind.

Now, with your eyes open, see if you can become very conscious of distance between you, the observer, and objects in the room. Become detached from what you are seeing.

Look at your hands. As you become conscious of them, they may begin to feel as though they belong to someone else.

Now become conscious of yourself, and place a distance between you and the things observed, so that things seem a little strange or unreal to you.

Practice this exercise of objectivity with your eyes open. Observe an object. Now become conscious that you are looking at it, without naming it.

Look at, say . . . a chair. Observe the tendency to say to yourself, "That is a chair."

Look at that chair. Observe yourself observing the chair. Put some distance between you, the observer, and what your eyes see.

You may have experienced this feeling of distance and detachment before, but never *realized* what it was— an extension of meditation.

Now begin to observe the extent of your reactions and involvement with the objects around you. Notice how little reactions and feelings keep you *close* to and identified with people and things.

Go the other way!

Be objective to people and things: that is, whenever you find yourself daydreaming or involved in a scene, become conscious that you are, become detached—with that sensation of distance between you and the world.

Without this kind of *realization*, you will never gain self-control. With it, you will gain a new perspective and direction. Different responses from those you've made in the past become possible.

Now, if you will, close your eyes again . . . and become conscious of the ache of your body's need for life.

Become conscious of your hands *through* being conscious of your forehead. Being aware of your hands, feel the ache of your body's need. And as you do this, you will experience a warmth beginning to fill you. Your breathing will change. You may feel an occasional popping in the bridge of your nose, as if your sinuses were opening up.

Concentrate on your hands; feel an increased warmth. If you do this consistently, you will sometimes be conscious of light emanating through your mind like a fountain of energy radiating and spreading through your innermost being.

You will *realize* all the principles written in this book and much more, without having to *learn* or memorize any of them. Without your having to remember them, they will be wordlessly present in your moment of need; they will save you from responding to evil. You will only respond to what is right in that moment. You no longer need to put your trust in memory, for you will have faith that you will see again when it is right.

You no longer need rehearse what you should say or do—your words and deeds will flow spontaneously from deep inner conviction, from the strength that comes from *realizing* what is right.

You will not fully understand what you say and do until it is said and done.

Allow your painful memories to surface in their own order. Don't dig them up willfully. When they come to mind, remain detached and objective to them. Your soul will not be stained by re-experiencing a sin that your memory recalls.

Remain objective so that you will feel only the guilt that is bearable from the past, not the tormenting guilt that comes from involving yourself in the events you recall.

You tried to deal with your conscience by escaping from Reality or forgetting error, but by doing so, you also lost the awareness of who and what was manipulating you. An so you continued to be manipulated.

If you choose now to *realize* your sins, you will also *realize* that sinning is a compulsion inherited through pride, which, in turn, fosters the growth of your basic error—your refusal to own up to the Truth.

The pain you feel is not so much from sinning, but from your ego's reluctance to see the mistakes you made that allowed the course of error to continue growing in you.

Face up to reality and graciously deal with manipulative forces. Divine Awareness will show you both temptation and its subtle power.

The counterdirection you need will come from the Light Who will cause you to *realize* forevermore.

You cannot believe the Truth unless you are willing to be aware of It. In your past attempts to escape from Truth, you have blindly believed and followed the lies whispered to your mind, for they supported your pride in its willfulness and self-righteousness.

Become objective to your thoughts. See deceit and who the deceiver is.

Your egocentric nature has an unrecognized need to doubt the Truth so that you may continue feeling secure as you play God. The strong pull you feel to doubt what is right comes from the invisible tempter, who understands your ego's inherent need to doubt the Truth.

Until now, you have been ignorant of this weakness in your egocentric nature. And this ignorance has made it easy for you to believe the worst—that you were hopelessly damned or that the sordid life you were leading was the one *you* chose. You have been too proud to admit that your life was not your own, which is the reason you have felt both responsible for and resigned to your choiceless choice.

You may even have taken pride in knowing that the worst was going to happen—as if this gave you one certainty in an otherwise unpredictable world.

Your premonitions of misfortune and danger do not necessarily mean that you will come to grief. Be conscious of them—they are warnings about your prideful life style—and this very consciousness will protect you from harm.

Formerly you used excitement to imprint pleasant memories on your mind in order to displace the effect of your bad memories. Your hypnotic enslavement to nostalgia seemed self-serving, because your awareness was hidden in your memories and you could not *realize* that they held you in bondage.

Nothing can save you from worldly hypnosis—the drawing power of sin—except one thing: Awaken from your dreaming and *realize* the truth about all of your ego weaknesses.

If you choose to awaken, have compassion on your manipulators, for they, too, are serving a hidden master in their own lives. Like you, they do not *realize* what is being done to and through them. Don't resent them. Be careful that you don't feel sorry for them either. Remain detached—unmoved in either way. See also that any love you may feel is a lie, for it is a common mistake to believe you love your corrupters or your supporters.

People you need, or whom you think you love, cause you much conflict. When they accept what is wrong with you, they allow you to maintain your belief in your innocence, and they help you move farther from the Truth—where they can exercise even greater control over you. They don't correct you; and you remain blind to your faults, sinning again and again.

And when you seek forgetfulness in "love" and become involved with *wrong* people, who accept you as you are, you develop either an insatiable craving for this false love or a fear of it—the very thing your ego needs to feel whole and righteous. Either way you are miserable.

To hold on to your false security, you feel obligated to prove yourself to your lover; you serve the wrong god in order to maintain a sense of innocence that you do not deserve, one that only makes you feel more guilty. You may even believe that your compulsive behavior toward people arises from devotion, duty, loyalty, love.

Because you have not been properly aware, you could not see what a lie you are living.

You must stop yearning for people who tempt you, who support your error. They have a lot going for them, because your ego can't or won't *realize* the harmful effect they have on you. Your tempter may provide so much pleasure that you find it hard to *realize* that he whom you think you love causes you as much conflict as those you hate. Often you really hate those you think you love.

You may have a need, which you think of as love, to find someone who will serve as a love-hate object. Why? Because you have been corrupted to exist on an *invisible* source of motivation and direction. If you were denied that source of motivation and comfort for your pride, you would be forced to *realize* your sorry state.

Your invisible master does not want you to *realize* the Truth, nor do you in your prideful state. How can you *realize* the Truth about yourself and continue being proud?

Your attraction to gross comforts lets you feel secure and allows you to lose your awareness of what is happening to you.

You have had only one freedom: the freedom from *realization*, which is freedom to do more wrong. Starting with unlimited freedom, you've arrived at unlimited despotism and abject slavery. To *realize* this truth without resenting it is the way to salvation.

Your salvation will begin as you gratefully *realize* the truth about your lie existence. "Ye shall know *(real-*

ize) the truth, and the truth shall make you free." (John 8:32 AV)

Become aware of the invisible forces behind your tragedy, sickness, suffering and hopelessness. The Truth *realized* in such moments will be life to you and give you very subtle direction in the world.

Remember—there is no cure from sin or counter-suggestion to its power *except* through your desire to *realize* and serve the purpose for which you were origi nally created.

Realize that you are vulnerable to wrong influences because of your pride. Even when you feel good thoughts, you are being deceived; they are a trick to pre vent you from *realizing* what is wrong with you.

Realize and be grateful for the Truth behind these words, and you will be set free.

Abandon excuse making. Never again defend your mistakes . . . even the smallest ones. Don't let the mo ment pass without observing any error you make.

A meaningful change comes about *at the very mo ment* the error occurs, but you must acknowledge it that instant!

Excuses block out the Light of Salvation. They sur face in order to preserve the sinning personality so that it can continue to worship its evil source. Excuses make the Truth out to be a lie, and the lie the Truth. And the more guilty you are, the more lying wisdom rises from Hell to take away your awareness of sin.

If you love your family, don't try to make them think they are wrong for seeing you as you really are. Admit your faults immediately . . . and not a second later. If you allow that special moment of seeing to go by, guilt may drive you into *acting* out what you should have done earlier. If you act in the moment, you are responding to the Truth, but if you play a role, you are the slave of pride's hypocrisy, and your dishonesty will eventually destroy your family's awareness.

* * * * *

Become objective to your thoughts.

Grow from an inner flow of grace, not by pushing against things as ego animals do.

Be objective to your thoughts. Leave behind the agony of decision making. Be patient. Wait . . . in time you will *realize* what to do.

Your pride needs much knowledge to think that it is God. Knowing and deciding things are agonies peculiar to pride as it plays God, trying to originate and organize its own universe.

Separate from your imagination and you will understand, rather than know.

If you are phony, see it.

If you see you are manipulating others, observe it.

If you find yourself manipulating someone before you *realize* it, admit your wrong motive to yourself. Apologize for it.

Disarm yourself. Give up the power you get from

people who are blind to your cunning. Feel weakness. Wait now for a new kind of inner strength to support you.

If something occurs that you don't understand, just leave it as an open question and wonder about it. Don't struggle to understand. If you struggle to understand or to solve a problem, your ego still believes that it can originate understanding. You have not fully discovered that understanding comes from wondering and waiting for God to make things known to you in His way. *Realize* this truth, and with this *realization* you will become patient.

Be still . . . then relax. Effort, guilt and panic will depart from you.

Wake up from dreaming! Be objective. *Realize* by the Light. Leave behind the confusion of your own knowing. Become nothing, that you might become something of God.

Don't be afraid of not knowing. The only thing you *can* do is abandon your ego refuge of knowledge and imagination.

Practice objectivity, and so live by the Light. You will be mysteriously nudged whenever you fall into excessive thoughtfulness.

Yearn to know the Truth, and so *realize* what lies beyond the retaining wall of thought and words.

Become aware of the ways in which life has shaped you, but don't be bitter about this discovery, and don't use it as an excuse to continue doing wrong.

Realize that you are not alone and that this is the

reason you know what is wrong with you. *Realize* that *you* can change nothing for the better. When you do not *realize* the Truth, your efforts will always make matters worse.

Remain aware of your problem. Resist the temptation to struggle with it. Struggle indicates a lack of faith on your part, a belief that you still think you exist alone with your problem.

By appealing to your pride and making you desire what is, in reality, frustrating to possess—by stimulating such ego reactions as greed—the alien identity has conditioned you. Your life is not your own; you are controlled.

You need to be saved. Allow yourself to *realize* the Truth, and the Truth will relieve you of your futile efforts to save yourself. Although they may increase in the beginning, your anxieties will diminish as you see and respond to the Truth.

Understand that you *realize* the Truth because the Light reveals It and that the Light within you is from God.

Should you discover evil within yourself, you do so because the Inner Light reveals it; therefore, don't be afraid any more. Have confidence. Face the evil in you; remain conscious of its presence, and the Truth will set you free.

The Light wants you to *realize* His Divine Presence so that you will not continue in your prideful way, taking credit for dealing with your problems.

Spiritual things are spiritually discerned. You perceive evil because good exposes it. Good is more subtle than evil. Whenever you see evil, know also that the Light is showing it to you.

Of course you will be fearful of what you see, but don't add resentment to that fear. *Realize* that you cannot struggle with it. Don't be afraid to feel helpless, yet be unwilling to abandon yourself to evil.

You ought neither to reject nor accept yourself. Just go on being aware of whatever is wrong, feeling compassion for those responsible for what has happened to you. They are as helpless as you are. Don't resent them for corrupting you or for allowing others to corrupt you, for the revealing Light is fully able to transform you as well as them, without any effort of will on your part.

Look, if you truly *realize* that you are helpless, that you cannot change your nature and that the Light is showing you this truth, you will also see that the Light will save you from evil and the awesome responsiblity of coping with everything by yourself. *Realize* this truth. *Realize* that in *realizing* your helplessness you will find help.

Be careful that you do not crystallize any *realizations* into thinking. When you *realize* what is wrong, simply see it without framing it into words. Don't even say to yourself, "Ah, now I know what is wrong!" Perceive in a wordless way the fact that you are helpless. See that of yourself you can do nothing. *Realize* your helplessness in a wordless knowing, and from your need will arise a wordless cry to the Saviour.

It is the evil in you, not *you* yourself, that is eternally damned and beyond God's forgiveness. But since your identity has fused with the sensual sin identity in your flight from Truth, you will experience the same pain it does in the presence of the Light. You see, it cannot tolerate the Light. Don't mistake God's judgment on the indwelling evil as judgment on you, or you will share in its blasphemy against God and will despair of finding mercy.

At some point there is danger that you might dare God to save you, but He cannot be tempted.

I warn you of these things beforehand so that you may be spared unnecessary pain. However, if you have already fallen, *realize* your error, and you will be relieved of the load you carry, which will both show you God's eternal goodness and mercy and save you from the subtle power of evil.

THERE IS ONLY ONE UNFORGIVABLE SIN: THE STUBBORN BELIEF THAT GOD CANNOT OR WILL NOT FORGIVE THE SINNER. Therefore, be alert to that phantom in your mind that spins negative doubts in order to serve its unrecognized need to doubt God. *Realize*, and it will flee from you.

Never struggle against doubt; merely become objective to your doubt feelings and thoughts. Become conscious that the unrecognized sin in every soul is the *inherited* inclination to doubt God, even His goodness and mercy, so that we can think of ourselves as gods—as being above the God we know exists.

For this reason, the force drawing you toward *doubt* is as strong as your inclination toward pride and self-righteousness. Adam's sin—the original sin—was that he doubted God and responded to temptation. *You inherit a compulsive inclination toward doubt and sin.* You sin and then doubt the Truth, doubt that you have been wrong. *Realize* then that it is not really you who doubts God. If it were, you would not be troubled by the doubts you see within yourself.

Realize that your doubts are wrong, which is the same as giving up pride and believing God. And when you believe, you will also learn to obey Him, which is all He asks of you in return for giving you salvation.

Realize that evil has always been present, sometimes masquerading as your conscience or as a friend who appealed to your prideful ego. Evil never wants you to *realize* its presence. After all, how can it mislead you if you recognize it?

As soon as you *realize* that it is present, it will often try to frighten you; it may try to make you think *it* is *you*—uttering such profanity that you will feel too ashamed to come to the Light. You see, if you believe that what it thinks and feels through you represents your true feelings, you may think that you will be judged as it is, and you will then judge God for His apparent injustice to you.

Remain objective to the curses and obscenities you hear in your mind, and sin will not stain you. Because you now believe that such thoughts do not originate with you, you need no longer feel hopeless or damned.

When you were consumed by pride, you assumed falsely that you originated thought. Become objective and you will see that only your pride with its limited way of seeing could believe that it was capable of originating thought. *Realize* also that your arrogant presumption that you were responsible for your thoughts made you feel guilty when things went wrong.

Always *realize* the variation of the basic lesson . . . do nothing but observe and *realize* what is not you. No evil can exist in the light of the soul's *realization*. It will not really be you who feels the terrible fear of God. It is simply you feeling what *it* feels. Do not stop meditating. *Its* fear of coming to the Light seems like yours . . . *it* fears that *it* will be *realized* out of existence, experiencing as *it* goes the Heaven that feels like the burning fires of Hell. (Restless nights mark a war going on inside you for your soul—but you will not feel tired the next day.)

Be careful that your ego does not become obsessed with observing the spirit of evil. Remember the subtle danger of believing that you are alone with any discovery, including the evil you perceive.

Whenever you think you are alone with what you are seeing, especially when it is unspeakable evil, it may become the ultimate fascination for you, making you seem to be as good as it is bad. You will become subjective, not objective, and your pride will cling to the resulting illusions in order to *realize* itself as God. The greater the evil, the easier it is for pride to know itself as God, for you to think of yourself as good.

Observe your helplessness.

Don't resent your helplessness.

Realize your needs—your need for life to soothe the

ache of being wrong, your need for patience. But avoid the tendency to formalize your needs into a wordy prayer.

Realize the need to understand, to love others unselfishly. And knowing that you need and that you cannot—must not—reach out to others or give yourself to them, wait patiently for the infilling of unmerited Grace. God knows what you need before you ask, and without the formality of words.

A holy need is a good need, for the love of God *is* a wordless yearning for Him. Such yearning is the only love man can know for his Creator.

Carry this observing, neutral, nonjudgmental but discerning attitude with you throughout life.

Keep your discerning awareness free from the distortions arising from anger and excessive study. Never again use knowledge to puff up your sense of worth, nor use it as a distraction or as entertainment. Instead, let the right kind of knowledge bring you to understanding.

Never struggle to learn anything, nor cram knowledge into your head. Learn by observing . . . and discovering. Scrutinize life for clues. Awakened by knowledge and facts, *realize* the Truth that testifies to those facts, remembering only what is effortless and natural.

Give up emotion and excitement as means of remembering and forgetting. Stop dredging up the past; doing so makes you become emotional and self-righteous. Don't reminisce and become nostalgic, wallowing in silly sentimentality. Don't look at today through the angry memories of yesterday.

Don't coerce people to accept you or your beliefs. You have no responsibility but to express the Truth. By doing so, you provide an example that stands in sharp contrast to evil. Be patient; let people make their own commitments.

Your responsiblity is to be truthful and forthright, to point out error in a timely way. Don't give sympathy; don't spare feelings. You are not responsible for saving anyone. If you feel responsible for failing, it is usually because your ego is playing God again. Saving people is selfish, the work of pride—a way of saving yourself by restoring your ego's self-image.

Be persistent with your admonitions, but *realize* that you have different responsibilities to your family than to strangers.

Correction must always be made without feeling or emotion, without thought of the outcome, *with firmness, kindness and patience.* Persist in the face of rebellion; give correction to your family and friends, even when they want to make up to you and pretend that nothing has happened. Do not assume normal relations with them until they apologize to you.

Never again rise to a dare or a challenge. If you don't know what to do, wait. Be patient. Remain aware and objective to people who intimidate you into making untimely decisions or who use praise and criticism to tempt you away from reason.

Calmly watch these pressure mongers until they lose the power over you that your resentment gave them. Learn this lesson well, and you will see beyond it to understand more subtle ones.

Don't dig into your intellect to get ahead or to answer problems. Be patient and wait until you are shown what to say, what to do and how to express your God-given talents.

Your only goal should be to remain patient and objective. When you are, you will find faith and with it the *realization* of what is right.

Yearn to *realize* what is good and right, prizing this above all else. Everything you do will be *realized*, for you are motivated by the Source of good. If it becomes the extension of what you *realize* is wise, work will become effortless, as if you were not working at all. Never again must work mean everything to you, nor must you throw yourself into work, for that is an ego-building experience.

Slowly but surely become conscious of all emotions and feelings that stimulate your ego to feel high and mighty. *Realize* that pride is the main cause of your anxiety.

Take special note of resentment—observe how it goads your ego into conflict with God.

Slowly shrink from experiences with people and things that stimulate and feed the self-righteous ego beast in you. See how all of your faults stem from your pride receiving comfort through anger and excitement.

No one can teach you the right way to feel. The way is within you, waiting to infill you—but only to the degree that you abandon the reinforcements to your ego life.

Lose the ego animal life; gain the spiritual life.

Become less emotional and *realize* the Kingdom of Heaven.

Move toward innocence by becoming objective to your thoughts. Yearn to *realize* and experience the missing part of your being, Whom you have longed for but have never known except as your conscience.

Realize innocence. Separate from the sin of taking thought, which allows you to escape from the Light of Reality; for as you float along in your imagination, the Light cannot enter, but darkness does.

Only through being aware, by not being ambitious, by being still—separate from your thinking-feeling self—can the Light enter and cause error to leave.

Why spend time worrying, scheming, planning, struggling, thinking—sinking forgetfully into your aroused, evolving, animal imagination and feelings—when you can spend the same time coming to the Light through meditation?

To *realize* honestly that you can do nothing of yourself precludes struggling; and realizing the futility of struggle frees your soul from its futility. Such *realization* alone is sufficient to relax and ready the soul for salvation.

Some day you will grow to *realize* Who salvation is.

Meanwhile, do what you can. Pull free from the morass of your own thinking, and you will *realize* the Light and allow the Light to *realize* His identity and purpose through you.

Faith is trust in higher knowing. It relieves you of

the need to have false confidence in yourself. When you place your faith where it truly belongs—in the Light within—you will no longer need to have faith in people. In the Light, you will *realize* whom to trust and whom not to trust, what to accept and what to reject. Faith, reliance and direction are reserved for the Light, Who gives you private counsel and deep understanding.

By the Light you will acquire that intuitive knowing described by the ancient prophets as faith. Faith expresses another facet of patience—a waiting without anxiety for the good you trust will come.

Be aware of positive affirmations, which are merely another way of lying to yourself. They stimulate the false hope you need in order to fulfill your ambitions and dreams and to cure yourself when your prideful striving makes you sick.

There are not many things to remember. Just be conscious that you must remain aware, close to the Light of understanding. Let It show you things as they really are. Once you experience this conscious awareness, the Light Who makes you aware will remind you whenever you begin to fall into your dream consciousness.

The meditation exercise is the means to this holy end. It teaches you how to maintain an attitude of no attitude; it teaches you endless patience, which enables you to face cruelty, persecution and pretense without flinching or hypocrisy, because you reflect only the goodness for which your soul stands still. When patience holds your observing soul still, evil does not enter.

Be still and know.

Be still. Let your soul be a lens that accepts the imprint of God's Divine Character, which is above sin. Let the Light project His purpose from beyond the stillness of your soul—a soul that is separate from the hell-stream of unconscious thinking.

Remain on this side of your thinking and never again will you be led astray. Never again will you be subject to, or attracted by, negative, morbid, perverse suggestions and directions from any source, nor will you be subject to the delusions or confused conclusions that are inherent in the thinking process.

Pieces of information will be discovered in the Light and fall into place all by themselves.

So there is nothing more for you to learn, just new things to discover. Grow now from *realizing*.

The Keys to the Kingdom are found in the meditation of a seeking soul.

*   *   *   *   *

In the same way that you are discovering how to *give* attention to your thoughts, discover now the magic of *giving* your attention *with love* to those who demand it, especially those who tease and pressure you in order to gain your affection—your family, your children, your wife.

Observe the resentment you feel when they force you to give . . . and let that resentment melt away in the

Light. Learn to observe them with infinite patience, that is, love that knows the proper measure of giving and withholding.

Become aware of resentment growing toward them, especially when they demand and get your attention in the old way. Give and deny with a different timing, with *their* best interests at heart ... not because you feel guilty for resenting them.

Being aware is really the same thing as *giving* your attention with patient, unmoving, Divine Love.

Love enters only through the portal of your objective, aware, patient soul, as you learn how to give your attention voluntarily, not compulsively.

Observe the resentment you feel and the blame you place on those who have aggravated you in order to get your attention and so have caused you to suffer many errors of judgment. Blame is guilt's way of making yourself seem innocent.

Observe the way that guilt arising from resentment obligates you to give even more attention and service to make up for it.

Become aware of distractions and pleasures that involve your attention, preventing you from seeing the fact that you are a slave to what fascinates you.

So become aware. Just learning to be consciously aware of your thoughts, your feelings—everything around you—will unlock you.

From now on, let kindness develop not from the old kind of obligation to relieve the guilt arising from your resentment or because you feel sorry, but because you see a genuine need. If you are helpful, don't feel good about it, and if you are not, don't feel bad about it. Don't swell up with pride or take credit for things well done.

Don't seek to please or fill the emptiness and loneliness of your being, nor soothe your anxiety with words of reassurance or with strange pleasures.

Every time you yield to a wrong impulse, you allow a false identity to grow inside of you, one that develops ever stronger cravings to comfort itself in the wrong way.

Be careful of this thing called love. Don't mistake sick, ego yearning for people and things for real love of life. It isn't; it is false ego need. And it is this weakness for people that can drive them away from you.

If you really love the Truth, you will become aware of your wrong needs and impulses. Resist: Observe your naughty desires objectively, quietly disagreeing with them without resentment or struggle until they lose their power to enslave you.

In moments of trial and temptation, be as calm and as patient as your seeking soul has been granted the power to be. Stand apart from what your body experiences. If it feels weak, if it trembles with fear . . . just watch objectively; don't add resentment. If you do not know what to do, then don't be afraid to realize that you don't know. If nothing comes to you, then nothing is what you are supposed to do. The moment will pass and you will be safe . . . strong in your weakness even as you were weak in your angry, animal strength.

Be wise; never again allow yourself to be entangled in worldly associations, friendships, cares and ambitions. Cultivate a friendly uncomplicated awareness through which all good can come.

From now on, whenever excitement, pleasure, dishonest appeals or feelings begin to capture your attention, the yearning of your soul shall be awakened, for it is no longer compatible with the stuff that pride, glory, dreams are made of. And in that moment you will be given the grace to make the choice that will free you from error.

Remain conscious of the feelings or pressures or intrigues that would normally involve you, no matter how strong their pull. Regardless of how right your feelings seem, you will become conscious of them when they tend to deceive you. And you will become aware when only your motivation is wrong.

From now on, your sole objective is to seek what will become the innocence of awareness, which is the opposite of the guilt that comes from running away.

Your true strength will come through the gradual realization of all your weaknesses.

Don't be too ambitious. When you see what must be done, don't roll up your sleeves. Don't be impetuous about doing good. Timing is essential. It is the evidence of where you are coming from: another facet of patience.

People know when you are a big ego trying to look important and when you are truly concerned about them. For this reason, never plan your speeches or moves, for whenever realization descends to become mere thoughts or words, the healing, the life, the purpose behind those words is lost. Your vain, self-righteous ego will strive and struggle, not realizing the harm it does. If it does see the damage it causes, it will try to make things better by playing God, but it will only fail again.

Rote learning never threatens your ego . . . the way *realizing* does. Don't be consumed with any kind of *learning*—read and listen objectively to these words until they spark an awakening and you see their meaning clearly. Don't try to hold on to your discovery. Don't try to memorize what you realize. Don't try to understand more about what you see. Merely let your realizations sort you out and clarify your thinking and then show you when it is timely to act.

Realization, not knowledge, is the language that the body recognizes and responds to, just as flowers and plants respond to the warm sun, not to words and memories.

If you *realize* anything at all, and you mistakenly think *you* are the source of your own *realizations,* you will be left alone, endlessly challenged by problems.

Just as the eye sees by the reflected light of the sun, so your aware soul perceives by the illumination of the inner, spiritual Light.

Realize. It is enough to *realize* that the Light within is the source of your knowing and making things new.

Panic exists only to the extent that your ego, which is consumed by pride, believes that it exists alone with the problems you see. The terror you feel arises from the awesome responsibility that this kind of evil knowing places upon you; you feel alone, abandoned and help-less. Consumed by pride, you resent these feelings and think you are obligated to change things. But since you can't change anything, you suffer the agony of *realizing* how insignificant you are.

Realizing is totally different from prideful know-ing; it is secretly embarrassing and humbling, but at the same time it releases you from the responsibility to change the world or yourself.

It is the Light Who makes you realize all folly, even the folly of thinking that you know the Truth simply because you have studied words . . . and that you can solve problems with facts.

You can never discover the Life or the Truth you seek by absorbing mere words, for the Truth comes through the *realized* meaning awakened in you by the words you are hearing or reading.

You will find *realized* meaning, and then meaning *realized* and made real, only to the degree that you stand objectively apart from words, so they cannot puff you up with pride, entertain and distract you from the Truth.

True teaching awakens you to the Inner Light, Who is a witness to the facts that pertain to the Truth.

To seek out Truth in words is to avoid Truth in real-ity. Never become excited when you *realize* anything, lest you become proud, lost—caught up in excitement, drawn away from *realizing what an actor you are. Never think you are the Truth because you know words of truth.*

Stored intellectual knowledge of Truth is nothing

but vanity and serves nothing but evil.

The Light in you is the ultimate witness to Truth—even to this statement of truth. The same Light that makes you realize is also the Light that will change things and lead you away from temptation and deliver you from evil.

The Truth is the Light by which you see. And in Its proper season, this Light makes all things clear and plain and removes your fear of making mistakes.

The Light behind your knowing IS NOT a set of rules or concepts that you can use to solve problems. It allows you to see—you simply see, and, therefore, you don't have to figure things out any more.

Don't conceive of God in your mind, for the invisible God cannot manifest Himself through the prejudice of an image.

You will come to know Him only by responding to what you realize is right, rather than to what you remember. Don't be afraid to forget your realizations as well as your accomplishments. You will realize again . . . even more subtle goodness when it is time for you to do so.

If you function from recall, you will be acting from the dead intellect and not from understanding, which is fresh and alive. You will be cut off from the source of life, which springs from the Spirit.

Therefore, never again follow word for word, but with a clear mind realize the Truth behind the words. What comes from thinking builds pride, but what comes out of neutral realizing awareness is holy.

Be patient about time and place; wait for the opportunity and the energy to follow through with your *realizations*. Do not let the thoughts that follow your first glimpse of Truth energize you, for the energy of the ego, which is involved in the scheming, planning intellect, is emotion. *But the power of realization is patience, calmness and love.*

Knowledge reinforces pride, but *realization* humbles. Whenever you *realize* anything, don't verbalize it in order to remember to make things happen. If you do take and hold such thoughts, you can recognize the work of pride, for you will experience emotion, panic. Just *realize*, that's all, and *realize* that you must trust the Source to give you an understanding heart in due season.

Never say to yourself, "I will or I won't . . . I can or I can't." "Can't" is often another way of saying "I won't."

If you have any goal, let it be to *realize* the Truth; allow all other things to fall into their proper place.

Don't will anything—not even to be well. Don't say, "Today I will succeed! I will do this or that!" Any act of willing will cause you to feel conflict and anxiety. You can only will to *realize* the Truth and to live by Its revealing Light, for this is the only exercise of the will from which good comes to pass.

Now, whenever you feel pressured to follow any strong feelings or notions, stand back; become objective. If they still remain after you have observed them and you feel no resistance from your conscience, you will discover the natural, effortless way to follow them.

The very act of becoming objective will dissolve your compulsion to act on unreasonable desires and commands, regardless of how they arise.

Your reaction to worldly authorities has made you emotionally rebellious or obedient to them; you have allowed them to condition your behavior, to come between you and the Real Teacher within.

While their advice may be quite sound, you must now learn to recognize your infantile rebellion against or conformity to the wicked pressure inherent in most worldly authority. Be in the moment . . . function from your own center of *realization* by *giving up resentment* against such authorities, who were themselves victims. Don't be upset and do what they say, or don't be upset and not do as they say.

Act from what you *realize* is right—don't react. If you *realize* that you are required to believe or do something wrong, don't resent it. *Simply don't do it.* You must be patient and learn not to get your energy from resentment, for the way you react is the key to heaven or hell.

You no longer have any obligation or loyalty to what seems right but is not or to what is obviously wrong. *Your only obligation is to what you realize is right.*

4 No i, Know 'I'

Every mistake you have ever made is the result of your lack of awareness. And you are unaware because you do not possess the special knowledge that enables you to see clearly what you are doing. This special knowledge, which I call understanding, is a gift from God, given to us as we abandon our egocentric desire to know ourselves as gods and yearn, instead, to know Him. Understanding literally means to stand under or among, hence to comprehend. We truly know only when we stand under the Source of all knowing.

There are two basic kinds of knowledge: intellectual knowledge and understanding about that knowledge. When you separate intellectual knowledge from understanding, you sow nothing but confusion and error, for you lose not only the realization of the principles informing and giving the knowledge meaning, but also the realization of what is wrong with any knowledge that is not illuminated by understanding.

True knowledge or understanding originates from Our Creator through the faculty of the soul inclined toward God. When knowledge originates from God, it serves His purpose, endowing His instrument with life meaning and identity. Since man is the instrument of God's Divine Plan, he must seek to follow the Divine Will in order to find the meaning of his existence; *he must not seek to play God.*

Understanding is the natural result of realizing. But if you are not content with understanding and leave it behind in order to acquire its essence, you are cut adrift—free to become like God—without even the realization that this is wrong. You are repeating the same sin that Adam committed so long ago in the Garden of Eden when he disobeyed God's warning: "But of the tree of the knowledge of good and evil, thou shalt not eat of it; for in the day that thou eatest thereof thou shalt surely die." When Adam ate of that forbidden fruit, he fell into knowing himself as God. As the serpent predicted to Eve, she and Adam did indeed gain knowledge of good and evil, but at the same time, they lost their spiritual discernment and their mystical way of knowing. Adam forgot understanding and became lost in the acquisition of memories, seeking to make himself feel like God

Just as Adam's desire to know himself as God prevented him from realizing what he was doing, you have not realized the implications of your actions, for you have inherited his pride. Without understanding, which his ego denied by aspiring to be God, Adam could not realize what he was getting into; and, without understanding, we, his progeny, cannot escape his legacy of sorrow, sickness and death.

We use learning to harden our hearts against the

Truth, to build our egos, to make us educated savages, to embalm us for the death that is part and parcel of the egocentric life. After all, how can we remember the Truth when we are immersed in knowledge for the express purpose of forgetting to do what is right so that we can do our own God-damned thing?

Because you lack understanding, which can prevent you from making one tragic blunder after another, your life is a series of mistakes; you are miserable. But how—where—do you find understanding? You cannot glean it from people or from books, although they may lead you to it. *Understanding is mysteriously present as you yearn to know the true purpose of your existence, as you abandon your self-seeking and desire to know yourself as truth.*

Do not confuse understanding with the ceaseless flow of thoughts that pass through your mind. In reality, those thoughts that come to mind in any moment of temptation feed your ego's hunger for glorification. If, in that moment of temptation, your soul descends into the stream of these seductive thoughts and accepts their images and promises of glory, you will lose sight of the truth about the temptation until you are truly ready to understand.

You always lose understanding when you lose yourself in your thoughts, and consequently you make your problems worse rather than better. Worry, by the way, is simply taking to and holding thought about your problems. Instead of stopping to realize the truth, you deny understanding by worrying and striving to work out everything for yourself, and so your prideful ego does not have to admit its wrong. Surely you can see that nothing will change for the better until you see the real cause of your problems, which are always grounded in pride.

Once your soul founders in the thought stream, it is forced into making self-destructive and self-defeating decisions. And you learn to fear making any decisions whatsoever because 1.) you are always worse off and 2.) you become more guilty and confused the more deeply you descend into your imagination.

Soon you begin to see that you are not really in charge of your destiny, that your decision making is the result of some furtive manipulation of your thoughts. You develop various psychological guilts, not the least of which is the guilt you feel for not being in control of your life. To combat this anxiety, you make a conscious struggle to determine your own course—even if it is wrong.

You weigh things carefully before coming to a conclusion, only to change your mind at the last minute, as if you were trying to outfox the error your decison would cause. You may even play games in your head. Coming to a corner, you say such things as "Shall I turn left or right?" On an impulse, you may deviate from your course just to be different, to feel you can determine something for yourself.

You can become so trapped in this egocentric process of decision making that you can interfere with your bodily functions. For example, you want to control your breathing so you try to develop some system of breathing. And, of course, you not only have trouble breathing, but you begin to feel guilty for doing so.

Choosing without Divine Guidance is the prerogative of pride. Such choices always involve your intellect and bring you into conflict with God, for you are trying to be a god operating out of your own self-knowledge; and by doing so, you are committing the cardinal sin—the sin of pride—and perpetuating Adam's legacy of death.

Remember that the soul that makes decisions is guided by the spirit behind knowledge and in this way is always in conflict with itself. Fortunately for us, God does not deny us understanding in this prideful state. But instead of being a gentle source of direction and motivation, as it is to the soul yearning to know the Truth, understanding manifests itself to the proud as the prick of conscience, as a constant source of conflict that calls attention to itself. For this reason, many of us first realize God's existence through the pain and anxiety that comes when our pride resists His speaking through our consciences.

Most of us are so grounded in pride that we disregard understanding when it manifests itself as conscience. Usually it takes pain—the palpable evidence of our error—to awaken us to the fact that we have a problem. But pain only makes us conscious of our problem, not of the underlying reason for its existence. It causes us nothing but misery, unless it triggers the desire to see the truth about ourselves, however traumatic that may be.

To recover the objectivity and poise you had just prior to your moment of failing, you need a shock opposite to the one that drew you down into the darkness of your wrong, upsetting you and blocking your awareness in such a way that you became caught up with your problem.

The countershock, or antitrauma, that you need accompanies your willingness to realize every fault you have. Once you recognize your error, you begin to awaken; and if you welcome this awakening, you will be released from your bondage to sin. First, you will see the truth about what is wrong with you, and as you see this harsh reality, you will re-experience a wordless knowing that parallels the verbal description of your error.

The spirit behind your faults will always assail you through your intellect and try to make you doubt the truth about them, to make you think that they are good. If you yield to this compulsive doubting about your true self, you will only add sin to sin. However, when your error is exposed to you and you accept it as error, you are released from your doubt-inspired confusion and despair.

And once you recover an objective viewpoint, you are given a second opportunity to deal with your faults. You see, the soul, when it assumes its proper function of awareness, inherits the power to deal with past faults, for it stands under God and is, therefore, impervious to evil.

But how do you become aware, recover that objective viewpoint that you lost so long ago? The answer is simple: by reversing the process that occurs when you are tempted. For every time you yield to temptation and choose wrong, you are less aware than you were the moment before your fall; but if your inclination is pure and you shrink from temptation, you become that much more aware, more able to see temptation for what it is, more capable of delivering it a mortal blow. And every time you respond to temptation properly, your state of awareness—or consciousness—will increase, progressing to a higher level.

Unfortunately, most of us block ourselves from awareness because we are so involved with our faults and our own thought processes that we cannot see what is wrong with us or where our errors originate. In our pride we assume that we originate them, and for this reason we grow extremely defensive whenever we are criticized. We identify so completely with the error that we take criticism of it personally; instead of being released from sin, we suffer as it is exposed, and this, in turn, increases its hold over us.

But what should happen when you see or hear the truth about your error for the first time? If you are in an aware, objective state, you receive a shock of understanding that stirs you to recognition. Recognizing your error as error, you experience humiliating consciousness about it, a quiet sorrow that permeates your being.

Most of us are given rebukes that could lead us to realize the truth about ourselves, but we seldom welcome them. You see, if the soul is not too identified and locked into its sin, rebuke can trigger its release from the problem. But if you do not welcome the realizations that can accompany rebuke, the shock of understanding only produces resentment, which further amplifies the guilt you feel because of your wrongdoing. And because it has rejected reality, your soul clings more tenaciously to the sin in order to gain some sense of security. Your problem, as well as your imagination, then becomes a refuge, offering you escape from the hard truth about it. For example, an alcoholic takes refuge in drink to escape from seeing the fact that he is an alcoholic. Have you noticed that you can criticize some people and they will say, "Thanks, I needed that," while others, identifying with the error, take it personally and react defensively? "I'm just a social drinker," "I need a drink for my nerves," "Alcohol is nature's tranquilizer," etc.

Even when you do recognize that you are wrong, you will not get any better as long as your ego resents the Reality that made it aware of its failing. Your resentment then blocks the redeeming Light of Truth and, at the same time, stimulates the development of the faults that give it a sense of security. And you feel not only resentment but also frustration because you do not realize that your hostility is directed toward God. Yes, you resent God, for you want to be God. But what happens when you play God? You are left alone, struggling hopelessly with and finding comfort in your sickness. Do you see now one reason why some people enjoy wallowing in their illnesses?

If we do not welcome the truth, the memory of a given temptation triggers the same emotions we felt when we first yielded to it. Consequently, although the temptation is not actually present, it evokes in us the same reactions and continues to offer us comfort. For example, you can relive love-hate sequences endlessly, relishing the sense of growth and the solace they provide.

Whenever the truth is unwelcome, you will be drawn into the darkness of the problem itself simply by thinking about it, and this, in turn, will strengthen its emotional hold over you. Eventually, your evolving sickness gains a stranglehold over your conscious mind. But your ego continues to exist without being aware of the truth; it can even believe that its degenerating body is rising, evolving to a state of perfection while your soul aspires to innocence.

In your egocentric state of mind, the truth always appears as harsh, cruel, wicked and heartless, while temptation in all of its forms appears as kind, good and pleasant. You see, the evil you have become involved with masquerades in appealing disguises. Perhaps the subtlest is that of the understanding and considerate friend, who comforts you and holds out hopes of glory and adventure to you. His façade actually conceals a devilish concern for your pride, which he puffs up with words of approval and condonement. Because your ego wants to believe this so-called friend so that it can preserve itself, you are blind to the truth, primed to be manipulated and used by him.

Perhaps now you can see why I cannot speak more directly about the Truth. You see, the kind of awareness you need can come to you only as you realize the truth *secretly, intimately, privately*—without words to tell you what Truth is. Speaking about a fault exposes it, just as a cry to a man poised to walk off a cliff warns him of impending danger. The cry is the important thing, and the alerted victim can realize or not realize the course of action he should take to save himself.

It is dangerous to study the Truth in any form; rather, error should be exposed. In this way, you are not robbed of the experience of realizing Truth for yourself. *Realization is a wordless shock—the cause of all meaningful change.* But your soul is not free to understand in the Light as long as it remains locked into lies, to the words and images that seem like truth to you. For this reason, these lies must first be exposed for what they are before you can realize the Truth.

When you use great words of wisdom to get high and help you escape from seeing your faults, you are intellectualizing truth. This practice is very similar to the way in which you deal with a problem in a truthful way. If you allow Truth to illuminate your understanding, you see both your problem and its proper solution, but if you intellectualize truth, you let the consciousness of it blot out the awareness of your problem. You become so mindful of memorized truths that you lose consciousness of your faults, which, of course, continue to exist and cause you trouble. And you develop a need for and a guilty fixation to these intellectualized truths. *You remain locked into your thought world,* and, *therefore, you are still not free from evil.*

Whereas the Light destroys pride, intellectual truths never threaten it, for they lock the conscious mind into delusions of grandeur and prevent the soul from repenting in the Light. Perhaps Satan's meanest trick is his ability to persuade a man that he is a good Christian because he believes in his own goodness and in a god who saves his pride.

Beware of going overboard when you explore the nature of error. *You need only observe it, not analyze it.* Be aware also of the quality of criticism you receive, for wicked people can rebuke you for reasons that appear valid; however, they usually chastise you for being virtuous, or they correct you in such a vicious manner that you rebel against their correction. And you cannot understand why this criticism makes you worse, not better.

You can also overreact to criticism in order to avoid facing the ugly truth about yourself. If you become sensitive to destructive as well as to constructive criticism and let it hurt you, you may eventually come to believe that criticism itself is responsible for your suffering, rather than your wrong reaction to it. For this reason you grow to hate and fear all criticism. *Never be afraid of valid correction.* Learn to realize the difference between constructive and destructive criticism by becoming objective. Realize that words of approval can be as wicked as unjust criticism.

The hostility you feel toward criticism is a primitive and ineffective attempt to keep it from touching you. More often than not, it is also the reason that the evil behind unjust criticism gets inside you.

You see, your initial wrong reaction triggers a series of incorrect responses in you. After you rebel against unjust criticism and do the wrong thing, you are in danger of accepting it in order to relieve the agony of your wrong reaction. First you resent the criticism; then you feel guilty and sorry because resentment is wrong; finally, you either believe the unjust criticism and/or become addicted to its wicked source, foolishly thinking that this will ease its pressure on you. When you are given valid criticism that is offered with a wicked intent, you will fall into this same trap—unless you become objective and separate the criticism from the person doing the criticizing. Many hellfire-and-damnation ministers are quite adept at giving destructive criticism, which literally enslaves people to them.

You should be Self-aware and, therefore, Self-correcting. You are fortunate if you have a true friend, one who loves you enough to hurt you and bring you back to the truth, for the truth about error can awaken you to reality. Such a friend or parent or true lover runs the risk of being hated, even persecuted, when he rebukes you. Criticism with love—correction—is probably the greatest gift one person can give another, but it is the hardest to give because it is the hardest to accept.

Allow this book to be a source of correction to you, but understand that the truth about error can only awaken you to reality. *It is the wordless Truth Who will save you from the evil you see.*

Whenever you think through a problem in the conventional, subjective way—by trying to analyze it and figure out a solution—that thinking process acts in the same way as did the temptation that caused your problem, first by upsetting you and then by conditioning you to be wrong. By thinking about your problems, you tighten their hold over you; you become a part of the very problem you are trying to solve. Unless you yearn to know what is right and to be objective, thinking becomes an escape that triggers irrational and compulsive behavior and a morbid feeling of hopelessness. The belief that thinking about your problems can solve them is the underlying principle behind many forms of compulsion. Only when you realize the truth about your problems, not when you think about them, will these compulsions be eliminated. All you ever accomplish by taking thought is to stir yourself up needlessly; you achieve nothing positive.

When you think about a problem, you elaborate on a fixation, which, in turn, triggers many weird feelings and desires that involve the consciousness more shamefully and deeply. You are caught in an endless cycle: You are aware of your problem because of the pain it causes; the pain causes you to think about your problem; thinking further complicates matters, and you see no hope of solution; the problem continues to cause you pain, and the cycle begins anew.

Remember, all suffering stems from the failure to observe in an objective way. In the objective state, the observer is not a part of the problems he observes, and because of this he is able to *realize* the solution into existence. He can look upon past memories and traumas calmly, without exciting himself.

The memories of your problem and the experiences

that caused it are connected, for memory is the glue that holds the sick personality together and keeps the problem alive and active, serving as an ego refuge. Memories are really just impressions made on your subconscious by the way in which your ego reacts to temptations and pressures. Usually resentment is a key ingredient in these reactions, and, therefore, it colors your memories. As you relive experiences, your conscious mind becomes more deeply locked into the problems you are remembering. Recall without objectivity draws you into your memories, sucking the life out of you. For this reason, people who dwell on their past try desperately to forget their problems when they discover that their constant preoccupation is making them worse. However, their efforts are futile because they are not objective, separate from their thoughts.

As you read about error in this book, surely you can see principles more clearly; yet I have not put Truth into words for you. Perhaps you can now understand what I mean when I say that to know the precise nature of error is to know the Truth about it. When you reach this point, you will discover the state of awareness that you knew just before you abandoned your principles for some form of gain or before you made an excuse and reached for pleasure and other insidious escapes. Jesus tells us that if we know The Truth, The Truth will set us free. This mystical awareness, which we all need, can come to us as the result of a rebuke given with the spirit of love. Such correction enables us to realize our error and to repent of our sins.

I cannot repeat often enough that thinking is not the same as realizing; it is a function of the intellect or, rather, a product of an evil intelligence beyond it. Understanding, however, does not belong in the realm of thought. So when you are corrected, you do not need to think about what has been said. Instead, you should allow yourself to realize the truth *instantly*. Just as memories are impressions of external experiences on your subconscious, so understanding is an impression on your consciousness that comes from an inner world of Truth. Through realization your "compulsions" will be of heavenly origin. The very act of becoming aware of your preoccupation with your thoughts and fantasies is the first stage on your journey toward the Light. To realize the truth you must back away from your error; only then can you view it objectively. As realization dawns on you, you leave words and faults behind. You are apt to exclaim, "Ah, now I understand and see what you mean!", then heave a sigh of relief, yet be unable to explain your experience to anyone.

Observe your weaknesses, then; feel them, but do not wallow in them. Your pride must be humbled so that your physical nature can also undergo a change. You may not have the self-control you wish in these first moments of truth. In the beginning, you may experience a trembling body, and your pride will resent its weakness, but soon that resentment will fade away, and you will remain observing your weakness. Time will pass and, before long, a similar stress experience will arise. You will realize that you are no longer responding as you were before: Now you are above the moment—patient and calm.

You begin to realize failings you were unable to see before, subtle faults you never dreamed you had. As you uncover your failings, you may feel that all you are doing is looking at problems, that you are not getting any better. But if you look carefully, you will notice that your whole life has changed for the better. If you ponder for a moment about your future, you will also realize that you have lost your fear of facing it.

The intellectually oriented soul must first discover that his intellect cannot solve his problems. You see, although he may indeed recognize his problem, his ego tries to make that knowledge effect a cure. For example, such a person knows intellectually that smoking is harmful. So he tries to stop himself from smoking, which, of course, he is unable to do. He then learns that he cannot command the effect he wants and tells himself, "I will wait until the smoking gives me up." But these words merely give him a license to smoke even more. Because the process of the ego-verbalized realization or recognition blocks the path of Light to the aware self, it is a source of terrible confusion until you fully understand what is occurring. All you need is objective realization— nothing more! You must acquire the ability to observe everything with the nonverbal kind of knowing that comes to you through doing the meditation exercises.

Allow me to emphasize this point. Suppose that you are sleepwalking and you awaken to find yourself poised on the edge of a cliff. Shouldn't the realization of danger be sufficient to spur you to take some evasive action? It isn't for some people. They take to thought; their ego steps in and causes panic. Functioning through their intellects, their egos are cut off from realizing, and they cannot deal with the situation calmly and sensibly. Such a person invariably overreacts and loses his balance.

We always evoke anxiety by taking to thought, which precedes an act of will—the evidence of the ego at work. How often have you awakened in the morning, feeling as if you were standing on the edge of a precipice, and, taking thought about the day, experienced fear and panic?

Whenever you mentally verbalize or visualize any move, even if it is the realized move, you will err, for you will be responding to your ego's limited concept of the situation, not to the reality of the moment. For example, recognizing that you are working too hard, you grow resentful and say to yourself, "I am not going to work so hard any more." You simply make an arbitrary, intellectual decision without realizing what is driving you, and since your decision is not grounded in understanding, you experience conflict.

But why do you feel anxious? Because your problem remains the same, and when you give up working, you discover the guilt you were escaping from in your work. In addition, you feel guilty because you were working in order to escape from your problems. To deal with the resulting anxiety and the pain it causes, you swing from one extreme to the other, bypassing the center of understanding. First you feel guilty for not working, deciding that your decision not to work so hard was wrong; then you determine that you should go back to work and work harder than ever. Because this decision is not right either, your anxiety level increases still more. Eventually, you become afraid to make any decision: You decide not to decide.

If you were in your center of understanding, you would realize what your basic problem is: In your pride, you want to impose *your will* on your life, rather than wait for God to show you His. Willing is an act of ego—even willing not to will. Once you realize this principle, your problems will dissolve and your anxieties vanish.

Give up willing things to happen; go through life without verbalizing and naming everything. Discover how to observe a beautiful bird without saying to yourself, "This is a beautiful bird." Learn to look at a flower without saying, "That is a flower." When you reduce something to a verbal or visual image, you block yourself from seeing the reality beyond the image. Unfortunately, most of us reduce not only things, but also people and events to images frozen in our memory. Suppose that you are angry at your child; in your anger you form a memory of his wrong. The next day you view him not as he is in the moment, but through yesterday's memory. He reacts to your prejudice, becoming more of a problem than he was yesterday; and you become upset again.

But why is the labeling and naming of everything you see wrong? It is the work of your ego, functioning through your intellect, a means of making you appear greater in your own eyes. You label everything in order to grasp and remember it. For example, you affirm that a flower is a flower, and this knowledge serves your pride, helping you to think of yourself as a knowing god; you then begin to think that because you exist, the flower exists.

It is surprising how many people secretly believe that if they did not exist nothing would exist, that everything exists because of them. The more they know or learn about the existence of things, the more they know that they exist, for this knowledge reassures the ego that it does indeed know and that because it knows, it is all-knowing. Of course, in our egos' separation from God, we are ceasing to exist, and our souls, through which realization should enter, are desolate. To escape from this wretched state of ignorance we fill ourselves with compensatory knowledge, memories and impressions, hoping they will make us feel that we exist—in glory.

If we were not so egotistical, we would see that we are duplicating, in a pathetic way, the Supreme Ego of the universe, trying to be the Source of knowing rather than being content to realize by It. We were created to realize life by realizing God. This level of realization places the ego in a state of awe and wonder, for realization is tantamount to worship. In return for that worship, God gives man His joy and approval, which is true eternal life, and shows him the correct way to respond to people and things. He also shares with us the intimate knowledge of His relationship with people and nature.

However, if you play god by affirming the existence of something—a flower, for example—you reinforce your egocentric state; you think of you, the observer, as the creator of that flower. You lose the awareness, the awe of knowing Him Who is greater than you. But with objective, observing awareness, you realize a greater glory than your own, and your observing is not dead but alive, profound and endless. You know that the flower exists because a Creator exists Who reveals to you His creation, the evidence of His creative genius; consequently, you lose all your delusions of grandeur and the guilt that accompanied them. The enlightened observer realizes that he knows things not because he is the knower of the known, but because he beholds them in the Light of the Supreme Ego of the Universe.

Remember the practical application of this principle, and begin to see your family in a different light. In your wrong way of viewing your wife and children, your ego affirms a judgment, and the memory of it then colors your next observation about them, reinforcing your previous judgment. You are always seeing today with the judgments of yesterday; and your family is always reacting to your judgment of them and reinforcing the role you play as god-judge.

When you observe your family in this wicked way, it has little chance to change for the better; if a change does occur, you don't see it, but at the same time you feel threatened by it. Your first vicious judgment continues to color the way in which you view them. Undoubtedly, they were out of order on the occasion that tempted you to make that initial judgment. But so were you; moreover, your verbal judgments not only feed your pride, reminding you that you are a god, but they also aggravate the problem so that it continually confirms your original judgment about it. "I knew he would do that again—what a brat!" "I don't expect much from her—I know she'll let me down." "He's always been the rotten apple in the family—I'm sure he did steal the candy, but what can I do?"

Man is the most malleable and contemptible creature in nature. He both passes judgment to make himself feel like a god and serves another wicked ego's need to see itself as god. Judgment is a part of the intellectual process, of affirming that things are because you say so. When someone passes judgment on you, you are changed in a negative way, for you continue to provide your judge with the reinforcements that make him feel right; and these, in turn, give him the excitement he needs in order to forget the guilt he feels for judging you. You are contributing to the growth of error in him just as surely as he is encouraging evil in you.

In the same way that you can become addicted to judging in order to forget the guilt of doing so, you can also become addicted to observing nature in order to escape the growing guilt you feel for "observing" nature in such a way that you think of yourself as the god of nature. As you behold nature in the subjective way, involving yourself with it, you are reminded that you, the observer, are a god. Eventually, you immerse yourself so completely in it that you truly believe that you are its god.

You can become so guilt ridden from observing

people in this subjective, judgmental way that you identify with them, often thinking that you are they. Have you ever noticed how you react to people you hate? You feel so guilty for hating them that they seem more innocent than you, so you cope with your guilt by "forgiving" them and identifying with the innocence you have attributed to them. You see, you suffer such excruciating agony as the god-observer that you become the observed person, place or thing in order to share its relative innocence and gain some relief. If you do not fuse your identity with whatever you hate or use to give you a high, you have no alternative but to face the ugly truth about yourself.

Give up being a god-judge! Allow yourself to realize, to understand rather than to stand over a situation. Realize that when your intellect feeds your ego the idea that it is all-knowing, you are left alone, responsible for your problems as you have always been, reacting endlessly and hopelessly to them.

Just as any father who loves his son corrects him, your heavenly Father will correct you and bring you back to Him—if you will let Him. Allow Him to show you *through realization* the truth about yourself and the Truth beyond. For a short while, these realizations will be painful to you, but soon you will discover the infinite joy of His love, the quiet happiness He gives you.

Any realization of failing on your part indicates the presence of God chastising you. You will also become aware of a previously unrecognized conflict with Him. Your hidden resentments toward God prevent progressive realizations and, ultimately, salvation; however, once you realize that they exist, they will disappear.

Let your pride suffer the humiliation that accompanies giving up the rote knowledge that made you high in the past; exchange this low kind of knowing for the higher, life-giving knowing that makes you truly humble. Don't be surprised if your memory becomes feeble, for realization has nothing to do with memorized knowledge. Learning in a mechanical way will seem pointless to you. Why? Because God does not want you to learn in a way that is not conducive to realizing Him; He wants you to live by faith, not be facts.

For example, your ego may hold on to the misguided notion that drinking is a disease—an ailment mysteriously visited upon you—and it uses this idea to avoid seeing the real reason for your problem. Drinking is obviously a fault, but as long as you let the idea that drinking is a problem envelop and protect your ego, you are using your knowledge of a lesser truth to avoid seeing the greater truth. It is a lesser truth to say that germs cause disease; the greater truth is that your degenerative state provides the environment in which they can thrive. You have learned to think of such things as migraine, ulcers, cancer, etc. as problems that need curing. But the cure can become a distraction that compounds your troubles as well as your anxieties.

Your pathetic efforts to deal with your problem create even bigger troubles, which you diagnose as causes. Your knowledge about your illness becomes greater and greater as do your efforts to cure it; you try the most sophisticated and complex means available, but to little avail. In the end, you are left alone, struggling hopelessly with your problem. The knowledge you thought would cure you has satisfied your ego, but done nothing to solve your problem.

You will not recover until you become aware of things as they really are and lead a meaningful life, one that testifies to your awareness of Truth. If you had lived in the Light, you would have the kind of awareness needed to meet pressure in the right way, and you would not know your present suffering as you do now—only by name. You would have no big, insoluble problems, for they would have been resolved long ago, while they were still small. You should be looking for the state of consciousness that does not allow problems to begin—an awareness that has no need to feel shame, nor to escape into and struggle in your intellect against impossible odds.

What do you really want? Do you want to be aware of Truth, or do you wish to go on being aware of yourself as truth? The more aware of Truth you become, the more the creative energy of the Light will focus on your problems and resolve them—and before your eyes will be the testimony that affirms that God exists as God for you to marvel and wonder about. And it is through this marveling and wondering that you will have eternal life.

If you sincerely desire to be aware of the Truth, you must first gain release from your enslavement to thought. The object of the meditation discussed in this book is to lift you out of the thought-feeling realm into the realm of realization, where your thoughts and feelings lose their hold over you as you are given understanding. And with understanding comes the grace enabling you to translate it into word and deed.

As long as you are content with being a mere collector of knowledge, you will not discover this realm of realization, for rote knowledge without understanding changes everything in a pejorative way, pulling you into your intellect, away from the Truth. You see, you can find the Truth in one of two ways: through understanding or by the pain of experience. However, if you rely on experience, you may never learn the reason for your suffering. You will never discover the Truth in your intellect, for it tries to rationalize and analyze everything; it looks into its storehouse of acquired facts for answers. But facts are merely facts, meaningless unless illuminated by understanding.

Understanding is similar to knowledge in that it flows from a wellspring of information, but the source is not external; it is implanted directly in the objective consciousness. Whereas your pride motivates you to gain and use knowledge in order to serve what *appears* to be its own egotistical purposes, understanding gives you the energy to move and have your being in such a way that everything you do testifies to the Truth. Because understanding awakens people instead of simply teaching them facts, it allows people to follow what they themselves come to realize.

It is imperative that you function from what you realize—that you know that you are known, that you know that you do not originate knowing, that you realize the origin of your knowing.

The proud person cannot understand because he does not want to, and because he cannot see, he does not realize that confounding thoughts that originate *through* him do not come *from* him directly. Because of this shortsighted viewpoint, the prideful ego has an endless variety of problems. His basic problem is that he feels too responsible for everyone and everything. In extreme cases, this burden may become so great that he becomes completely insensitive—even to his proper responsibilities. The very nature of pride is to play God, and, as God alone in the universe, the prideful person is *forced* to accept the guilt for everything that goes wrong, although he may rebel against this and try to reject his guilt by projecting it elsewhere.

By taking the responsibility of sin upon ourselves, we are really simulating God's forgiveness of our sins. And by playing God, we compound our sin of pride; we become more guilty instead of more innocent. Whatever you do to find innocence causes great guilt because you are really holding on to the pseudoinnocence of your pride.

You will find true rest and innocence only in desiring to realize God; you will never find it if you continue to know yourself as God. You can be saved only by allowing God to take the responsibility for your salvation upon Himself, for in Him there is no sin; in Him our sin ceases to exist. God has a plan to remove sin and pride from the world, and you will realize what it is as your yearning to know God leads you to become objective.

God offers salvation to all of us, asking only that we repent. When you repent, you literally turn away from sin toward God, and you regret your wrongdoing: that is, you acknowledge your errors with sincere remorse. You place your trust in God instead of in yourself, and He renews you; you become a new man. Repentance occurs in two stages: First, you realize that *you* have been trying to resolve the problem of your guilt; second, you regret your sin of pride, which is the sin of sins, the one from which all others flow.

Probably you believe that you created and are responsible for your pride-sin nature. In reality, you have inherited it; you do not choose to sin—*you are compelled to do so.* Because you think that you do have the power to choose, you attempt to remedy your errors by indulging in self-incrimination. By heaping blame and accusations upon yourself, you believe that you can purge yourself of your faults, and to hasten your purgation you add a large dose of sadness. But don't you see that any effort on your part to make yourself innocent is an act of pride, which only makes you more guilty and morbid?

Realize this truth. Give up your efforts to save yourself, to make things right; and stop blaming and damning yourself and others. Once you see the futility of struggling and cease trying, you will relax; and as you relax, the sin of trying to remove sin falls away. You are still left with your sin, but you no longer believe that you are responsible for it, and you realize that you have sinned because of the compulsive nature of your pride toward sin. You were born a slave to sin, and your nature has come down to you through your parents from Adam, who fell from grace because he yielded to his pride, disobeying God in order to be Him.

Now as you realize why you are helpless, why you cannot save yourself, the responsibility for what you have done wrong—indeed, for what you may be doing wrong this very moment—passes to God, Who takes your sins upon Himself. Suddenly you feel released, for it has become His responsibility to save you, and when your salvation is God's responsibility, not yours, lo and behold! Not only does the guilt of your sin pass from you, but so does the sin. Search the Scriptures to more fully comprehend this mystery, which is fulfilled directly in you when you seek.

Playing the role of God causes you many awesome and painful consequences, which I hope bring you to realize the nature of your ego's striving. You see, because you have never been able to realize, you were not able to realize the nature of your pride, nor could you realize its destiny or the terrible price you pay for being its slave.

You must also realize that your desire to know yourself as God has been the primary reason for your intellect's restless acquisition of knowledge. I am not implying that you ought to give up intellectual knowledge or memories, but I am saying that you should not use them to serve your pride. Knowledge and information should awaken you to realization, triggering an "Aha!" experience in you; and when they do, they will cease to be important to you, for you understand the principles behind them. Your intellect has just so much capacity to store knowledge, and when that is filled, it bogs down, backs up or breaks down. Memories—of facts, experiences, people, etc.—yield meaning and fulfillment only when they are illuminated by understanding.

By knowledge I mean names and know-how. Certain knowledge is useful because it brings you to understanding, but once you have gained understanding you can forget it because understanding is the basis for its existence.

You see, the ego sets itself apart from understanding in order to remain proud. It compensates for its ignorance of God and, consequently, its awareness of its desolate state by acquiring knowledge about Truth; it simply amasses words and concepts and tries to live by them. Because it has learned in a mechanical way, it is unable to be objective. And for this reason, the intellectual ego deceives itself that it also understands, mistaking words or concepts for the Truth behind them. When the ego, in its pride, tries to apply this bogus understanding to problems, especially to personal ones, its efforts backfire, causing even bigger problems and anxieties.

Although the egotistical person claims he wants to solve his problems, he would be lost without them, for he thrives on them. Be honest with yourself for a moment. When confronted by a problem, aren't you secretly delighted to be excited? Don't you accept the challenge it presents in order to prove your great knowing to yourself and others? When you respond to such a challenge, you are really giving in to the temptation to be proud, and this, in turn, *causes* a failing to occur in you so that you are in trouble even if you should prevail over the situation.

And your ego enjoys wallowing in its own failing. Perhaps you have noticed how active your mind is when you run a high fever and how you tend to hallucinate or daydream the higher the fever becomes. Your fever is, of course, physical evidence of some sort of failure on your part. In a similar way, people with bad habits can never see what is wrong with them, because they are so involved and caught up with their problems.

The failing of the soul always activates a degenerative process, which catches the soul in a spiralling downdraft. And the soul becomes subject to the metabolic processes of its own failing. When a man dies, you can see him slipping helplessly away into the mire of his degenerate, feeling, thinking self. Some people are dead—victims of this hideous process—long before they are pronounced clinically dead.

And what sets this process in motion? The ego. In its desperation to know itself as God, it avoids understanding by merging with the images that multiply out of its own degeneration. The more we react to our problems, the more the thinking process develops; and the more we *think, the more we think we are*. Whether we amass knowledge, whether we run a fever or whether we worry, we are, in effect, finding more knowing and, in knowing, more pride and, in more pride, more failing and, in more failing, more knowing. We are trapped in a cycle of degeneration that can end only in death.

Now do you see why it is imperative that you stop hiding in your mind—in its swarm of ideas, facts, fantasies and memories? Stop hiding so that you can realize a new way to think and to know. Abandon your ego supports and your prideful way of knowing; allow yourself to be given the gift of understanding.

Understanding requires that you know God as God and yourself as nothing; and when you do, something will come through that nothingness, just as you came to "nothing" through being a something. "And whosoever shall exalt himself shall be abased; and he that shall humble himself shall be exalted."

5 Understanding the Word Made Flesh

The title of this chapter is not a metaphor—it is meant literally. Understanding is knowledge made live, and it is only in this living form that it is ultimately useful to man. Knowledge that is separated from the awareness of its source is dead; and, far from being desirable, it is a source of great harm, in that it offers a counterfeit of the reality man was created to seek.

Out of the original stillness came the hurricane of all material creation. Out of the Timeless Center came the movement—the primal energy—of time, and out of time came light and matter, and the mass of matter lagging in the time stream became space for matter and created things to move in time. The universe is the architecture of God's creative genius, and man is God's personalized expression of Himself: the visible, material reflection of His invisible, spiritual self. The material body of man, the living counterpart of the soul created in God's image, was assembled by the creative gathering power of the still soul. Even as the heavens and the earth were spoken into creation, generated from His eternal stillness, so our Creator breathed life—His Divine Identity—through the still soul child of Himself.

This soul of man belongs *in* but does not rightfully belong *to* this earthly realm; it belongs to the Creator of all realms. The body was formed around the soul like metal filings around a magnet, out of the dust elements of the earth; and as the dust gathers in the rays from the sun—a spectacle both material and ephemeral—so man is part heaven and part earth. Creation was to have been the setting for the jewel wherein the expressed purpose of creation was to live and venture through time and space, being eternally renewed on an endless adventure of discovery in the universe, living endlessly as God lives eternally. The purpose of the soul's adventure would have been to observe and so to learn of God, to witness and marvel at the immensity of God's creative genius, to be *forever mindful* of His grandeur and His greatness and by that mindfulness and worship to receive His sustaining approval—everlasting life—for an endless voyage of perfection through discovery, eternally renewed and awakened in the soul through the awareness of the Creator.

Then something occurred that disturbed the stillness of man's soul and altered its relationship with God; and so this first soul, torn away from its original ground of being through pride, sank into the changed substance of its created physical self and became lost in space with the sands of time flowing restlessly through the gaping breach of its own disobedience. The evidence of this failing, which all mankind has subsequently inherited, is the restlessness we feel in our souls to this very day.

We are told in Genesis that man's first disobedience concerned his ambition to know of good and evil, and that account is not myth but truth, for the mere knowledge of good and evil serves only one purpose: It is the basis of judgment—a prerogative of God. Such knowledge is an empty and useless thing to a humble soul obedient to the guidance of God's will; therefore, to know God—to re-establish that lost relationship—the soul must abandon its ambition to retain and expand its knowledge of good and evil; it must become still and separate from its fallen, earthy nature. As children of disobedience we must now yearn to know God as much as the first man yearned to know *himself as God*, or else we cannot discover what we must know to live forever; and this special knowledge—understanding—comes through stillness, for stillness is the place where understanding is. Where there is no knowledge there is knowing.

Children of disobedience come into existence proud, mortal and finite. But as children of obedience you are remolded through repentance from within to fit the original pattern. And this miracle occurs by means of the resolving power of the Light, through the lens of the still, obedient, objective soul: humble, immortal and infinite.

But what assurance do we have, other than external

evidence such as Scripture, that we can be reconciled and restored to the original state? Awareness. Our assurance is the simple fact that we are made aware that we exist in an imperfect way. How can you be truly aware of the cause of your imperfection and remain imperfect? You cannot! But remaining unaware of a faulty existence, a soul cannot mend its way; and pride proceeds from birth to death, unwilling to be aware of its original failing. Its only "awareness" is of its own glory and is based on false knowledge; and false knowledge is ignorance. In the New Testament the term for such ignorance is the Greek word *agnosia* (the origin of our English word,"agnostic"). It is the negative of *gnosis,* which means seeking to know spiritual truth in the sense of an acquaintanceship with the source of that truth. It is this special kind of knowing—understanding—that is the very center of everything I am trying to say to you in this book. LIVING KNOWLEDGE, WHICH IS UNDERSTANDING, IS BEING AWARE NOT ONLY OF THE WORD AND THE MEANING OF THE WORD BUT ALSO OF THE PROCESS THAT REVEALS THAT MEANING AND THUS OF THE VERY SPIRIT ITSELF. SUCH AWARENESS IS TRUE UNDERSTANDING: THE WORD MADE FLESH IN YOU.

You cannot experience this awareness and continue to believe in your own glory: An ego-centered life is no longer possible. For this reason the proud man seeks to escape true understanding and to clothe himself with false knowledge in which he can find the security he needs to continue to exist in pride's way. Through this dead knowledge he seeks to elude the Light that would reveal his error. And so the ego remains in a state of perpetual disobedience sustained by its belief in false knowledge. Moving away from the Light, the blind, ambitious egocentric exists in the realm of the intellect where knowledge becomes the thing believed, for there is no Light to reveal either the lie or its deceitful source. The lie can exist only in the realm of ideas; it cannot withstand understanding.

Merely to observe any vain idea is to destroy its force and effect. You cannot possibly preserve a false idea while observing it for what it is. But, fearful of the Light, you can move away from it toward the realm of the idea itself and lose yourself there in fantasy, much as you can become lost in an absorbing screenplay.

Thus do vain men live in a world of make-believe, where the ego-appealing lie, the cherished belief, is reality, and where the truth is but a dream.

But as Light shines once again upon any subject, It awakens you to knowledge—understanding—an awareness of the Light that created it. Your memories will, therefore, cease to consist of ordinary knowledge such as thoughts of pictures, sounds and those experiences that are produced by the shock of trauma. Instead, you will have something of God, Who inspires an understanding of Himself through the objects of His creation. The God who originally created the object created it not only for its utility, but also to testify to His existence in the soul of the observer.

To appreciate art we must have in us something of

the artist, although that something is never as great as the artist himself. The artist continues to create for us, and we continue to appreciate his work; and when we develop an appreciation for art we can also develop an identification with the artist. Thus does our loving Lord of all science, art and craft lead us on our way to infinite perfection through infinite appreciation of Him by revealing Himself through the concealed thing. For us, perfection lies in our infinite awe of our perfect Creator.

It is, therefore, in our growing awareness of created things that we discover infinite knowledge of Him; His marvelous works inspire in us something of His eternal identity through which we experience eternal life. *Here then is the fruit of the tree of life: intimate knowledge of God.* It is as different from the fruit of the tree of knowledge of good and evil as night is from day, for that *knowledge* consists in the false belief that we are or can become gods by acquiring intellectual knowledge—dry concepts and categories. Such knowledge, which makes you proud and self-righteous, is not only the point of separation, disobedience and judgment; it is something deeper still, for it is from knowledge without understanding that all the judgments of pride are made. A judging soul is always in conflict, for man was created to be guided by his Creator, not to choose his own path, based on the faulty judgments of pride.

To acquire knowledge, then, out of the mistaken belief that through it we can frame the judgments necessary to make the decisions that will resolve our problems, is a malignant error. Such knowledge so acquired is dead. It may be sufficient to repair a clock, but it can hardly satisfy the needs of a living being. Only understanding—living knowledge—is equal to such a task. Understanding comes only when you begin to abandon the misguided belief in the efficacy of knowledge, the faith that, through knowledge, you can be saved. Surely, you have discovered that the more you worry, scheme and plan to solve problems, the more you make matters worse, and that the more you strive for more knowledge, the less clear the solution seems to be. But abandon knowledge as your savior, and behold! Like thunder and lightning flashing across the sky of your mind, comes living knowledge to fashion a new race of men full of common sense and wisdom—men like Jesus, who was the first of this new race.

Understanding is often written about in books, yet it cannot be gleaned from books in a way that is conducive to life. For that reason, this book is not meant to be a book of learning or wisdom. Its primary function is to admonish your way of life and hopefully to lead you to its rejection. It is meant to serve as a guide to show you how to put down your ego life supports and to pick up your true life. There is no need to try to teach you specific fragments of knowledge; the new life is there, *waiting to unfold* as you put down those ego crutches. Under no circumstances should you endeavor to learn or devour the contents of this book. It is written by way of another's understanding, and so it is second hand to you and, therefore, dead as far as you are concerned. It is, however, indirect testimony that first-hand knowledge does exist. These words should serve only as a catalyst to awaken you from your dream world so that you can move and have your being from true knowing rather than from mere rote knowledge. The letter of the law is needed only because you have lost the Spirit of the law, but the letter cannot save you—it can only lead you back to the Spirit, which makes the letter unnecessary.

The more aware you become, the more awareness inherently understands how to resolve problems: You know intuitively what to say, do, give up, dissociate from. And you find that shrinking from what is wrong is the same as being obedient to what is right. You find that through awareness you are drawn ever closer to God. The proud ego looks down into his own intellect for answers, but the true seeker abandons the intellectual process and is left with a dullness, a questioning and a yearning void that God answers with the very essence of understanding.

The egocentric man is afraid of the Light. He prefers the dark theatre of his own brain in which there lurk the kind of lies that help him to save face. He prides himself on his own mental prowess and cunning. He is forced to work harder and harder in order to clean up his own mess; but he calls staying busy "progress" because he cannot (will not) see that it is not progress. To the degree that you are willing to abandon your faith in knowledge, pride ceases to be and things are then seen in a clear light of Truth. Problems are resolved as if by magic. Here in this objective state, in the full awareness of God through His Son, there are no decisions to make, for there is no need. The first and only decision your soul can make is whether to seek the Truth, the highest knowledge in the universe, the *logos* from whom sprang all things. The *logos*, who created man to be aware that the Word is with God and the Word is God, created him to appreciate the Godhead infinitely through his witness to all the marvels of His creation. To attempt to achieve any other objective than seeking first the will of God is contrary to the divine intention, and therefore it causes guilt, whether you succeed or fail in your endeavors.

But pride offers a counterfeit salvation. The ego shields itself from guilt with the fabric of excuses, and such a mind becomes less and less conscious of its own guilt and more subject to temptation each time it errs in its judgment. And because you always lose awareness of the truth of what you have done each time you fail, the process tends to repeat itself until you finally make *the* fatal mistake and are caught forever in the "hunter's trap" of the evil one, who has been stalking you stealthily from the day you were born.

The process is beguiling in its simplicity. The moment you err, your soul tends to become aware of its failure, and you experience this awareness as self-consciousness. The immediate effect is a feeling of inferiority, guilt and resentment that leads to a rejection of being aware. The impulse of pride is to escape the humiliating criteria; and so, gradually, you lose awareness, escaping into a feeling-based thought world. Your next judgment is then based on this reduced state of consciousness, and your error is greater. The escape process is repeated to the very end. Inexorably you lose sight of all the delicate wisdom and the principles by which internal problems can be resolved and external problems prevented: the understanding by which comes the true health, wealth and success.

Your mind has a kind of genetic intelligence of its own, which, if it is not directed properly, will run away with itself, producing problems instead of solutions. By its very nature it requires guidance, and if you do not direct it and supply it with correct information, someone or something else will; and this misdirection is another cause of your confusion. Although your brain has a special ability to gather information through the senses and to compute answers to certain types of mechanical problems, it cannot compute a cure for illness.

Your conscious mind is able to perceive that, for example, by standing out in the freezing rain you can contract pneumonia. When the soul apprehends this fact, it activates your mind to bring your body in from the cold. This is a very basic example of how understanding or, simply, applied rote knowledge can change your relationship with your environment, either to prevent or to cure a simple illness. Provided that there are no other complications, once the cause-effect relationship has been changed, the genetic intelligence of your body can go to work solving the rest of the problem for you. Healing, you see, has not so much to do with the action of the will or intellect; it is a natural function of the body. Just how the body performs this miracle is not terribly important right now; what *is* important is that you see some kind of order. Recovery from illness is effortless and automatic once the body's destructive relationship with the environment has been altered. Your future well-being will be measured in terms of how well you can understand your improper relationship with life, nature, friends, enemies, food, sex, etc. A recent scientific experiment may help to illustrate this point.

A fatal dose of poison was administered to a cat, and, of course, it died; but a second cat given the same dose was immediately placed in a sleep state, and it recovered. I understand that this experiment was repeated several times with exactly the same results. If this is true, there is a moral to be learned from those poor cats.

But do we really have to look at the cat experiment to see the truth of this principle in our own lives: that the mind, in its worry, tends to interfere with the genetic intelligence of the body? Now, I am not speaking about miracle cures, although I believe them to be possible, but a gut-level, plain, God-given common-sense truth, which, when applied, seems like a miracle cure. It is surprising just how many people do not have enough sense to come in out of the rain!

If you do not understand that the natural state of the body is one of health and that illness is produced by your interference with this natural state, you will continue to become sick, and probably you will try to worry yourself well. Faith in this remedy or that often reduces the worry and allows for a recovery, and people believe that the treatment made them well; therefore, they go right back to living the kind of life that made them sick in the first place. Most courses of treatment are designed primarily to placate worry, and for that reason, a great many people recover; but there is a limit to your body's ability to cope with standing in the freezing rain, as it were.

To carry the analogy one step further, let us suppose that the problem confronting you is as simple as standing in the rain, and suppose also that you could in your own lifetime become tough enough to compensate as animals do—perhaps develop blubber or a mat of thick, woolly hair all over your body. The undignified result of this sort of thing would be that you would have become less of a human being by becoming more of an animal; certainly you would be far less like the image of God that you are supposed to emulate. It follows, therefore, that any physical compensation or adaptation has something to do with our lack of understanding.

You become sick because your ego-based relationship with your environment is wrong. Stand back, then, and observe what your relationships are. Alter your body's ecology, and your body recovers naturally. The only miracle involved here is the miracle of understanding.

A proud person cannot allow himself to understand and still remain proud. But when your ego is too obstinate to admit that it is wrong, then the tendency is to avoid understanding so that you may also avoid shame and guilt, and the fruit of this evasive action is worry, which will ultimately bring you to an even greater sickness. Should you be "cured" by some means that leaves your faulty relationships unchanged, you would be heading toward an even more serious problem that one day *nothing* would be able to cure. At that point the worry will also become incurable, and, like the cat in my previous illustration, the worry itself will kill you more efficiently than the disease.

There are certain religions that teach you how not to worry; they show you how to keep your mind on pleasant, lofty concepts so that it is endlessly distracted and thus unable to dwell negatively and destructively on its problems. This approach, too, can work for a season, but such fools still do not have enough sense to come in out of the rain. By distracting the mind with affirmations, chants, mantras and the like, they are not likely to find the common sense they need to alter their relationships. Such pious, high-minded fools often die from the most vicious, malignant, degenerative diseases, because they do not know how to be conscious of their problems without worrying about them and making themselves worse. So they die, desperately denying that their illnesses exist. It is always so: The ambitious, unenlightened mind is challenged to solve the problems that come into existence because of its unawareness, and then it literally worries itself to death, or, if it does not worry as a means of dealing with problems, it fails to give them the healthy attention they need.

The kind of living knowledge that is valid in human experience must spring from the understanding heart. Understanding may bring with it knowledge, but understanding cannot be synthesized from knowledge.

You can have knowledge, you can deeply understand that knowledge, you can collate knowledge and put it to work based on understanding that springs again from common sense. Look at this example: One plus one equals two. Now you can *see* ahead that one plus two equals three. Knowledge alone does not know what to do with itself. *It is only when you apprehend the process that makes you aware of knowing that knowledge becomes valuable.* Knowledge should enter the mind by way of understanding through the lens of the soul. It is not good enough for me to tell you that you should come in out of the rain; you really must see this for yourself. As a matter of fact, if you fail to see it, the faculty of understanding tends to atrophy so that you will become dependent on others to tell you what you should know and do. The trouble with this approach, of course, is that these people are just as lost as you are, and, without understanding, you will not know what or whom to believe. There is a limit to the value of external direction. Rote knowledge can cause rebellion against rote living, for it is always a guilt-producing compensation for not having understanding, and the answers that such knowledge brings can only substitute for the truth of understanding. A man dies from misguided faith, faulty relationships and debilitating dependency on people and things. We were designed to ultimately have such a relationship with God, Who gives understanding to him who seeks, not useless information. We must learn to depend on the leading of the Divine Knowing revealed to us in our moment of need, just as we have done in the past with books and people whom we believed knowledgeable.

When a man has solved a problem with understanding, he also becomes aware that if he had more understanding he could have met that moment better than he did; this is because the truth leads to the Light, and more Light is ahead, for when you give up worry through true faith, then you receive answers. Being closer to reality through that exercise, you then see by disturbing hindsight how much better it could have been done, This kind of hindsight then operates as the next foresight, and true hope and faith progress on their journey to the Light. The ego, deceived by knowledge, experiences a similar but deceptive hope and growth process. After an ego solution it is also easy to see how much better things could be done, simply because the right answer was mishandled, or else a new problem has been produced, which requires new knowledge to solve it. And so the proud ego moves on, restlessly following the ever increasing spinning of his thoughts, seeking vacations and distractions in the mistaken belief that if he could only relax and slow his spinning thoughts, he would have the knowledge of how to deal with them and the problems they represent.

The true solution for this dilemma is found in meditation, which is not a slowing down of thought but rather a slowing down of the soul, which allows it to draw apart from the thoughts in the mind so that it can observe the thought process. The soul that is carried along in the stream of aspirations and illusions that arise in our intellect under the pressures of time and space is torn loose from its foundation of being. Such a soul is a helpless prisoner of his body in the material universe, a stranger lost to a strange, harsh dimension that really should be subject to him.

Thoughts and dreams run on the energy of emotional power. You react, you feel yourself think, and then you act out of emotion-powered thought. The surge of power you feel when the "thought pod" ripens and bursts appears to be originating from thoughts that also seem to be originating within you. The behavior patterns that emerge from reacting, feeling, thinking and acting are earthy and base, for this cycle bypasses and effectively precludes reason. Meditation neutralizes the rush of emotion to the head and prevents further reaction to pressure and the natural stresses we encounter as we fall to temptation. When you remain unruffled and poised, a certain dignity enters. Sufficient objectivity and power is provided to prevent an emotional reaction, thus staving off yet another agonizing turn of the dehumanizing cycle of nature. Even though you do not react to the pressure, however, the problem confronting you still remains. Your soul, having used patience as a shield, has also stopped worry dead in its tracks. Without reaction and emotion the animal computer ceases to function in a compensatory way, leaving you with a need. *Such is the nature of concern as opposed to worry.*

Concern evolves out of patience, even as worry comes from impatience. From concern, meaningful spiritual answers arise, just as the formula for failure emerges from worry. Thus, the seeking soul becomes objective; it gains patience and self-control; it does not react, and so it does not need to worry. It is aware of problems, and it is full of genuine concern, which is compassion. Such need is always met by the Holy Spirit indwelling in man.

As nature provides for the animals' identity and for their need to adapt and grow, God provides for man; God is man's relative and his relative ground of being. When He answers your needs, you feel a stirring, an impulse, a deep sense of knowing, and then a surge of power, and—suddenly—you discover that you have acted truly. Marveling at what has transpired, you then find excellent reason for everything that has occurred, but the negative counterpart to this process of education is rationalization and the excuses you find welling up inside you to explain away your mistakes.

There are then two kinds of knowing and learning, which come about through two different kinds of reaction: one based on pride and temptation, the other on humility before God.

When the proclivity of the soul is ambition, its drawing force is emotion, and the stimulus to emotion is stress. Stress or pressure then stimulates such a falling man and sets on fire the wheel of nature in him. A man's body is sensitive to stress to the degree that his soul is failing. The beast in man rises, that is, it compensates, on each occasion of the soul's failing. And so it comes to pass that when a person responds to pressure emotionally—and that is the only way a failing soul knows how to respond—that ungracious emotional response causes a flurry of thought to appear in the mind; for it is the brain of the creature that is responsible for computing an answer to each new stress situation. This flurry of thought stuff rises to envelop the soul on the occasion of the soul's failing. Thus, each failing of the soul finds the consciousness absorbed in the increasingly active intellect.

In animals, this thought process produces favorable psychological and behavioral answers to stress. It is not so with us. The animal character that appears forces other people who respond to us to go through a similar kind of agony, and the net result is that we are confronted with yet a bigger problem. And how do we react to this one? With an even greater emotional reaction and with an ever increasing flurry of thought, worry, scheming and planning to overcome the problem that we have unwittingly created for ourselves and others. With each reaction to its own projections the soul becomes that much more absorbed into the activity of the intellect. If the ego refuses to face the Light and the Truth, then the soul will identify with the evolving animal self, which is coming into existence through the failing that leads to worry, while the worry itself leads inexorably to failing again.

Pride, the original failing of man, has left us sensitive and answerable to stress. That original failing, which separated man from the means of responding in any way other than as animals do, forces all mature adults to compensate and be drawn down through the evolutionary stratum in a compulsive way. The order for man born of woman is response first, then excuses, worry, analysis and so on. This excuse-making process implies that pride is still trying to make every worry look right, still playing god, in other words: and *this is where your real failing exists*. There is only failing and rising; but when the ego is too proud to admit to the fact that it is failing through its responses, it will then come to see its downward attraction into the intrigue of its animal cunning as a sort of progress. In the minds of proud men caught up in this carnal process, worry, rationalization, imagination and a blossoming intellect appear to be glorious things. Such foolish men welcome danger, intrigue and trouble as a kind of adventure—they enjoy the stimulation of their reactions to challenges, because such emotion contains the seed of compensating, carnal life qualities. In other words, we can learn to enjoy being upset because it appears to promote growth.

It makes little difference whether such people enjoy danger or are terrified of it; they seek it just the same. Those who enjoy the excitement of challenge and thrive on the apparent growth are really developing in the same way as those who are cowardly and terrified of stress, because they sense the truth about such development through displacement. The adventurous, aggressive-type ego stays ahead of guilt by means of challenges and study. The fearful deal with anxiety through an endless process of worry—a recognition not only of the terror itself but also of the fear of being unable to cope with what one is becoming through one's own reaction. If either of these types of people lived in a world where everything were perfect, where there were no problems to upset or challenge them, they would doubtless discover that all their risings were failings, and then they would be obliged to rock the boat, to stir up necessary excitement and intellectual activity so that they could escape from and stay ahead of such a discovery. Every emotional response, then, produces a twofold effect: One is the illusion of growth, and the other is escape into a flurry of ideas that can make you believe that you are becoming more intelligent. Emotion stimulates that flurry of intellect, which serves as a high, and the ego escapes into that high from the truth of how low high really is.

Remember that the soul itself is incapable of originating thought. By taking wing on emotion-activated thoughts, we attempt to elude the truth of our failing and helplessness; and at the very same moment we discover security in the false belief that we are rising above our problems. And so we never really solve our personal problems at all; we compound them, even as people who respond to us wrongly compound both their own and our turmoil. I cannot emphasize this factor enough: Emotion triggers a process of deterioration that seems like rising when it is actually failing.

A vast majority of people actually enjoy worry and strife because in reacting to the problems (often those they themselves have projected), they have more and more occasions to lose themselves in what seems to them to be an endless and glorifying elevation. When at last you separate your soul from the activity of your intellect, you can see clearly how stupid you have been. The truth is a divine paradox: The more highly you think of yourself, the more stupid you really are; but, the more stupid you see that you are, the wiser you have become.

It is for this reason that in your meditations you will go through periods of feeling lost, stupid, foolish, dull and small—your memory will fail you. But after those moments have passed—and this may take hours, days, even weeks—you will suddenly be able to function from a much higher level of knowledge: understanding. After such experiences you begin to realize the difference between emotional thinking, where you reach down into the gut level of intellect for answers, and the higher way. You will feel the pull on your soul to answer to problems in the old way, that is, to race along with your mind looking for the ego security of any kind of answer; but you will resist, and behold—a true answer appears!

In the beginning you will make a mistake or two, suffering the pain of reacting and being drawn down into the world of worry and analysis. But the pain is good, because it will drive you to a higher ground where you will then enjoy the short, painful experience of being stupid-smart, rather than being your usual smart-stupid self. The smarter a man is in this sense, the more arrogantly dead and dull he is. Who makes himself great shall be humbled, and who humbles himself shall be made great. This is not to say that there is no place for the intellect. On the contrary. But remember this rule of thumb: The intellect should spring out of understanding in the Light. True knowing comes out of the soul's acknowledging that it does not know. The less you know, the more you may understand and know; the more insecure you are, the more secure you really become.

In the past all of your imperfect judgments have proceeded from imperfect knowledge, for in your pride, which is separated from God, understanding is lost. In such a state there can never be true enlightenment to guide your way, only imperfect knowledge that shapes your imperfect judgments. It is natural to fallen man to use intellectual knowledge *about* evil to gain power; and any knowledge about good will be used to remind you of how religious you are. Therefore, beware of the study of good as well as the study of evil. Do not pore over religious facts as if they could save you; they only bear witness to the truth that saves. Shrink from carnal and wicked knowledge, and you will begin to become objective, and you will flee from your own hyprocisy.

How then does one learn? First, you must give up your anxiousness and hurry to learn, for that is a product of ambition, and you must not absorb knowledge ambitiously as a substitute for understanding. In your seeking to know, be patient; realize that you don't even know what it is that is good for you to know. Desire to know what is good for you; scan the pages of this or any other book looking for clues that can *awaken* you to the awareness of who you really are and what is wrong with the way you are currently. Trace your faults back to your ego; see how you have acquired imperfect knowledge to make your imperfect judgments, which have and do now sustain all of your fantasies, dreams and illusions about yourself.

That we need a special knowledge in order to grow there is no doubt. Questions about life must indeed be answered, and decisions must be made either in perfect humility or in imperfect knowledge; but separated from perfect knowledge through pride, there is nothing left but the ego's groping in the darkness. Just as true knowledge is the understanding of all things in the Light of God's presence, excuses and lies are a form of imperfect knowing. Judgments based on such faulty knowledge give rise to short-sighted answers, and we cannot see that the very problems we are trying to solve in this fashion have come into existence by just such knowledge.

Some of us are blessed to see how dry the well of intellectual knowledge is, and, therefore, we find it difficult to study in the traditional way. Every decision that is based on rote knowledge is productive of guilt, which, if it does not cause a compulsion to learn, can produce a fear of knowledge, judgments and decisions, not only because the outcome is always more humiliating but also because of conflict as the original sin repeats itself in us.

You have been, and perhaps you still are, falling for the old line that promises that through greater knowledge, striving and hard work you can achieve the exalted state and become something of a god yourself—the belief that through knowledge you can clean up the mess you have made for yourself through your glorious striving. But seeking greatness is really nothing more than seeking to elude the guilt of seeking greatness.

A common misconception is that the opposite to evil knowledge is good knowledge, just as you have in the past believed that the opposite of hate is love. But I have already shown you that there are two forms of love and hate: one love-hate relationship revolving around evil, the other, true love-true hate revolving about God. Just as it is true that you cannot find true love-hate until your ego recognizes and repents of the fake love-hate syndrome that sustains your false identity, so it is that you cannot find true knowledge of good and evil—discernment—until you vomit up the intellectual knowledge of good and evil—judgment—that sustains your pride.

Do not stand in the way of the Light to be that light; give up judgment and begin to discern by the Light. You must separate your soul from the prejudices of cultivated knowledge through which you attempt to escape from God in order to view yourself as god. Surely, you can see the distinction between understanding good from evil in the Light and deciding on that distinction for yourself in the darkness without the Light. Examine closely the delicate razor's edge—the distinction between judging and discerning—and see how knowledge can phase into understanding, leaving you totally without an externally based source of information. Withstand the temptation to judge, realize the incompleteness of your knowledge, and behold, you can discern good from evil in a new way. Be henceforth relieved of the burden of intellectual study; learn now by observing, retaining knowledge effortlessly in the Light. The value of certain knowledge, if it is not studied or crammed down your throat, is to bring you to the Light, so that you can realize what is before you; and when knowledge has brought you up to the Light of knowing, which is for you understanding, knowledge in its imperfect sense ceases to be for you. There must be no more word-for-word memory of what is written in this book or any other so that you can find a never ending understanding of what no book can teach. Smoothly recited, regurgitated words and phrases will block growth, so stand back, flee from dry rote knowledge, also observe false knowledge in your mind, the lies, the illusions, the fantasies and treasuries of judgments. Let repentance of these be sufficient.

In the Light everything serves the purpose of the Light. Suffering, poised to become the tragedy of the future, takes on new relevance because it it were not for that suffering from your judgments of good and evil, you could not have come to repentance. How can you experience the futility of your own knowing unless there is a greater knowledge by which you can know that futility, a Light that makes you aware that your judgments are wrong? Therefore, since there is an inner means of knowing that knowledge and striving are vanity, it must also mean that the same Light is trying to tell you to stop striving.

It is in the moment, when you become aware, that you must acknowledge the truth of what you see. Do not run away; you must continue to stay in the Light so that, as your awareness increases, you may also become aware of the process by which you are being made aware and ultimately of the very Presence Itself, Which is the source of all awareness. In the moment when you find yourself becoming emotionally and mentally involved, worrying, analyzing, scheming, planning, dreaming, you will be made aware that you are doing something wrong, and at that very moment you *are* no longer involved ambitiously with your own mind. What happens in that moment is that you become obedient to the Light that has always been trying to make you aware. Moment by moment you will be reversing the process of escape that you have used in the past. From now on,life will be a tug of war between daydreams and awareness. At certain points in your daydreaming you will find yourself being made aware of being in the, dream state, the various mental currents that have enveloped you, and in that moment there is a little more freedom, understanding and control over the problems of life itself. *The moment you become aware that you are not aware is the moment of truth.*

It is essential now that you discover how to discover for yourself, for if you cannot, you will not grow up as a child of the Light to live in the projected world of good that is called the kingdom of God. Paradise is a mental state before it is a physical one. *To learn, in the purest sense, is to discover the universe in such a way that every discovery awakens you to marvel at its Creator.* To marvel and wonder is what man was created for. To live in perpetual awe is tantamount to the worship of God,

144

and to worship God is to be loved by God. Is not this worship precisely what we seek for ourselves when we pathetically play the role of God, saying to the world, "Look at me; look at what I've done!" God is the Supreme Ego of the universe, and our imitation of Him is evidence of our separation from Him, and that results in conflict with Him in our consciousness. Immutable physical laws are evidence of a law giver. Science, mathematics, languages are all far more spiritual than you might ever have suspected. In all things there is evidence of God; and He, being within, testifies to His creation, and this testimony can excite us in a special way. Instead of being caught up in the thing or the knowledge about the thing discovered, we can be caught up in the Spirit that makes such realization possible. Discovery of how to discover is an exciting and endless adventure, for to be excited only as a seeker can be is to respond to the revealing, indwelling presence of the Holy Spirit.

To respond to the spirit of revelation is to be reborn, to be replenished and nurtured by the Spirit that came by the very first seeding experience. This is especially true when you read of God's message of salvation through Jesus the Christ. It all really begins here, and it goes on forever. When Christ said to Peter, "Upon this rock I will build my church," he meant that the body of God is to be made up of people who see for themselves and who are taught by no man.

Discovery is quietly exciting; your awakening involves you with who made you aware and introduces into you something of His divine nature, *just as tempta-*

tion does when it excites you with a lie.

Wicked, ruthless preachers in sheep's clothing will teach you many things you should be discovering for yourself. Thus do they effectively *rob* you of that inner discovering experience. Of course, they preach truth, and they are knowledgeable (too knowledgeable), but it is in the prideful, devilish, intellectual sense. Their motive is to confound and confuse you to show how great and successful they are. Tempting you to follow suit, they choke you with untimely knowledge, using the very truth that can save you to kill you. The devil himself can appear as a ministering angel of God, ushering men to "heaven."

Those who seek truly know enough not to seek. Such knowledge that uplifts and refreshes the common egotist is dry and boring to such a soul. It is because you are not ambitious for knowledge that you will eventually understand.

To know that by knowing you cannot know and to give up striving to know is the greatest of all basic wisdoms.

BE STILL, AND KNOW THAT I AM GOD.

6 The Negative Influence of Positive Thinking

All positive suggestion is negative suggestion in disguise. To be healthy and proper, suggestion must be original and intuitive. The closest you can possibly come to giving someone a suitable positive suggestion is to awaken him to a principle or a fact—and even that must be timely and intuitive, or else your advice becomes an external direction to the other person and can become negatively or hypnotically charged.

There are many different ways of impressing upon our minds so-called "positive" ideas, ideals and beliefs—and *all* of them are wrong. You may be hypnotized into believing that you are Napoleon or acting like a Christian, even though neither is true.

Tempted, cut off from the life that flows from reality, we either excuse what we have become or else we seek out idols who seem to embody our lost identity and we mimic them. We are either wrong people who excuse our wrong or wrong people who act right; and I suppose the latter is the lesser of the evils, if the façade is not used as a front for wicked behavior.

True perfection only comes into being when the inside matches the outside. When you make inner contact with your real self, that self comes into being as a real person—a truly right individual who is no longer in turmoil and who does not need to pretend. By this same inner relationship, your faulty self gradually becomes right through and through—and all you need is a change of heart.

What does the Bible say about this? "Cleanse first that which is within the cup . . . that the outside . . . may be clean also." Once this inner relationship is established, there is no longer any need to work at excusing and pretending.

Just as it is wrong to pump yourself up with superficial positive suggestions in order to achieve a goal, so it is equally incorrect to praise your children as a means of making something out of them. Praise literally lifts them up—builds their egos—and drives them into conflict with their true selves. They become dependent on praise as a motivating force, and later, realizing the enslavement and the damage that praise has done them, they are compelled to hate praise as well as the sycophants who flatter them. This judgment also further breeds conflict.

Words have no therapeutic value except that they can, skillfully used, nudge your attention toward the threshold of your Real Self. The mind has no way of transmuting a sound that represents a thing into the thing itself. Occasionally one hears about so-called "miracle cures" achieved under hypnotic trances. Actually, these "cures" occur through an accidental referral to the patient's Real Self. In other words, the patient recovers miraculously because a certain type of hypnotism is so close to the process of meditation that sometimes the mechanism is triggered that changes the factor or hypnosis into a true meditation, and so the person becomes whole, and that is the real basis of the cure, not the therapeutic suggestions.

On the other hand, those who take the usual course of hypnotic suggestion sometimes experience the transference of symptoms (an apparent cure) or the temporary displacement and relief from morbid worry. It is not unusual for a victim to forget, temporarily, what his problem is. When asked how he feels, he will cheerfully affirm, like a pretaped cassette recorder, "Why, just fine, simply fine. It's just like a miracle!"

So-called religious revivals and crusades often produce this sort of effect. The excitement of the gospel music pumping in the background and the emotionally charged appeals of the preacher stimulate the victim to put aside his fears and guilt. His brain circuits, overwhelmed by emotion, blow his mind clean, and he forgets his problems. But these apparent cures and others like them are not real, and they never last long; sadly, the victims are led even farther away from becoming real human beings by what appears to be their salvation.

This chapter deals primarily with understanding the negative aspects of positive suggestion, in the hope that through true insight you will be able to untangle the maze of confusion already woven in you like a tapestry that you call "personality." From a clear understanding of how the problem forms, the real solution comes.

Even as all positive suggestion is negative suggestion in disguise, what is called "negative suggestion" can be a form of constructive criticism; but only with the proper timing, intuition and the force of love can such criticism destroy the grip of false belief on the hypnotized mind. Once freed of the negative influence at that point in time, the victim can come to his own senses and begin functioning from within his own center in a true and positive way.

All truly positive suggestions must emanate from within the individual himself. Education, manners, wisdom, wit, love, understanding, industry, talent and grace—these are all waiting to unfold from within. Impress a person with the selfsame things that he should discover for himself, and you will destroy him. Expose him to knowledge so that he might be awakened from within, yes, but don't shove it down his throat! Through impatience, overeducation and motivation, you separate him from what true knowledge and direction is all about.

Protect those you love from the infiltration of worldly rhetoric and hypnotic pressure, and they will unfold from within like a flower. Your awareness, wisdom and true timing can reach into their minds and neutralize the effects of pressure, often before it can materialize into action, and neatly nip potential errors in the bud before they take root. Little overt direction is necessary, but if it is required, it should be only of a kind that awakens your loved one to subtle, dormant principles of life through which he can see his own way to move and have his being.

With infants and small children, the motivation and direction needed is largely simple discipline—for example, the protocol of eating and cleanliness. You may have to remind a child patiently a thousand times to brush his teeth until this duty, lovingly discharged, penetrates into his awareness and he recognizes that need for himself. You can avoid all of this bother, of course, by frightening or upsetting him so badly that he will mechanically assume his "duty" forever in the name of "self-reliance," but is it? The unloving, impatient person, eager to rid himself of the burden of responsibility, will push, bribe and motivate his children, and in this way change them into confused robots.

The true authority is within; those who are truly linked to that authority in themselves understand the very delicate process of slowly introducing their children to their own centers of dignity. If you have such authority in yourself—that is, if you have abandoned your ego life—your offspring can follow any suggestion from you without any danger whatsoever of becoming conditioned to an authority outside themselves, for the love coming through you is in concert with the understanding of life in them.

So obedience and agreement with that kind of direction is the same as obedience to Self. As the child grows, physical transference to the same identity within himself is a much simpler matter.

Unfortunately, most parents and teachers condition the child to answer to the pressure of outer authorities, and thus they separate them from their Real Selves. Once this conditioning process begins, there is less and less direction from within and more authority imposed from outside, on which children either learn to depend or else rebel against.

In this way, we become increasingly a society of outer-directed beings involved in relationships with leaders and authorities like the one we should have with God. And so begins a journey into darkness, confusion, chaos, suffering, tragedy and, finally, death.

Hold fast! You are on the road back, but first you must explore and fully understand the nature of error on your journey toward grace.

The text you are following serves as a constructive criticism to argue against the false belief and confusion that so-called "positive" answers have kindled in your mind, to awaken you to the dormant principles that quicken you to action.

The need for those silly affirmations, which advocates of "positive thinking" suggest that you tell yourself, indicates a deeply buried disturbance, a defect of personality with which you don't know how to cope. This "positive thinking" is the same as lying to yourself, and accepting it is the same as being lied to. It is either something you are taught to do, or else it is simply a futile, desperate attempt at self-direction. A lie may pose as the truth, but it soon reveals itself for what it is by the fruitlessness of its message.

After the first wave of lies has thrown you off center and got inside, you need more lies, which you call "truth," in order to placate the trail of guilt and hopelessness it leaves in its wake. Positive thinking allows you to grow continually worse by helping you to think you are better off. Denying that anything is wrong or affirming your rightness is not a cure for what is wrong with you; it is a malignant ego sickness in itself because it prevents your getting well.

Suppose, for example, that you have accepted a negative opinion of yourself via the condemnation of your parents. Suppose also that to offset this abuse, you labored your entire life so as to prove yourself to people and make them "eat their words." Now look at what you have done. Do you really believe that having people think you are great is the reverse of having them think ill of you? It is not, because the second lie (your greatness) affects and sensitizes you more than the first lie—the contempt that originally condemned you.

Though you didn't want to believe the first lie was true when you accepted it, accept it you did. And that is the problem. Why did you accept that low opinion of yourself—and what is the weakness that allowed this negative thought to get in and eat away your insides? ONLY WHEN YOU UNDERSTAND THIS BASIC WEAKNESS WILL YOU BE RELIEVED OF THE FUTILITY OF WORKING YOUR ENTIRE LIFE JUST TO PROVE YOURSELF TO OTHER PEOPLE.

God does not operate where there is an image—good or bad. Neither must you have the audacity to conceive

Him in your mind in any shape or form. When you have put aside all images of yourself, you become correctly related to your true self. You are then whole and protected from all manner of negative criticism. It can't get at you, or rather, between you and your true positive self; consequently, you will feel no obligation to prove yourself to anyone or to disprove the world. You are free to live a truly productive and rewarding life. On the other hand, when your ego is challenged to make something of itself (you) by your response to criticism, you labor in vain and earn nothing but a greater condemnation by your own conscience. So regardless of how people might pump you up, it becomes increasingly harder to believe them. By accepting praise, you not only become dependent on the god of praise, but also you become more sensitive to condemnation. Why? Because you have not cured the original sensitivity to the negative and because your ego is striving after a glorious image of itself.

Furthermore, you are worse for trying to cure the effect of one lie with another—the so-called "positive." The positive suggestion is not a cure for your negatively suggestible state; it is simply another lie that your ego clings to. In other words, you become more sensitive to words—including negative words—more externalized than before, more suggestible than ever. Your ego life develops to become based on images and lies that revolve about temptation.

Suggestion involves a two-stage process: 1) Suggestion in the form of outside condemnation becomes internalized because of a little-understood weakness of character. The emotion you summon to keep the suggestion out (anger, resentment) happens to be the very emotion that lets it in! 2) Suggestion in the form of praise contains its own excitement value and renders you even more suggestible to the negative word.

In plain English, if I told you that you were stupid, and you then worked your head off to induce me to tell you how smart you were—well, how stupid could you get? Your entire life would be wasted proving yourself and working for approval. Finally, after you are utterly exhausted, people will damn you anyway, and, feeling confirmation in yourself because your conscience now tells you that something is truly wrong, you resign yourself to what seems the inevitable, negative truth about yourself. You give in to what seemed right from the start and submit yourself meekly to punishment and what appears to be your destiny.

Remember this rule. Your emotional responses always make you disobedient to the internal world represented by your conscience. And so you begin an imperfect relationship with the tempter in his various guises—one of his forms makes you wrong, and another helps you to feel that all is well.

If, when you react to an unfair accusation, it sticks in your craw and you try to cough it up, you must go on accepting that lie until you see your original error— where you went wrong. Your battle to offset its effects only makes it come true that much more easily. That is why we have the Fifth Amendment to the Constitution in America—because the average person does not know

155

how to deal with a false accusation. It is not unusual for a victim to become so upset and excited that he can be made to believe he is guilty of a crime he did not commit and confess to it and accept the punishment.

We all come into the world subject to the lie because the inherited nature of the ego is lie-oriented. The ego is bound to its sense of self-worth through lies until you see the futility of this kind of illusion. Your ego craves words of praise, and it is threatened by criticism.

By now, you should have fully realized what ego is: the spirit in man that denies the Spirit of Truth in order to be in that exalted state that only God possesses! We resent our deficiency and crave to feel sufficient, and since the only way we can satisfy this ego craving is the lie while we are in this state of being separate from God, we go on revelling in lies and resenting even the valid criticism that, if realized, could institute the process of salvation.

It matters little where the lie begins, whether you begin life in a negatively charged oppressive family atmosphere, in one where you are always being encouraged, bribed and pumped up, or the usual combination of both extremes. You resent your despicable family for not giving you praise. Praise is what you crave from the cradle to the grave, and because it is the wrong thing even to want, you are unhappy because you are guilty. The result of craving love and being rejected is guilt—but so is being accepted and glorified. The craving for praise stems basically from your wrong ego nature trying to assert its righteousness and claiming its "divine" due.

The serpent in the garden once told the first members of the human race that to disobey God and eat of the tree of the knowledge of good and evil would make them become like God, and as the first man fell for the glorifying lie, our own propensity, as his progeny, is to keep hungering for and falling for the lie—the lie that helps us think, no matter how low we sink, that we are gods in our own eyes. But the lie keeps breaking down in the inner light, and we see how much more lowly and inferior we have become in the process; but still our egos keep reaching.

So, as your actual inadequacy grows because you are growing in the wrong way, the craving for the lie increases as does your frustration, especially when you get what you want.

Suppose you have an ambitious mother who promotes and encourages you to be a great violinist or a wealthy business tycoon. Your vulnerability to her suggestion has something to do with your ego desire to be great, and the temptation is irresistible. You see, any idea that promises greatness seems good in your eyes. Once you become motivated by positive suggestion toward the goal of greatness, you can't stop, because the moment you do, you feel anxiety, uncertainty about what you have become and the direction in which you are traveling and that your ego cannot admit is wrong.

As you mature, the momentum may be taken over by an ambitious wife, one who cares about your money and power, but not about you. As you get nearer what you think of as the top, you become more guilty and uncertain. Craving assurance, you get it, but when you do, it drives you into conflict with yourself. One day, at a point of diminishing return, every positive suggestion, and even the good things you own, become negatively charged. Your mind and body revolt against the encouraging lies you need to bolster your morale and against your material possessions, because they are clearly sensed to be a cause of pain. You become like a spoiled child who screams for his own way, and when he gets it, screams even louder because what he really needs is correction.

Since you have nothing else except empty praise and motivation when the pendulum of dissatisfaction swings, you gravitate to poor surroundings and lowly, discouraging people; and perhaps you refuse to work toward anything at all.

At first this feels like the more honest thing to do. You might even want people to be mean and negative toward you, hoping that will cancel out the curse of glory and the good life. But it doesn't.

In your meditation you will be able to see and give up your craving for praise as well as any support you have demanded for a way of life that wasn't your own to begin with—a way of life you thought was your own because you refused to admit that it wasn't. Remember, whatever is right for us to do doesn't need any support; and when we are right we will not need to affirm or to hear affirmations that we are right. What is more, we are not threatened by criticism, because we are no longer lie-oriented.

What lies at the root of all of your problems, then, is that your ego, wanting to be God, hates Him and wants to be self-sufficient apart from the Truth. And as you damn the conscience that loves you and tries to save you, your own rejection of that loving correction becomes your own damnation, because you are rejecting reality and life so that you may continue lying to yourself and believing you are more than you are. As you seek a better self-image, your conscience nags you with guilt, and you resent it. Resentment of the truth breeds further guilt, and the process snowballs. The better you try to feel about yourself, the worse you actually become. How then can you deal with this state of mind?

1) Stop fighting yourself—your conscience. See it as the friend it is and don't resent being shown the truth about yourself. Stop making self-images. See that the part of you that curses God is not really you at all but an implanted identity—an evil you have identified with that is trying to stop you from becoming objective.

2) Don't resent people who reject you; and, furthermore, see the folly of chasing after people for their image-building affection or acceptance.

3) Don't resent those weak individuals from whom you can easily manipulate praise. Manipulated love is not real love, and you blame your frustration on their withholding and cheating you of real love. Of course, if they had real love, they would not play this ego game with you at all.

4) Don't hate people who praise you to get you to serve them.

5) Stop reciting those foolish "positive" affirmations.

6) Change your vocation or else your motivation for working at it.

7) Be aware that everything that seems like security is just as destructive as insecurity. Although you were probably raised under one extreme or another, perhaps alternating, don't resent your parents for their mistakes in your formative years.

8) Be careful not to gravitate to the kind of environment that corrupted you while you are looking for a substitute parent to hate or love.

If you are unable to get praise, the only thing you can be sure of is condemnation—so the chances are that you will have learned to use rejection as an ego advantage: You will have learned to give your ego the comfort it craves through the excitement of judging others. Even though your underlying motive is to solicit praise, your desperate, clumsy, clawing ego earns you contempt instead. You then learn to damn those who reject you, so that you can get higher on resentment instead of praise. Damning those who damn you becomes a form of ego security. God damns the guilty for not praising Him, even as He loves whose who love Him. Your imitation of His divine prerogative is the source of your error. The result of damning people—judging and resenting them— backfires into a growing feeling of self-condemnation. ("Judge not, lest ye be judged.") We then fall into the habit of damning people to forget our own damnation, and, growing even worse as a result of being judgmental, we damn ourselves and feel utterly hopeless. Or, perhaps, the guilt of resentment drives us to seek the praise of those we have judged; then they take advantage of us, and we judge (hate) them again. If you will stop grasping for love and praise, you will not feel the need to condemn. Whether you seek praise or salve your ego's wounds with the balm of resentment, you are ultimately driven into conflict with God, the Supreme Ego, Who alone has the right to receive praise or to deliver judgment. The way in which most of us first learn that God exists is by playing God and experiencing conflict with Him in the form of conscience, until we repent.

Only through our emotional response to it can a negative suggestion be implanted in our minds, and this is especially true when that response is one of resentment. We finally accept the negative person and his suggestion as a means of assuaging his pressure and that of our own guilt, which grows out of resenting that pressure—of resisting without grace. We conform to outside direction as a means of dealing with pressure and guilt, and we are thereby rendered both suggestible and gloomy.

For example, a mother damns her son and screams into him the suggestion that he will grow up to be a drunken bum like his father. He resents the suggestion, but the burning hatred of his judgment of his mother corrupts him and makes the suggestion take, and it finally causes in him that same guilt-anxiety condition that drove his father to drink. Slowly the idea of drink becomes more attractive to him, and he yields in order to resolve the agony of conflict.

Many diseases and so-called "inherited" illnesses are transferred in a similar way through an emotionally charged climate in the home. In these cases, there is no genetic transference, although, perhaps, the same genetic weakness may exist. Rather, we select or else we are overwhelmed by the dominant personality—through emotion—and we assume the same identity and habit patterns, thereby setting the stage for the same kind of illness. Sensing the identification with our parent, we can begin to fear that we will die of the same illness or suffer the same fate in some other way. Worry then gives a sick attention to, say, the heart, so that there may be heart-attack symptoms long before the attack strikes, and if the heart happens to have a genetic weakness, the emotional pressure expresses itself at that point.

Let me restate that hating wrong can make you feel right, and as long as you have something to hate, the guilt for hating does not actually catch up with you. Women who have damned and nagged their good-for-nothing husbands into their graves feel the same kind of terrible guilt the day their husbands die. That is, on that day, they suddenly become aware of a morbid fear. Then they discover the same damnation in themselves that they have pronounced upon their husbands. At some funerals, the bereaved widow has to be forcibly restrained from leaping into the yawning grave by solicitous relatives—and with just a little exercise of the imagination, one can see the reason. 1) We identify with the person we need to hate, so a part of us dies and goes beyond with him. 2) There is also a physiological tendency to follow our identities as well as a psychological one to follow whatever supports our ego's sense of well-being.

Remember this rule of thumb: Whatever gives a sense of well-being is actually tempting us and taking our identity away in exchange for its own, and that is why we follow.

Just as our attempts to achieve security have led us in the physical world, so do our departed securities—the spirits of the dead—lead us into the next world. Sometimes we can manage to lay hold of a new form of security to help us keep from slipping away, but in clinging to that person or thing we heap coals of fire upon our heads and theirs. We love them because we need them. They may be tempted to love us back, but their love hurts us more than it helps. The security they offer becomes the cause of our greater insecurity, and in the process we may even feel better than we deserve to feel, but we still feel unworthy, damned by all the good things our lover and savior bestows upon us, and we have only death to look forward to for escape from the growing pains of existence.

We can fear life with them because we can only get worse, as well as life without them. We can hate them for loving us, and our hate draws us just as near to death as it does when we cling to them in love.

The key to overcoming all of these morbid thoughts is again gradually to give up your unholy need for ego comfort as well as the resentment against the failure of the lover's remedy. On the way back, it is invariably resentment that must be dealt with first. If you were infected by prophets of doom, beginning with your parents, it was your resentment that made it all come true. Resentment tempts you to become like those people whom you hate. Resentment building on resentment also sets the stage—the sequence of causes and effects that eventually makes the suggestion stick because it proves itself out and forces you to accept the label.

For example, if someone keeps calling you crazy, you would be very sensitive-resentful toward the word, "crazy," and you would be very reactive to words and glances that you could construe as implying a judgment of your insanity by others. You might even look for people to insinuate that you are crazy so that you could indulge in the dubious pleasure of resenting them. Remember the rule that resentment is a judgment of others, and judgment provides us with a temporary sense of superiority and ego comfort. But resentment, since it also produces guilt, also eventually produces uncertainty and mental confusion; it makes us sensitive as well as suggestible and traps us into a state that is actually inferior to the rascal who tempts us to judge him. Resentment that makes us high also makes us less aware of what we are doing; so we blunder and make silly mistakes, we fumble and generally make fools of ourselves. Then we see people's expressions—they stare at us as though there were something wrong with us. Again, we resent the implication, but that is more resentment, judgment, guilt and loss of awareness, because we are high on judgment. Getting high on judgment is the only way we know to avoid feeling or knowing that we are stupid, inferior, confused and crazy. But when we come down from our high, we see that we are all of these things and more.

See how easy it is eventually to accept completely the original suggestion that got into our minds? Temptation, you see, makes you weak, inferior, responsive, obedient and, perhaps, like the person who tempts you. Resentment is one key to your conditioning and misery. Resentment is also the temptation to judge so that you become more nearly separated from reality and, whether you like it or not, more sensitive and obedient to the wishes of the tempter. Your ego, attempting to rise above what is above you, without the grace to do so, sets you on a downhill course—all because you are tempted to overcome what will overcome you in the end. The agony of resistance becomes so unbearable that we must give in to a person or idea for relief. If we overcome, we are what we hate, and if we don't, we are bound to serve what we hate.

We become guilty mostly because our egos resent a bigger ego that is the power we foolishly want to be. That contemptuous thing always manages to stay ahead of our judgments of it. That contemptuous thing that teases us to judge it is the basic cause of guilt, not the suggestion itself. A suggestion sticks fast only when the sin evolves through emotion to match the label. Although it may not stick for some time to come, in the sense that we have not yet resigned ourselves to it, the stage is set. The main reason for being threatened by name-calling is that the negative idea assaults the bastion of our egos, which you remember is built out of great and glorifying ideas of itself.

Have you ever wondered why you were so sensitive to words, constructive or destructive? (You notice more in the negative form.) The ego is built on exciting ideas, and fantasies are assembled from the words we need to hear. Naturally we resent people who fail to look up to us and who, instead, condemn us—but that's how guilt forms and begins to associate with the word. We only feel damned by the word because of our resentment and judgment against the tempter and his word, and that eventually develops into either his prophecy or likeness because of the force from the source of motivation. And so it comes to pass that if we go on hating and judging, we eventually come to the degenerative stage that matches the word. And then we are forced to resign ourselves to the "truth of our fate."

So one day you may be acting a little strangely, and a well-meaning friend may say something like, "Yes, my mother experienced something like that before they took her to the mental hospital." Zap! All at once you have arrived at your own personal predestination. There is no more resistance left. The last suggestion has such impact that it forces you to resign yourself to your lot because 1) it is obvious that you are crazy, and 2) the only recourse to the pain of resentment is acceptance.

There is at that moment of truth an overwhelming tendency for your soul to accept people and ideas that you have been resisting all these years—to receive or even welcome and not hate any longer the spirit that has been shaping your destiny, your body, for its home.

People tend to resign themselves to death in a variety of ways. Sooner or later the positive effects of medicine and the doctors' assurances fail to work. And the victims are that much more advanced in their error and sickness because of such medical help. Why? Because in getting better we are allowed to live longer to become even "wronger." The longer we live, supported by the doctor's love, with pride, ambition, hate and false love, the more guilty we become and so the more damned we really feel for getting well. So when we become sick again, as we surely will, there is a tendency to hide in the sickness from the trials and tribulations of facing the world. We can be afraid to get well because, if we do, we fear that somehow we shall become more guilty, and we also know that as a result we shall be more sick one day than we are currently. Sickness, then, becomes a form of false security for our egos; however, I have shown that there is no such thing as security—because any security makes us just as guilty as the sin we are hiding from!

For example, you meet stress, you fail, so you become a coward. Now, rather than become more of a coward, you avoid facing experiences that reveal your fear—but not living at all is as guilt-producing and fear-producing as not living properly.

Sooner or later all encouragement backfires, not only upon you but upon people who serve it to you. You feel that somehow they have failed or betrayed you—

and so they have, for not giving you proper correction.

Your child nags you for his own way, and you give in. You are then just as guilty for giving in as the child is for demanding his own unreasonable way.

The greatest demander of love of them all is the sick person, for he is also desperate for life; the closer one is to hell and death, the more unconscious power he has to lead and tempt others in order to get his own sick way. Now when you acquiesce to these sufferers, you are unwittingly drained of the storehouse of life and the homage that you have wrestled from others, and in giving up your life, however unwillingly, you begin to degenerate and embrace sickness too. At least, in this way, you will be able to recover from others the malignant energy that you were forced to give up. The king is dead. Long live the king!

It is absolutely wrong to sacrifice your life substance to the sick, if for no other reason than that you make them more sick in the bargain. No wonder you feel somehow responsible when they die. This is also why you feel so helpless, guilty and sick yourself. An experience with a sick mother, for example, can set the stage for the same illness in you. Cancer is a typical disease in these circumstances.

The "helpless" condition of the sick person cries out for help, and help comes. You serve the sick, and when they die, you take their place of "honor." The sick person will praise you for what is really your compulsive service, so you obtain that much-longed-for illusion of worthiness as you give up your energy, resentfully. Now, when your beloved invalid dies, you are lost without the praise you have grown accustomed to, and you become aware of your guilt, and your weakness becomes sickness, bringing with it a pathetic demand and appeal to obligate others to begin serving you just as you have served. Sick people are wrong people. Neither hate them nor cater to them; correct them.

Remember that the first reaction to a demand is resentment, and the second is therefore, guilt. Third is suggestibility and sickness. Finally, there is identification.

For heaven's sake, give up resentment against everything—your lot in life, your entourage of sympathizers, your doctors—and also give up your need for and your acceptance of sympathy and love, by degrees, of course. You must come to have an attitude of no attitude—an attitude without self, images of self and without judgments. Here the Light of God dwells—His image and identity come alive in you, and you can sin no more.

7 Dealing with Morbid Thoughts

Every ego comes into existence fixated to an increasingly conscious ideal of perfection—pride. Revolving around that false, godlike idea of perfection is the will to ultimate power—the compulsion to judge and to demand homage.

So long as the conscious mind stubbornly retains this ideal of perfection, which it believes to be its own, it is subject to dreams and wish fulfillment that, alone, can satisfy and give idea form to that ideal that operates on the more abstract conscious level. The ego clothes itself in whatever dreams most closely fit its unformed ideal; but, since each ideal of perfection is itself imperfect, the only way in which the ego can see its own being as infallible is through illusion or dreams. Without them, it is forced to face the reality of its own imperfect and pathetic state.

In other words, like gods, we think that we establish our own definition of perfection, and then we proceed to fool ourselves into believing that we are attaining it. And so we grow in our imaginations until the soul's imitation of God matures and comes into direct conflict with God. At this point, instead of helping our egos to grow, as they once did, resentment, judgment, praise and flattery give rise to an intolerable pattern of conflict and guilt. Conflict with God, which produces all guilt, then forms a part of that conscious ideal of perfection that we bring into this life with us; but, instead of enhancing it, the guilt of ego striving mars that ideal of perfection. And the more we struggle to offset the stain of guilt, either by getting high on judgment or, at the other extreme, by eliciting praise for ourselves, the more we come into conflict with the true God, and the more guilt mars that pattern of our own ideal of perfection.

Remember that the ego consciousness obtains its seeming reality from unconscious dream stuff. Dreams cling, as if magnetically, to give form and a sense of reality to the wayward soul, because that is the only reality it can have and the only reality it desires to know. Unfortunately, this dream stuff will also cleave to all of the negative aspects of the soul's pattern—guilt. And guilt then draws to it ideas of unworthiness, inferiority, failure, punishment, damnation, dying and so on. Out of these come the various sorts of fears or phobias.

None of these psychological symptoms, which, incidentally, can lead to complicated illness, premonition and calamity, can be removed from the unconscious mind until the individual soul repents of its secret wish to aspire to the Godhead. Each time we attempt to offset or to escape from the guilt of playing god, we stain the soul with new guilt that, in turn, draws a pattern of negative ideas that give form to the guilt-ridden ego. Negative morbid thoughts begin multiplying like rabbits, because the subconscious mind comes up with thoughts that match not only the ego's need for glory, but also those that cling stubbornly to its actual imperfection, caused by seeking glory that it does not deserve. Pride, which precedes any failing, always falls lower in its attempts to rise higher. Every high is a new low. Each high involves descending further down into a world of dreams and being contaminated by experiences with sensation and temptation.

The ego, by its own plan of perfection, always makes itself a cripple, because it stands outside God's perfect plan and at variance with Truth. It is, therefore, wrong. It can never be right; so in its cravings to be high and mighty, there is added unto it only guilt and inferiority—a gradual falling away from what perfection truly is.

As long as the ego remains stubborn and hardens its heart against a greater truth than itself, it will call on illusion, the stuff dreams are made of. The actual guilt of this process of trying to be right results in an aftermath of gathering up morbid thoughts that crystallize around the real image of the guilty soul like iron fragments around a magnet. A partial list includes fear of falling (because we are), unworthiness, failure, disaster, punishment, illness or dying. These and many others are the outcroppings—the symbols of what is really happening inside. Each produces its own imaginings, which set the stage for the real thing to happen.

Again, the more we try to rise above, or to compensate for, failings and guilt, the more we experience inner failing and guilt. Later on, we become afraid to compensate any more. We give up because we know our own efforts only bring a growing sense of failing, futility, failure, disillusionment and guilt if we succeed. So we actually fail because we are afraid of success and its attendant guilt.

We even make ourselves ill so that we can think that there is something wrong with the body instead of its owner. In refusing to suspect the real reason within, we come up with ideas (compensations, really) that help us throw the blame elsewhere, something like a physical ailment, but never a spiritual one! Proof of this becomes a kind of relief to the soul—proof that we are still all right and that the body alone is wrong. Many disorders, from hypochondria to real illness, are induced by ego folly, that is, by searching for what is wrong with the body rather than ourselves. Not all illnesses are imagined; they don't always have to be. But if we become really sick, we make it work for us and are afraid to give it up. We are afraid to get well because we would have to give up our refuge and be forced out into the world to fail again.

When we look beyond our bodies and project our guilt onto others to blame them for our unhappiness and failure, that blame becomes resentment and then judgment; and judgment becomes more guilt because it pumps us up like a god, producing soul stain, greater hysteria and a wider variety of symptoms as well as a growing imagination in our constant search for new scapegoats.

Projection can become paranoia, in which all fault or evil is outside us and wherein we imagine that people are plotting to overthrow or destroy god (us). We judge them; we take defensive action; we hurt others before they get a chance to hurt us, and we end up always more guilty. And the cycle begins again; this time there are even more people against us. There have to be to offset the truth that there is more and more wrong with us inside.

None of these illnesses or other related morbid states can be cured by sympathy—that makes for far more guilt because it feeds the ego—or by drugs and medicine because they also feed the notion that the body is wrong, rather than the soul. Nor can stubborn, hysterical ideas be removed by affirmations or hypnotic suggestion, because the actual condition of the soul draws all those sick ideas back again after they have been apparently removed. The same holds true with drug-shock or electrical-shock therapy, which are both guilt producing. Nothing on God's earth can remove persistent, self-destructive ideas until the soul faces the Light and repents, stops striving for power—gives up judgment and comfort from the guilt of judgment, along with the craving for human love, the need for glory. All of these produce the stain of guilt that draws morbid thoughts.

Remember, even though we may succeed in drowning ourselves in various pleasent fantasies, the morbid-thought process is not far behind—and it forms the basis for the need for new fantasy. The morbid thought becomes *much more a real part* of the ego self than the need for fantasy is. Fantasy is the need of the ego to escape from the morbid knowledge of what it is still becoming through fantasy. Morbid thought eats away at the supposed benefits of illusion, making the ego crave more illusion.

We are really much more vulnerable to negative suggestion than we are to positive suggestion. The aftermath of every positive stand is a backlash of blacker, foreboding belief in the worst about ourselves, things to come, or the world. Our plan for glory does not work; "our" plan makes cripples out of us, forcing us to resign ourselves, protesting or surrendering, to the "truth" of Death, the gateway to Hell's "Heaven."

It is the Pied Piper of Hell with his pleasant "in" sound that has led us rats to our glory-seeking end.

Running from the Truth's Light in a vain attempt to *be* that light, we are drawn inexorably to the gates of death—by accident, illness, tragedy, grief or by our own hand. See how easy it is to accept the inevitability of death as a part of life? We are forced to resign ourselves to Hell's last claim, just as we cannot help accepting morbid thoughts of sickness and the morbid conditions that follow one after another to tragedy, thence to death itself.

We are drawn hypnotically, screaming, struggling—first in the mind center—there actually protesting like a convict being dragged to the scaffold, or perhaps managing just one more fantasy, as we draw close to doomsday. We see the Pearly Gates open for us on the "other side"—only to hear them clang grimly closed behind us, awakening us in death, where there are no more images and no more escapes from the harsh reality of Hell itself and the spiritual face of our once unseen comforter-tormentor.

Who was it who said, "The wages of sin is death?"

Do you see now the relationship between ego and the morbid state of mind and body? Morbid thoughts merely reflect the state of the soul and portend its future. THE CURE LIES IN IDENTIFYING THE PARTICULAR GUILT OF THE SOUL WITH EACH FEAR AND ANXIETY.

No use raising false hopes by uplifting your spirits with rosy positive suggestions to be well. There is simply not enough instruction in such ideas as, "Get well, be healed, have courage" or exhortations to repentance. Repent we must indeed, but that word, "repentance," must be loaded with more meaning before we can understand how it is done. Only through objectivity can we come close enought to the Light to repent.

When we repent, we are more open to believe in the good that does happen and in salvation from death, because true life shines at the end of the road we travel. We shall have given up pride and made ourselves part of God's Plan, and we shall have stopped trying to set up our own kingdom.

So come up out of hiding in the dark world of thought, illusion and fantasy into the Light of Truth that you might be saved from morbid thoughts that portend death.

The heartbeat of your meditation practice is your desire to know Truth and the Plan greater than you and yours and to stay objective to the thought stream. Here you will come to know yourself by God's indwelling Light. It will take years of resisting to conquer the tendency to be pulled into rosy thoughts, negative thoughts and gibberish, but with each measure of success, you edge closer to self-mastery and greater understanding.

Separation from your involvement with the thought process as well as the comforts that sustain it is the basic tenet of your meditation exercise. Every involvement with your thinking represents a previous encounter with some form of temptation (evil) or an escape from the truth concerning it (also evil). Looking at these persistent thoughts properly is the key to your change; but as long as your conscious mind remains locked into those memories, meaningful change is impossible. You cannot be tempted as long as you remain objective. Falling down involves losing conscious altitude and being locked into a level of flesh growth that includes the memory that holds everything together—repeating and building the error anew on itself.

You cannot gaze objectively at any thought without causing that thought to break down. Take any thought—a pink elephant will do. Sit back now and look objectively at the image of a pink elephant. See if you can hold on to it. You can't; it breaks down.

This principle holds true for any idea. The only way you can hold on to a meaningless or negative thought is to float along with it, but then you will not be objective. You will not have the presence of that Inner Light shining through your still soul to break down the image, and without It you will remain a prisoner of your ideas and past conditioning.

It is the practice of sick minds to fantasize and employ their dream material as a dreamboat they board to move away from the Light of Reality, which their egos will not bear. Many religions promote this common, infantile practice of escape, which, incidentally, affords immature egos a shield against the Light to allow for growing up. The ego, you see, cannot grow to full animal stature in the Light.

If you will observe carefully, you will see that everything children do is ego-based—*as the ego glows, their body grows;* unlike animals, children must grow egotistically or else they cannot grow properly in a physical way.

Children develop vivid imaginations that shield them from the Light as they grow; they are also very impressionable and always for the worse. They have little or no *objective awareness* to protect them. Protection implies the objective ability to look at ideas forming in the minds and to stare intently at the source of wrong ideas with the same kind of gaze. Protection from undue influence is the role of the objective, loving parent. Unfortunately, most of us don't have, and are not ourselves, loving parents.

Approaching physical maturity, most of us get stuck halfway between childhood and adulthood—our egos are afraid to go on to face the truth about our supposed maturity.

While the guilts of our early childhood are not really our guilts at all, the ego's tendency, desiring always to be right, is to shrink from the truth concerning them. As we grow older and tend to be more aware, we also feel defensive about the sins inflicted upon us by our parents or what they neglectfully and unlovingly allowed to happen to us. Complicating a series of such traumas is our hatred of parents or guardians for perpetuating the crime against us or sitting in silent consent with, or not protecting us against, corrupting influences. We almost surely have deep-seated hatreds going back to birth that trace directly to parents' cruelty or to their neglect—which festers into guilt as we grow tall enough to approach the Inner Light. But remember, none of these sins visited upon you constitutes *your* guilt. As a child, you could not have prevented these things from corrupting you; you also had no other way of dealing with misfortune, no recourse but resentment, or a clinging desperately to symbols of security, even if they hurt you. Giving in to tyrants who make the pain of hatred toward them unbearable is a common form of loyalty.

These and other problems formed in childhood ARE NOT YOUR GUILTS AT ALL; they are really projections of your parents' sins "visited" upon you. As the Scripture aptly states, the sins of the fathers are visited upon the third and fourth generation of those that hate the Lord; but mercy is shown to those that love the Lord and keep His commandments.

Pride, being what it is, will defend what it has become before the Light—and that is partly, perhaps mostly, where your real guilt lies. Tempters and tyrants of all kinds have the egos of the people working for them. They tempt, goad and license people to commit crimes and atrocities, and then the people will defend "their" actions—but they will also justify and defend their tempter, whom they emulate or look to for assurance for what they have done or have been made to do.

Enemies can look like friends, and friends can look like enemies—just as the Light experience can feel like Hell if we are proud. That moment of truth inflames the old enmity between man's soul and God, and a devil crouches on your doorstep begging to give you support and comfort. That is why sick people flock together— and why when we fail in any endeavor we are prone to run to the more lowly, loathesome types for comfort. We need someone to tell us that we are all right when we are not.

Cultures claim the very young for their own because they know that when they grow up they will defend their wrong way as the right way and thereby sustain the culture. The only way in which you are going to be able to learn to cope with all of these ego pressures is to find a way of observing the ego objectively—a way of seeing illusion *as* illusion by comparing it to the testimony of truth that is within you and that you must discover.

The meditation exercise, which I have discussed elsewhere in this book, is designed to teach you how to become objective and aware. When you practice it, be careful not to fall asleep, and don't be afraid of distracting noise. The worst thing you can do is to *resent* distraction. Learn to use any noise or distraction as an anchor to help keep you in the present moment. Focus your attention—actually learn to *give* your attention to, say, the blaring television, and learn to listen to the dialogues or the music *without letting it register in your mind.* It is a marvelous practice, for it is precisely the way you will need to learn how to listen to foolish arguments *without forming counterarguments* and without letting them register.

In the past, everything made an impression on you. You are loaded with all kinds of impressions, arguments and memories that have weighed heavily on your conscience, that never had any real value to you and have no business being there inside your head in the first place. So now, become objective—*don't let anything inside or outside, whatever it is, hold your attention captive.* Acquire the knack of *giving your attention.* Whenever you find yourself lost in the argument, or getting interested in a play, or drumming your fingers with music, stand back. Come to your senses! Keep it all out there, literally. Don't allow it to get under your skin. Watch out for irritation that will really pull on your attention; give your attention first to the irritation and then, as you calm down, to the bothersome idea. Sounds or sights get under your skin when you use them or allow them to irritate you and otherwise distract you.

Remember, what excites or irritates you away from yourself will always get inside you and end up as a memory, a wrong experience or trauma, causing anxiety and guilt to form. After meditation with that TV blaring loudly, you should be unimpressed, unable to remember what went on, even though you heard every word clearly. Yet while listenting in this objective state, should you hear something profound and meaningful at that moment, you might find a place for that.

Heretofore, you tried to block people out by attempting to ignore them, and you accomplished that by fixing your attention elsewhere; but if it worked, *somebody else* would get to you, and often you would be hung up with that somebody else as a means of running away from people and things that bothered you. It isn't long before the thing or person you have used to divert your attention also begins to bug you and makes you feel nervous or guilty.

After you have failed to meet any experience properly, you may find it difficult to meditate for awhile. Don't try at this point; let the emotion run its course and *suffer the consequences* for a short season. Then meditate.

Most of your discoveries about yourself will be during your daily activities. As you approach your usual duties, you will notice something wrong, compulsive or mechanical about what you do. Observing this changes the outcome. Many discoveries will be made as you perform your day-to-day activities, but behind it all will be your meditation exercise that is teaching you to approach everything with a new awareness.

Be apprised of a very subtle danger in observing once suppressed emotions rising to the surface. Just as your ego can be distracted by and fascinated with negative surroundings as well as caught up in pleasant situations, so can the mind. Hating wrong people as well as what is wrong in the world can make you feel right. One can make a practice of observing wrong people and gloating over what is wrong. One can observe phantoms of the mind in exactly the way one does the things outside. Observed memories, though, are usually playbacks of those experiences with the real thing.

It is possible to fool yourself in the practice of meditation. You can very well appear to be observing thoughts, allowing the bad ones to surface, and in effect you can be watching them faithfully, according to the instructions. But remember the vital difference between observing a thought stream from an OBJECTIVE point of reference, standing aside as a person might on the bank of a river watching a boat go drifting by down current, and getting into the water, floating down the stream alongside the boat, gawking at it. The big mistake is to get into the thought stream and drift away from the light of the present moment and become fascinated with watching the boat.

A morbid thought can be just as much of a distraction as a pleasant one—perhaps even more so. When we are unable to turn away from our morbid thinking, we tend to use it as a distraction from knowing just how wrong it is (and we are) and so neatly avoid the failure it represents.

Our pride invariably craves negative situations as judgment food. Frequently it is a situation where we were not involved with the error (another's). Observing others gives us a sense of objectivity, apartness from problems, therefore a pseudosense of righteousness. Externalizing in this manner, observing outside wickedness in the time-space continuum pulls us away from the Light, from observing our own faults, and we become busybodies, world-watchers and world-worriers.

The same holds true with memories of such experiences and, of course, with the problems that underlie them. We can drown ourselves in self-pity, so to speak, which is to say that we can go floating downstream with our memories and forget what they mean in terms of failing. In forgetting what they mean, there is ego relief.

Used as a distraction, any morbid thought or memory can be quite effective in keeping us from facing the Light of the Presence. Fascinated by evil, both inside and without, we can see *only* evil and no good in the world except the observer. What a comfort that is if we still desire to play god!

Be careful! Don't be trapped when these morbid thoughts rise—stay away from them—remain in the

Light of the Presence. Don't slip your moorings; stay apart from these thoughts. If you happen to get caught up with them, it might seem as if you are meditating correctly, because at least they are out in the open, and they are indeed being observed.

You will be fooled *only* because of your unrefined intent that allows you to fall into the river of your mind, and if you are very obstinate, to drown. Again, be warned. Don't go thought-riding in the rapids of your mind in any shape or form—especially with the morbid ones. It's just another cop-out, an escape; and if you are not careful, you will believe yourself to be heading toward a God-sent date with Death's destiny in dignified, almost rosy resignation. You know the line, "It's better that I leave this world. Everyone will be better off without me. I am only a burden to my family," etc., etc.

Another danger when flashbacks bring out buried feelings of hostility toward, say, your mother is a sudden feeling of warmth and life enveloping you for that person. Beware!

It is not unusual for children to "love" whomever hates them as a means of getting their "love" in return. Secondly, resentment is a primitive and ineffectual first line of defense against cruelty; but resentment results in guilt, which often can only be relieved by having the opposite feeling to hate—yielding to instead of resisting the hated object and generally surrendering one's self to it. This can lead to a life of surrendering to people for feelings of "love." All kinds of scoundrels take advantage of us this way!

Be careful not to mistake the catharsis and the release of that warm feeling for the discovery of genuine love. There are two kinds of catharsis—observing released feelings of hate and, behind that, observing *released* feelings of *false* love. The ultimate aim here is not having any feelings at all, one way or the other, toward anyone. You may have experienced a warm feeling around certain people as though it were a love experience—or perhaps you didn't know what it was. Now you do. Giving up those warm flushes toward people (for the "love" they give you) allows for the inrush of God's sustaining approval—also warm. The false kind of "love" toward a person or thing prevents God's love from enveloping you and saving you from all this error.

Let me remind you that the conscious mind does not think during the meditation; it merely observes, which means that you, the observer, are not part of the thought process *at that time.*

The observer cannot possibly "think." He only observes thinking in the usual sense. The soul is caught up on a higher plane, and the knowledge received there does not become thinking until it touches down lightly upon the mind once more.* For this reason, the meditation brings awareness of knowing something very profound, yet one is not able to put it into words, nor is it necessary to do so.

Within the observing experience is also the standard by which we compare the thoughts passing by the

---

*We stretch after each meditation to activate new influence of the soul in the body.

field of the observer's vision. If the meditator is not meditating correctly, he is swept along on a thought stream. As he is carried along with the idea (it makes no difference what the concept might be), he is borne down into the world of imagination and past experience and in this state forms a flurry of new false conclusions about what he is *subjectively* "observing," and that causes ideas to multiply like rabbits and leads to many kinds of confusion and guilt.

Repentance is utterly impossible in this subjective "observation" state because we are unable (or unwilling) to compare the past experience that we uncover with the indwelling Light of Truth. Instead, we compare experience in this state of *regression* (going into the past) with the prejudices of the soul—in other words, with what the ego wants to believe about those past experiences. A powerful thought stifler like a mantra can be utilized to carry the mind away from the truly objective state. Once the mantra, with its implied standard, is drummed into the mind and becomes an effortless part of our thinking, the wrong meditator clutches desperately to that "saving standard" and goes drifting along re-exploring the dark recesses of his mind. And then he comes upon hidden memories of the past that he was unable to face or cope with before, but with his mantra he can. He looks at a memory. He sees a scene where perhaps his mother was being cruel to him as a child. He sees his own resentment, but does not see anything wrong with that. Just before he gets to the resentment part, he experiences a warm feeling toward his mother that he promptly misinterprets as the discovery of divine love—which he later tries to feel toward everyone.

The warm feeling happens to be that childish way of overcoming intolerable resentment. As a child, he learned how to "love" what he hated to keep from experiencing the excruciating agony of hating. That never did work either, so he turned to drugs or drinking to cover that. Another use of a mantra is to achieve total oblivion—a refusal to think of anything at all.

Now in that moment of false meditation, going back into the past (to "better" days), he uncovers and re-experiences feelings of "love" toward his mother, which his ego—looking for evidence of his own goodness—interprets as divine love radiating from him toward her, instead of looking at the underlying hatred that gave rise to it and the worship of all that is wrong with his mother and other rotten people, including his guru.

The mantra or any other nonsense that reinforces the idea of the inherent goodness of our egos makes this kind of selection possible. The Light of Truth shows objectively the folly of all experiences and causes us to repent, to vent and to give up both errors ("love" and hate) rather than cling to one or the other. We can cling to resentment as a form of righteousness, too; some religions even teach *that*.

The mantra as well as many other religious beliefs allows you to look at past experience according to the implied standard of the mantra—which is easy to do because the mantras we chant or the affirmations we recite take us away from the ultimate standard that shows all things as they *are* and that would bring mourning, repentance and salvation *from* the problem, rather than from the knowledge that a problem exists.

The foolish meditator never experiences true repentance. His ego does not want to be humiliated; it may see what is wrong, but does not recognize it as error. He can never feel true shame because he looks at the problem by a false standard of comparison that he carries into his dream. Only the Light can make us sorry enought to experience true repentance and change.

The true meditator comes out of meditation clean, purged of the error and problem. At that time an entire new mode of thinking flowers in his mind as the soul touches down once again to sit on the "throne" of the mind, there delicately poised in command of all he surveys. At that moment, thoughts rush upward to give form to all the meaning gathered in communion with God's Holy Spirit. Our mind is alive with new wisdom, and this, too, multiplies like rabbits, one insight leading to an ever greater spiral of true insights, which become the building blocks of a new universe within.

Morbid and negative thoughts have only one basic origin, namely, the soul's weakness: pride. This apartness from God's protective circle of grace, which pride brings, allows these dark thoughts to enter our consciousness.

At each succeeding level of the soul's descent to hell through death, the mind is more vulnerable to negative suggestion, and the body is more sensitive to stress. The more sick or degenerate we are, the more negatively complex we become. We develop a tendency to *believe the worst* because of the overwhelming evidence that confronts us; for the egocentric mind is not a creature of faith but one of proof—and the proof of our error is always mushrooming up before us.

But in a remarkable double-think process, the same pride in our nature tries desperately to disbelieve the evidence presented to it.

As described, morbid and negative thinking takes place at different levels of descent—for example, the ego is very suggestible in a special, subtle way that makes the body more brutish; then the brutish mind is sensitive, impressionable and gullible to any idea because of the soul's separation from Truth. In its failing state, the soul has a need for lies, and that is a further failing and departure from reality. Then sickness and tragedy follow, to provide even further negative influence upon both mind and soul.

Before going into detail, I want to make you aware of a sequence of morbid thoughts based strictly on an attitude of consciousness that has nothing to do with suggestion, direction, evidence of failing or premonition.

It is just possible, if you are like the vast majority of people, that you will discover something very awesome—which is a basic discovery when you meditate—and that is: You have hated God!

Disbelief, doubt and hatred are part and parcel of our egocentric state of being. A state of war has always existed between you and God. But as you stop running, truth catches up to you and illuminates the error more fully, so that you experience that enmity with God known as conflict.

Conflict exists before we realize what conflict actually means in its deepest sense—conflict is war, you see: an unholy war between the soul and its Maker.

Don't be too alarmed to realize this fact. You are not alone or eternally damned because you have hated God—it is sufficient to be sad or sorry, even embarrassed, and that sorrow becomes repentance. Repentance, you see, is the same as capitulation—a surrender or yielding of one's will to God, which in turn means joining forces *with God.* This discovery can lead to sadness and result in a cessation of hostilities between you and God, which brings peace of mind and a new way of dealing with life as a matter of course.

In your apartness from God, you were sustained by God's mortal enemy, and by virtue of your separation, you were in effect serving Satan. So while you were fighting for your true self, your soul (consciousness) was immersed—spiritually, mentally, emotionally and physically—in an unholy alliance with the Prince of Darkness. That is the reason why you were so vulnerable to negative suggestions, no matter how positive they seemed at the time—*the source of ego comfort itself is hellishly negative, and all its assurances and support were themselves lies!*

If you have doubted God's existence, it is only because your ego has had a need to doubt. You can see the doubt thoughts looming in your mind when you meditate, and you must learn to reject them. Don't force yourself to believe in God; just reject the doubt, and you shall both know and see God.

The deep guilt caused by doubting God often drives people to extreme compensations, and they will be moved to affirm strongly that God exists—this, too, is heresy! It's like saying that if you did not affirm God's existence, He would cease to exist—which is just another way of proving that you are greater than He is! Worse yet, you think that you are His creator, better than God for having made Him—this, too, causes self-exaltation, greater conflict and terrible fear that makes you want to scream louder and louder that God does or does not exist (as though your screaming would disguise your feeling superior to Him!)

Morbid attitudes and negative thinking are all due to the awareness of the soul's own failing, like negative self-knowledge. All kinds of weird suggestions come homing into the mind as we draw physically and psychically closer to death and Hell. Morbid suggestions flit unbidden into consciousness without rhyme or reason, and we spend most of our energies trying to push them back out of sight, where we won't have to face them.

Then there is the kind of morbid thinking that arises out of the supreme audacity of making judgments about God's goodness and justice. You tell yourself that God has got to be some terrible Super-Being with little mercy (something like your secret self, perhaps), and that is why you are afraid to face Him—that attitude alone is reason for terror!

You even go as far as judging God openly by your

own unloving, unforgiving standard, He can't possibly forgive you, you tell yourself—so you damn Him for His incapacity to forgive you (really your own unwillingness to forgive others). So long as you think this way, you compound your own feeling of damnation, which grows to utter despair—a perfect example of how morbid thoughts arise from the soul's impoverished condition. The funny thing is that what makes us feel so rotten is really God's goodness; we are damned only by our own damning. All we have to do is realize how wrong we are, and the Heaven that feels like Hell becomes, at once, heavenly.

Then there is the negative thinking of doom. As the soul approaches death, it can not only sense but also see tragedy and disaster ahead. In other words, such experiences may have little to do with imagination, but thoughts such as these can arise out of a sort of psychic precognition, from seeing what may lie ahead.

The moment the soul cries out to God, the door to these scenes of the house of horror shuts—and this kind of morbid thinking is quickly resolved.

Unfortunately, the incorrigible ego will also cry out at these times of psychic distress, but his cry is heard by the very one who has dragged him down into the abyss of terror looming before his mind's eye. The horror of being "helped" this way, drawn in helplessly by your very cry for help, is too terrible to describe. This infernal cry is to the only "god" the egotist has ever "known and loved"—this "god," who is the one who has helped you to think that you are God, is the Lord of Hell whom you see at that anguished moment! As an egotist, you *cannot* cry to the true God, but only to the "lesser" one, who apparently serves your ego in this life. In your egotism, you won't know how to cry in any way other than to cry for what has led you to Hell.

And, at the last, what has saved you from yourself claims you for his own!

8 The Real You and the 'Not You'

Now that you have seen how the emotion of resentment becomes the medium for all manner of negative suggestion when you are upset, let us consider how this emotion sustains your pride and gives evil the power to use you as a pawn in a devilish conspiracy.

You will never be well until you learn to stay calm and in your center—a condition that keeps out error and suggestion. Realize that resentment is the soul food of pride as well as the substance of your brutish conditioning. Repent of your anger and thus fast from the stimuli that feed a prideful, brutish existence, and then the Light comes shining in, flooding your mind and body with the essence of the Light. You will then move and have your being in a positive way that will also bring a whole, new and beautiful world into existence.

But from anger, resentment, hate, impatience, hurt feelings and the like arises a mist in the mind that blocks the Light of understanding from coming through and gives form and direction to a base and gross identity. These unruly emotions not only build pride, but they go on through the portal of the ego to crystallize into the kind of person who will express the will and purpose of the hell's angel, who is charged to support your pride.

Every time you are angry you make a judgment. Anger is the handmaiden of judgment; one can't exist without the other. To the degree that you repent of anger, pride ceases to be pride because it can't continue as pride and repent at the same time. Anger must diminish because it is no longer compatible with or acceptable to the repentant soul. At this time, the Light will come streaming in to purify all memory of sin and to exorcise things of the darkness.

The evidence of every judgment you hcve made is the crystallization of the tempter's nature in you. In other words, you have become like what you have hated—the tempter became your environment, and you became the product of your reaction to that environment. You must no longer hate the sinner. "Hate" instead the sin, for you can effectively hate sin only by not judging (hating) the sinner. The sin in the sinner tempts you to judge; it traps you into being just as hateful as the sinner and to be filled with the same kind of dark spirit.

Have compassion, therefore; love your enemy—by not hating or judging. You should not, however, *force* yourself to like him. Observe the error—yes!—be aware of what it is, but don't condemn the person who commits it. In this way you starve or defeat the error operating in him. Feeling no feedback from his temptation, the error grows weak, feels observed and lets go of its victim. How your beloved "enemy" will respect you for this!

By hating the sinner, you are really in accord with the sin in him. To be tempted to hate, you must first have had an ego need to judge, and the tempter merely sense that need and brought it to light.

But never for one moment believe that you have no control over your hatred. You have control to the degree that you can admit and be sorry for the secret pleasure you find in hating! It is the denial of your faults to yourself that keeps you bound to them.

In the beginning, it was an initial shock wave of temptation that altered you, and it is the shock wave of your reaction to each new temptation that perpetuates your corruption. Shock is a trauma that displaces your real identity with the spore of a new one— an identity that craves to judge others. In your egotism and guilt, you defensively think of this tempted identity as the real you, but it is not. When the "not you" takes up residence in your body, it teaches you to be defensive against Truth. Were you perfect at birth, you would also have been immune to change and resistant to temptation; but instead, you have an inherited proclivity to pride that is awakened and continually stimulated by the trauma of judgment or any other excitement offered up to your ego.

In that so-called "awakening" you really fall asleep to reality—you become unconscious to the truth that the pride you feel isn't yours at all; instead, it is a subtle, evil entity that has gained entry to your body in order to feed and enlarge itself on your substance, in much the same way that a wasp or fly larva grows inside its caterpillar host. You must know this truth! Were it not for temptation, your potential error would remain dormant and never come into being. And if the error had never grown and come to light, we could never have come to repentance, nor could we be saved from sin. So evil has a value: It brings your weakness to light so that it can be known whether or not you will repent.

Evil is nourished by the emotional miasma of foolish egos. Evil operates through the medium of a tempter by making you feel proud—but eventually it is not you who lives, but only evil who lives through you! At that point, *you* become a tempter.

In reverse: It is not you who should live but God, through Christ, Who lives in and through you.

Awaken! Realize the folly of pride. Repent, so that the Light of God can be fully realized through you. You will not be existing merely for yourself, but as a medium of His will and purpose. You will literally die to sin and come alive in Truth—or else you can choose to remain dead to Truth to be "alive" to the service of sin. Such a life is an illusion of pride, and in the Light of Reality it is seen to be death.

In the Light, you will eventually see "it," the "not

you," the judgmental self you have thought of as "you" all of your life—the self that has catered to you, comforted you in your vain pretenses, and led you into rebellion and escape from reality. It is this "self" that mutters curses against God and makes you think that you are thinking foul thoughts so that you will be too ashamed to meditate, become still and come before God. Don't be fooled! Know it is the NOT YOU—you must see that it is not you who mutters these curses. How can you know? You know because the real you is ashamed!

It is not so much for the pride you have that you are guilty, but, rather, it is for *wanting* to be proud, because, in the end, it will never be you who is proud, for you will have ceased to exist—served up to that that tempted you to pride from the beginning. The Prince of Darkness will glory in your suffering.

From wanting to be God, you fall to provide Satan his power, and Satan's feast is the combined judgments of all mankind—one man's judgment against another.

Emotion, then, has constructed for you a brutish and sensual body in which something sinister dwells— the NOT YOU! And this "not you" feeds on and operates through what is left of your altered soul—the part of you that is not yet truly committed to God, still wishing to be proud.

Perhaps the most important thing you must now realize is that EVIL HAS NO POWER OF ITS OWN. It exists only through the power you forfeit to it by way of pride's ambition. Evil grows when you are tempted to use it to urge your ego toward the forbidden and again when you seek escape from the guilt over what you have done. It uses your attempted use of it!

Evil cashes in on the life you obtain from being emotionally close to people and things. Nature is commissioned to endow animals with vitality; but through man, nature's vitality passes over to energize the work of evil. While it is true that all life comes from God through time and space, only man in his vanity has the capacity, through error, to give some of nature's power over to the devil.

Satan is the fallen spirit that lives in and through people just as God ought to live in them. By sustaining proud men in their illusions and grandeur, Satan steals their animal life to sustain himself in power and authority over them. He shapes men's bodies and draws souls to himself. Devoid of any life, he is endowed only with ths cold negative polarity to draw life into himself from the people he tempts. His power comes only from disobedient men and women. Remember: Your reaction to temptation actually causes a change for the worse at the very moment that your ego hopes are raised.

So fallen man, through his ego need, lives anxiously in his animal body on borrowed earthly vitality, giving energy over to the spirit of evil as no other creature can. The flesh form we assume (for us it comes via maturity from childhood, while for Adam, it was a fall into flesh) is meant to be restored and then translated. We are ultimately meant to become as Adam was at the beginning before he fell and gave up authority and power by yielding to the wiles of Satan; but because men keep seeking assurance for their pride and its continuance, they continue to give up power to evil through the women they use.

As we are restored, we shall one day have access to the Tree of Life deep within the soul so that we may partake of It and live forever. The power of the Holy Spirit leads our spirits to God, through the intercession of Jesus Christ, His First Faithful Son. The closer we come to God in our spirits, the more the enlightened spirit is quickened; and as the spirit quickens, the soul is able to give life and power to the body so that it also becomes transformed. After we have finally repented of all our sins and recovered, we shall be restored to natural health and resemble Adam and Eve in their fallen state. Then we shall live out our lives in purity and goodness, serving God while awaiting translation. As the soul rises in consciousness, it carries the body up along with it.

On the other hand, as the soul is tempted and led in the opposite direction, it moves closer to evil. Through the tempting experience, the quality of bodily life is slowly altered pejoratively. The body draws closer and closer to hell through the realms of nature and matter, with a spirit of deception leading the less and less conscious soul, providing false comfort and drawing the life from you as you obtain it from other people and things in nature.

Resist evil with the energy of true enlightenment, and the devil and devilish people will flee from you.

The heaven of eternal life or hell and infernal suffering hangs in the balance—the inclination of the soul toward good or evil. No power on earth can save you from this god of darkness; it is the proclivity of your own mind that decides your fate. Your own ambitious yearning for power and glory draws the Prince of Darkness to you just as if you had crooned sweetly for his presence, and this same vanity renews again and again the hellish bargain: your soul, your physical substance of life, in exchange for your glorious heart's desire! Eternity traded for a few moments of ecstasy, power, glory, self-righteousness and judgment!

It is the style of your early conditioning that determines the path your corruption takes. If you were born in Borneo, for example, you would have made a "good" cannibal; if born in Moscow, a "good" communist; and if born in Amman, perhaps a "good" Arab terrorist planting bombs in Israeli airports. That being the case, what should you see about your present "good" loyalties?

Surely you have seen by now that all social orders are a conspiracy against the individual. All societies are pyramids of power structured of tempted people who collectively serve the evil that operates through their figurehead politicians, the strongest (weakest) and most ambitious of them all. Unless you are prepared to abandon your race, your cultural orientations and identity, you cannot be saved.

Let me restate the principle again to enlarge the concept. When you are pressured or excited, you react—and in that reaction you give up energy to the tempter who holds up or upholds the pattern of your ambitious dreams. The wrong grow very strong on the strength you give them through your weakness—your need for their assurances.

As you react with excitement and give up power, an exchange occurs; simultaneously you receive the spiritual identity of your corrupter, and at that moment you become a little bit like that person, and you support the system operating through him. If you look carefully, several things are happening at one time: 1) You are·reacting, deteriorating and giving up strength; 2) there is a projection process going on; the tempter's nature projects into you and beyond to form a miserable world; and 3) your potential of true identity is assimilated, absorbed and devoured by the tempter, who represents the social order that spewed him out.

The embryonic identity you now posssess is a displaced one, a wrong and a guilty one—above all, it can be so proud that it can't admit it is wrong, and it will be defensive against the truth. It is a child of its cultural corruption—a child who will cling to the parent culture and the evil operating behind the scenes for continued patterns of its growth.

Remember, comfort—false love—is just as much a temptation as temptation itself; and what culture has planted, it carefully nurtures into the image of itself to serve and to cling to the purpose operating behind itself from this invisible hell.

Returning to the point: Your original identity has been sacrificed, exploited to power the false ideals of the system operating through the tempter, and he, in turn, is a victim who serves "his" energy, which he has got from you, to power someone even more ambitious than he himself. Virtually a military chain of command is formed with power, life and energy plundered from the youngest and weakest upward, passed along the chain to the strong man at the top. From the top, the corrupt cultural identity is passed down the chain until it reaches the bottom. We grow in rank in this military chain of command as we are big enough to bully or tempt another out of his life and true growth.

Now the basis of the power of your immediate superior officer is your ego fear of facing the truth, because the moment you try to stop serving (reacting) and going along with him, he will withhold the pattern of your ego growth, identity as well as hope, the possibility of "promotion," hope of power and glory, which until the dawning of Light is the only hope and the only game you know. So the moment you lose social approval, you are overwhelmed by the terror of guilt and despair.

But guilt is unbearable only as long as we want to remain proud. The shock of seeing our enslavement to the establishment through which hell is served can make us truly sorry. I am NOT speaking here of the grief that comes only from being a loser.

Such a shock can lead to repentance and change your identity at the core of your being. This is the kind of change that also renders you dependent on the Light Who gives you back your displaced identity and makes you a new creation. In return for that new identity spore, you serve God for His sustaining approval instead of the Devil's. Unfortunately, this same shock can drive you back in to the Devil's comforting arms.

If we all resisted temptation through repentance, false systems would fall, and a new, perfect system would rise, with each person containing and nurturing one small part of the plan of what the new culture is to be. As the individual flourishes, so will the social order become more perfect and elaborate, each serving the will of the invisible Source and Leader—God the Father through the Prince of Peace, His Son, through Whom men are reconciled to God.

Currently the invisible Prince of Darkness rules on Earth through the lives of sinners, who cannot refuse to serve him for fear of losing their glorious illusions and false righteousness. You cannot help the social man. He already has all of the "help" he wants.

So in your ambition, you are tempted (changed) to serve a spirit more haughty than your own. In other words, there is really *no such thing as your own ambition.* That is why all goals are frustrating, futile, debilitating and guilt producing. He who tempts you to play god is god over you.

The same principality that enticed Adam to reach for the forbidden and took away the very advantage he promised to deliver is the same who tempts you to, for example, get rich quickly and then lord it over other men.

The cardsharp and the con man stay ahead of the victim's ambition. The hope of getting ahead is held up, and the foolish victim keeps stumbling after it. The con man always gets the very advantage he offers to the stupid, greedy, ambitious ego. That's how we can learn to be like our tempter. When we discover the secret of getting ahead, we tempt our brother for advantage over him even as another "brother" hovers over us, taking every advantage away from us, at the same time *projecting* more *knowledge* (justification) to take advantage of our less fortunate brothers.

Through your ambition you are part of a dog-eat-dog world, and *all* cultures serve the fiendish intelligence that said at the beginning, "God lies; you shall not die, but you shall become gods and be able to judge good from evil yourself."

So we are born inheriting death as part of life, and the Devil *projects* his hell on earth, operating behind a mask of social order—and it still lies and still leads!

The irresistible yielding up of energy is directly related to your ego need for illusion. If you are attracted to charming, personable people with a need for them to like you, that is sufficient temptation to cause you to give up energy to them in exchange for the ego support you now unwittingly require. Or look at it another way: Your need for approval has failing and ambition somewhere at the back of it. Look at this need. Be willing to give up "friendships"—and then be sure you don't fall into the *resentment* trap! It is another high that causes you to deteriorate and give up the life energy these "friends" need. Everyone has been motivated out of his life and identity, and almost everyone is in turn a motivator.

As a motivator yourself, you plant your identity in

your victim, and your victim supplies the strength and power to the identity that others further back in time have imprinted in you.

The power of worldly authority lies in the energy we are all forced to give up to these authorities—and *your overreaction, your helplessness, fear, paralysis and your trembling before them is proportionate to the level of your fall.* Your most immediate superior can be one of these people who puts you on and makes you feel comfortable and superior—or you could instead be caught up through the medium of poetry, symphonic music or a chemical substance. Your heart palpitations before these indulgences is evidence that you still look to them either for a goal, something you want or merely for approval.

Remember the rule: *Whatever* gives you a high, puts you on, gives your ego a life or moral support, *whatever* comforts you in any way at all, unfailingly reduces your awareness of what is wrong with you. But the level of your physical existence comes down, too—you always become subject to and the slave of whatever produces this sort of illusory effect. You are forced to serve that person, endowing him with energy for him to give you the homage and ego satisfactions you crave.

The *solution?* First of all, you must give up your victims! If you don't, then you remain part of a food chain—a victim of those who can still victimize you. They will take the energy you take from your victim. So repent of your proud, vampirish, sinful nature—and *give up* your victims, your children, husband, wife, etc. As long as you tempt others for advantage and life, you remain unprotected in that dog-eat-dog world. As long as you tempt, you will be too bloated with worldly delight to have room for God's saving grace. Realize this in the Light of Truth, and you can shrink back from harming others, and no more harm can come to (or through) you.

Of course, you will become weak—but such weakness becomes a yearning, a mind/body agony for true life. Admit freely to your victims what you have done to them, the tricks you have employed to upset, rule and have your way with them. Explain to them also, especially to your children, that what they have become is mostly your fault because of what you have failed to represent to them.

Have you driven them to drugs? Take most of the blame back upon yourself. Show your child how you have merely projected your guilty identity into him and stolen his relative innocence and youth. Remember, the rule is constant: The tempter always changes places with the victim; the victim becomes you, and you become the victim.

Adam had the highest place of honor and dignity; but, because he was ambitious to be more than he was, he was tempted—and instead of evil and nature being subject to him, he became *subject* to evil and nature. And so it has been ever since. We, his progeny, keep repeating the same scenario. The evil that got into others tempts us in the same way, and they get our power and apparent innocence while we feel their *guilt* . You rise in the inverted pyramid of society only to the degree that you obtain the strength of the masses. Wicked authority needs your strength even as you need its approval.

So, after repenting, give up two things;

first, your victim(s),

then have the courage to give up your entourage of "friends"—you can do that mostly by being honest with them.

All is resolved in the Light shining through your objective (less active and more aware), conscious self.

Don't fall into a dialogue with "your" thoughts—just watch and see how even they try to *tempt* you to deal with them. Sometimes the spirit in charge can fabricate the most elaborate arguments against such things as your worthiness to come before God (and just who is worthy?); or it tells you that you are not meditating for the right reason so as to stop your meditating to God completely. God almost never talks or reasons with you as spirits do—God is Light, and His Light teaches mostly by shining on things and exposing evil for what it is. He shows clearly where to go, what decisions to make and gives generally a whole new dimension to your observation of life.

The old physical conditioning with its nasty spirit of deceit cannot exist long in the presence of Light shining through the soul. There is little more to do but watch either with a spirit of inquiry or with wonder. Evil things are afraid when they see that you *honestly* don't know how to deal with them and that you inquire of God.

There will come a time when "IT" will come out of you, perhaps contorting your features as it leaves. As it comes out, it can fake almost any ectoplasmic form—

usually a dark, deteriorating and hideous mass and sometimes an animal identity you have appropriated or identified with, such as a pet.

Remember the rule again: You are not to deal with people, thoughts or even the spirits you may observe. Merely watch and thus stand objectively, fearlessly aloof so as to allow the Light to do His work with you merely as the medium and the observer. For Heaven's sake, don't be upset, afraid, worried, or impatient—that will be your ego moving back into the fray.

You will marvel at what transpires through you— and somewhere in all of your wondering you will find more faith in what you do not know than in what you do! You will discover trust that allows the Will of the Light to save us from "ourselves" and to transform our world from darkness into Light.

Temptation, then, is always a demand for energy. If you do not cancel the pressure of such a demand with true love, you will lose your very guts to the hungry tempter, whom you can never hope to satisfy. Your response has something to do with realizing the form your ego desires to take—a boss, a judge, a lover. He or she is your authority only because of your ambition.

Every tempter has a two-fold need: The corrupt part of his identity will promote your ego and demand your life and energy in exchange, while the decent side of his soul (if it exists) hopes that the best of you will come out to oppose him. The decent side (again, if it exists) is a prisoner—it is buried under thousands of layers of corruption, and this decent side cries out for freedom.

Do you see why it is so vital to separate the sin from the sinner? It is the sin operating through its captive that tempts you to respond and finds its mark in your ego need to judge or to be praised. That response draws life from you and feeds the error growing up in that tempter. So it comes to pass that the sin, now bigger as the result of being fed, demands and gets more soul food.

You see, there usually is a dual need in every problem-ridden person confronting you—one part wants to devour you, and the other wants you to destroy the monster that holds him (or her) captive. In this St. George-and-the-Dragon episode, the fearful maiden in distress waits in the tower with bated breath while her suitor attacks the monster—and if he loses, the dragon gets her too!

The world of hell prevails through your impatience, and you become sucked in and changed—recruited into the service of Hades. You too become a prisoner locked in the tower and in turn must wait for a victorious St. George who may never come.

Or—you can hold the Light within, be repentant, and suddenly you are "St. George" (the Christ Light is in you), and you sally forth as warrior of God against the dragon still lurking in enslaved mankind.

Pride always responds with excitement and in the presence of temptation fails. Humility doesn't. The more pride you have, the more you need to respond. Pride, through the emotion it needs, is the only portal through which hell can enter the earthly realm.

It is sufficient for you to realize what your resentment and false hope mean in terms of pride. You must wait to *be repented* . You cannot make yourself be sorry. The presence of the Light in which you stand, as a result of your persistence to know the truth, will affect a God-produced sorrow that leads to salvation.

To the degree that you have compassion for your enemy, neither liking nor hating what is in him, to that degree you will prevail over temptation operating in and through his mind and body. And to that degree also you will project a new world that God has prepared for those who love Him.

In a battle between two beasts, the stronger one drains energy from the vanquished, but if you have ob-served animal behavior very carefully, you will have seen a pecking order of losers. A big dog tears up his op-ponent, who runs away with his tail between his legs— and as soon as possible finds a victim of his own to pro-voke for the *energy* he lost in the previous fray. Re-sponse to danger causes the loser in nature to *give up* a sort of life energy. In animal life, survival of the fittest is the rule.

Just as there is a pecking order for chickens, there is an entire hierarchy of pecking orders for natural life. The lowly must serve ecologic vitality as well as physical bodies in the food chain.

And there is a pecking order of hell on earth.

Now if you look very carefully, you will see that the pecking order of hell begins with the uncorrected female as the center of the family circle. The psychological crav-ing men have for women is connected to the assurance that is needed for their ego (animal) identities—the result of an original temptation and exchange, and later perpetuated through a guileful, dominant female.

We always crave what corrupts our souls—the implanted embryonic hell identity in man screams and craves to be nurtured, and men are forced to serve their life substance in exchange for those ego assurances. Women are superior to men in the sense that they lead. Women excite and threaten men—women are also "friends" of man. Men develop as the result of some form of female support, and their miserable world of "success" is based on the pattern men project, which depends on whatever it is the woman is *required* to continue projecting.

Awareness of his base animal identity makes the ego of man very self-conscious. He doesn't see what every woman can—that the "love" he craves from her only makes a more unprincipled animal or weakling out of him. He doesn't realize what is happening to him through all his love affairs. He is unaware that he is worse off for being "loved" and that as his ego gets bigger and more guilty his body becomes more gross and brutish with each successive "love." A man loses something of his humanness in his ambition, and this loss occurs just at the point of his sexual support.

An ambitious fool believes his ego "love" (enslavement) and craving for the female is good and that his achievements are noble—and the hell operating through the female lets him go on believing it: *His kingdom come depends on it.*

Behold then the mystery of life! What temptation plants, temptation "loves" and nurtures—hell "loves" its own—so you see there are two kinds of love and motivations, because there are two spiritual sources—good and evil.

The primitive "love" from a woman that motivates men is really temptation operating through her, shaping the man to the specifications of hell on earth. Satan is a guileful woman's god, and woman is man's god—the head of a reverse projection of the righteous order.

The mysterious, essential need that woman has for a man is not sexual, but one merely associated with sexuality. It is really hell in her craving for his vital life force—power from and over the stupid and wicked fallen male. Hell leads, a woman demands—and the male obeys. Behold! The present misery of the world is a projection of a perverted, inverted, heavenly pattern.

See how hell has succeeded in creating a "man" in its image and bringing forth a "woman" out of "man" as a helpmate for him. The "man" referred to here, of course, is the masculine, dominant woman fashioned out of the decay of the male identity and essence; the "woman" is what has been regurgitated as a feminine "man." That is why all men feel inferior to and threatened by woman and why they are always making monkeys out of themselves trying to prove themselves as men—and never quite making the grade.

Without the intervention of understanding, in due time *all* men and women become sexually and spiritually exchanged to varying degrees. Ultimately what we see, if we care to look, is an exact replica in the negative (reverse) of God's original order of creation—which was the Spirit creating man, then taking woman out of man in order to do His will, to project His purpose abroad on the face of the earth.

A woman is unique in this respect: She is and was the source of what man is today, and because of this arrangement her ego is excited by and dependent on his failing. This is another temptation.

And so it comes to pass that ambitious men crave love, and when they get it they become more craven, unprincipled beasts. A woman's craving for love is a vampirish ego need for his life essence, which he is forced to give up in exchange for her approval. As a woman is exicted over a man's weakness (lust for her), she obtains power, and this is what attracts her to a man. It is often, of course, mistaken for love for him.

A man browbeats, enslaves, degrades and exploits other men for advantages and to recover life force and then yields it all up to his demanding wife as payment for her approval. In the pit of iniquity, fallen men degrade one another and fight amongst themselves in the pecking order of animals to obtain life. The more sophisticated, cunning female-oriented or female-exchanged males live on the energies seduced from other men—but the less sophisticated ones glean life by working close to nature and loving the excitement that comes from animals, pets, drink and drugs, and so on.

Society, then, is built on a system of families exploiting families, with the ambitious, demanding woman draining life and energy from her equally ambitious husband and children. The family unit in turn is exploited in business, government, school and church by ambitious men driven by the demanding women they need to maintain their ambition.

When you find God's grace through repentance from your desire to be ambitious and proud—then you will be fulfilled by true life from within. This kind of life has no need for the life of others; neither will it give up life to others.

Down is up in the Kingdom of Hades. A male is always dependent on and inferior to whatever it is that builds his ego; he is always used by what he tries to use. He can't beat the house with any system or trick because the odds always favor the house.

This is why decent women suffer—and also why wicked, ambitious women are delighted to play the game to the hilt.

Men, you adore her with your cunning love to get back what you lost, and you lose again. You hate and degrade her to feel pleasure—and you are more guilty than ever. You pretend to worship her, bow down and debase yourselves for her approval, to buy back your self-respect, only to discover you have again sold yourselves down the river. You are no better off for all your efforts. Her approval is only a deception, for the moment you accept that approval you are worse, not better: less, not more. So then you hate her and make fools of yourselves—and then you love her and make bigger fools of yourselves.

Remember this principle! Hell projects by tempting, teasing, comforting and eliciting a response. It impresses its identity and its plan into its victims, and the victim gives up energy life in the heat of excitement to pride.

Here are a few positive actions that will break this dilemma.

Men: start by being less ambitious and not making woman the center of your existence. Don't chase her, trying to get back what you have lost. The self-respect any temptress could give you would be illusory at best.

As you meditate, your compassion for your wife's plight will very slowly become stronger than your sex desires and your physical need for her. You see, the quandary is mostly a *man's problem*. The *pride* in man requires woman to play the role of temptress.

The *woman's dilemma* has been how to deal with the man's demands, his obsessive sexuality and his making her a monster and an ugly, shameless whore merely for his ego and physical pleasure taking. It is often sufficient for a woman just to *realize* the part she has played and to desire to play the game no longer, regardless of any advantages she may appear to lose.

If she stands her ground steadfastly, she could conceivably lose her man—but then what will she have lost? Only what she should not have had in the first place. But if her honesty awakens her man to his shame and he is sorry (grateful) and respectful, they will learn to live happily ever after.

The woman has a comparatively small problem—

one of security, but a man will experience quite a lot of difficulty with his base thoughts and desires.

Do you see now the importance of a man-centered home?

With the Spirit of God leading the man and God's love in man correcting the woman, the way is easy and sure. The man no longer falls to temptation, nor craves-hates his woman through whom it comes—but in effect he calmly says: "Put the apple down, Eve. There's a good girl."

9 Implanted Identity

Whenever you become stimulated emotionally, the source of that excitement implants something of its identity in you. Then a strange thing occurs; instead of being terrified and revolted by that particular experience, you can become attracted to it, fascinated by it, even needful of it. You can grow to love the most despicable, degenerate people, places and things and never see anything wrong with your associations.

Literally, you are changed every time you respond emotionally. Whenever you experience a shock, for example, you actually become a little bit like the shock source. A little bit of that environment impresses itself upon your nature, displacing your true identity and disturbing the other relationships you had prior to that shock experience. This spore, engram or false imprint is really a new and sinister form of life that cries out for the condition that spawned it. It is for this reason that you may begin to notice a strange fascination for and agreement with conditions or people you resisted before the trauma. You find that what was shocking, repulsive, or horrible one moment has become a bizarre pleasure or an uneasy comfort the next. Our bodies can become irresistibly attracted to things that once repelled us.

But as your life begins to revolve around the originator of the peculiarities of the shock object or person, shock is no longer experienced as shock; instead it is regarded as a comfort and is equated with growth. It becomes the source of energy from which you live, and it begins to motivate your every action.

So the shock, trauma or emotional response that you first regarded as enemy becomes a friend—unless you learn to resist it properly.

Let us examine the mechanics of this process in detail through an all-too-common example. One day your son or daughter comes home strangely different, as a result of an experience of this type.

Increasingly, from that point on, you feel that you don't know him any more—he has changed—he doesn't love or respond to you as he once did. Instead, he is completely caught up with some friend who does weird things that don't seem weird at all to him. With each passing day, he becomes more like the friend and less like the beloved offspring whom you thought you knew so well.

Now, instead of rescuing their children from this influence, it is not unusual for parents to be so shocked that they also become like their weird children.

The sly tempter who lies at the base of the shock

has much going for him. He knows that once corrupted, his victims will not only become physically dependent, but also psychologically dependent. It is the nature of every proud ego to defend itself against the knowledge of failing. The ego simply cannot admit being wrong and still remain proud; no matter how degenerate it becomes in the process, the ego mind must always allow itself to believe that any change is for the good—every movement an improvement. At this precise point of need, the subtle tempter enters and agrees with and provides for this psychic need for lies.

Thus, there is a bodily need as well as a psychic-psychological one to be met by the corrupter-comforter, who quickly changes roles for the purpose. While the ego is wallowing in its lies, it is not conscious of the evils being perpetrated through its mind and body. You really come to believe that you are being loved by this considerate, understanding, kind, comforting friend, because he does seem to fulfill all your needs. You do have all the lies (which seem like truth to you) that you need to excuse all the sensual seeds of the fiend growing up inside you. The Devil is indeed understanding and generous with his children. What Hell plants, Hell carefully nurtures.

Corrupted people, in their compulsive way, become very loyal to their wicked teachers, because their given life depends on their leader's continued existence. To attack the leader is like attacking the followers—they are identified! You may well discover that your own children—if they have responded to pressure from you—will climb the walls when you begin to change for the better. Their corrupted natures cry out for you to continue to be what you were before in order to support what they have become. Your projected identity in them will try desperately to torment you into being your old, base self. Your children find comfort in your former rottenness, and they cannot cope with your new-found grace, and if you become upset with them, you will find yourself slipping back into that old familiar role.

Do not fall into the trap of thinking of yourself only as a victim. You are also a corrupter—a tempter of others, particularly of your own children. Every time you react emotionally toward them, subject them to pressure or try to motivate them improperly, you are laying the groundwork for their eventual destruction. If your child comes home changed, you are responsible for hardening him, and if you react to the change by becoming upset, you could very well change with him.

In your fallen state, you have only two choices: to resist or to conform, and in *all* hostile resistance there is always the seed of eventual conformity, whether you see it or not. Remember this rule: Resentment is a reaction to temptation, and that resentment can build to become the shock that one day will change you permanently. Meanwhile, your feeble, angry resistance (resentment) feeds the error in your child or whomever else you are reacting to.

Under this system, if you desire to change someone, let us say a criminal, you must represent a greater force or shock than the original one that changed him into a criminal in the first place. Otherwise, your flimsy resistance only hardens him and strengthens him in his role Why? Because he would be able to tempt the life out of you. In your failure to change him, you would actually be feeding his cause. And you would become a little like the criminal yourself in the process.

A great many well-meaning policemen get hooked in this way, and they become bitter, very much like the animals they deal with. Without even realizing it, the underworld has gained an unwitting ally in a policeman's uniform.

The problem then is this: You cannot change anyone for the better, including our hypothetical criminal, by means of any kind of shock you are capable of conjuring up, because you cannot shock the hell out of anyone by conventional means without converting him over to the particular brand of hell that is in you. The exact opposite of what you attempt occurs. You respond with hostility and, through that act, give up power that supports the evil, while you undergo a change and become a little like whatever it is that you are fighting. It is in this way that men become what they fear or hate the most.

And an exchange is always taking place whenever one person reacts emotionally to another, so that you are always in constant danger of making others worse and falling yourself.

The only shock that can change a man for good is the shock of Truth. Only by being awakened to an awareness of Reality can any meaningful and lasting improvement occur. Therefore, you *must not try* to create change in others, for to do so is to act from pride. When you do not react and try to change others on your own, whatever it is within you that does not fall for the challenge *is not of this world,* and its very presence in you can provide the necessary shock to bring about the good that you desire. This is a very important point, so please bear with me as I say it again in another way.

Whenever you do not resist or resent the evil in another, when you do not try to outwit the alien "resident authority" in your opponent—*at that precise moment* when you do not respond or accept the challenge to your ego—something that is not you, something of incalculable force, becomes manifest from within you, and the mere presence of it can reverse the process of sin. Only that force has authority over hell on this earth. To convert another person through the force of your own personality or cunning is simply to create a slave to the evil within you, and nothing has really changed.

How, then, did we arrive at this sorry state in which the most we can do, of ourselves, is to trade sins with one another, and how can we escape the consequences of such lives?

In our formative years, impressions are made upon our minds that affect our entire lives. This outside influence should not be, because from it we are bent—forced in directions contrary to what our inherent proclivities would otherwise have been.

In order to come back from being an Englishman, an Arab, a drunk or a cannibal or whatever you have become to what you might have been, you must first understand the mechanics of change from the negative point of view. I have, therefore, divided this chapter into two parts: 1) the mechanics of the problem and 2) the techniques of dealing with the trauma of emotional reaction and shock.

Neurotic behavior and cravings should be traced directly to an unrecognized need to gravitate toward the source of an original shock. In fact, criminal and other types of rebellious behavior depend on a series of substitute sources to sustain them. A person so afflicted may unconsciously display an obnoxious, irritating habit or mannerism in order to draw upon himself the type of critical response from his environment that originally seeded his neurosis. The emotional response with which most people react to such behavior traps them into providing the necessary environmental reinforcement to keep it alive. For example: A child is called "stupid" by his classmates, and, although he resents those remarks, he soon finds himself behaving stupidly. There are two reasons for this apparently paradoxical behavior: first, because he has become a victim of suggestion through hostility (which is the basis of suggestibility) and second, because he needs reinforcement to maintain his hostile response—by behaving foolishly he tempts his peers to call him names and from these recurring incidents he draws the emotional energy to sustain himself in the new, hostile way he has come to know through his angry response to the initial temptation.

If he now tries to behave normally again, he discovers an unbearable emptiness—a void that must be filled with something, and the only seemingly satisfactory answer that comes to him is to experience more of the emotion that corrupted him.

The rule is that emotional shock displaces our identities with something of the nature of the shock and then causes our entire lives to begin to revolve around the peculiarities of the shock source itself. If you were shocked or tempted to steal, you would soon find yourself craving support for your new thieving identity, for without constant reinforcement from outside yourself—from your environment—the implanted identity would cease to exist. Depending on whether you were hooked by rebellion or conformity, you would be obliged to behave like a thief in order to elicit either the criticism or approval that is required to sustain this pride-related, emotionally begotten identity.

This principle is consistent as far forward and as far backward as you care to explore it. Before this chapter ends, I propose to give you more than a hint that it also applies to the primal shock that altered the nature of man to that of a male who clings to a tempting female for the support of his displaced life.

Returning to the example of the child and his tormentors, we discover, on close examination, the classic psychic pattern of sustaining force supporting his compulsive behavior: *judgment.* The child's pattern of behavior is an archetypical one that is set in motion *through* the action of others *tempting him to judge them.* His own hostile response, then, becomes the vehicle by which the suggestion establishes itself in his mind, and precisely that same hostility tempts him to take the role of judge. The error imparted by the tempters to their victim now beckons from its new home and demands that the cycle of provocative behavior-goading judgment continue in order to replicate the cruel circumstances of the original trauma and thereby reinforce the child's fallen identity, sustaining his secret judgment on his wicked associates.

Similarly, any form of foolish or eccentric behavior is in fact a trap designed to excite you to ridicule another, to make you a source of trauma by means of your judgment and, consequently, to provide a basis by which others will be tempted to judge you. Observe your reactions in the presence of an eccentric, a hippie, a drunk, a junkie, or even someone patently rude. If you react in any way to these behavior patterns, you must learn to overcome your response, or else you will remain trapped by your own judgment into supporting their peculiarities, even as they support your tendency to be judgmental. Just as professional counselors cannot afford to respond favorably or unfavorably to their patients and retain the ability to help them, neither can you respond to those around you and provide anything other than a further impetus for their continuing abnormal behavior.

This principle is particularly visible in the parent-child relationship. For example, a young man grows up with a compulsion to expose his genitals in public. In one such case, the behavior was motivated initially by

his mother's reaction to her discovery of the boy mastur-
bating. He could have survived the embarrassment of
the incident and grown to normal manhood if his
mother hadn't howled with disgust and created a traumatic, emotionally charged scene that gave rise to a pattern of resentment on the part of the boy toward his
mother. (Resentment, you will recall, is also judgment
in which something or someone by his wicked emotional reaction impels us to undergo an emotional
trauma or shock.) From that moment on, there exists
not only a compulsion to masturbate, but to do so in
public. Why? In order to produce the intensity of disgust
that his ego has come to need for the support of this new
way of life—a way of life that came into being because of
the boy's judgmental reaction to his mother's emotionally based judgment of his action. Exposure then becomes the means by which reinforcement and energy
are obtained to support the only way of life of which he
is now aware. He finds surrogate mothers by exposing
himself to other women, most of whom can be expected
to be disgusted just as his real mother was originally.

When your own perverted need tempts a person to
tempt you, that temptation is no longer experienced as a
shock, as it was in the beginning. Successive temptation
seems like love and security. Woman did not, of her own
initiative, originally tempt man; she was tempted to
tempt him, and men continue to demand that women
remain something that is not meant that they should be;
and they levy this demand because of their continual
need for a source of support for their fallen identities—a

source that, by comforting them and accepting them as they are, will allow them to feel better without requiring them to *be* better.

Another example: You may find yourself attracted to a man who has the same peculiarities as the father you hated in your childhood. You may even marry him for no other reason than the dubious luxury of hating him in order to sustain the personality within you that came into existence as a result of your former feelings of resentment toward that parent. Naturally, while you are in the throes of dissecting the flaws in your newly acquired beast, you see very little wrong with yourself. In fact you feel very secure and almost saintly by comparison. You may even experience a relief from your anxieties and a strange, uneasy sort of peace. Yet your very indignation toward the folly of others traps them into being the base you need to support your own error. Your fault has come into existence through the wickedness of judgment, just as that of your victim (who now forms your base) arose from someone judgmental, *just like you*. We all have an urgent need to duplicate the situation that caused the evil to develop in us, if we are to continue to exist as evil has created us. If you learned to smoke in a locker room, were humiliated in a restaurant, or had your first sexual experience in the back seat of an automobile, you will find yourself drawn to such places for reasons that may have puzzled you—until now!

When boy meets girl (nagging mother) and girl meets boy (product of nagging mother) they complement and complicate each other. In our faulty marital state, we all fortify each other's neurotic tendencies. Just as the school children in our earlier example got their kicks from taunting and the victim got his judging their wickedness, and just as the children could not observe their own error, neither can you see the error in your own ways. By acting like a drunk, a junkie or just a plain, red-blooded male, you are soliciting support for what you have become, and whenever that is in error, then the error seeking comfort in the ground of its being produces a terrible conflict in your soul. It is primarily for this reason that women climb the walls in the face of unprincipled, oversexed husbands who are seeking in their wives the original source of shock that changed the first man into an uncertain male—a male who goes on to become very suggestible and loyal to various other forms of corruption and compulsion.

This, incidentally, is why we must have strong laws such as the Ten Commandments, strong parental discipline (hopefully with poise and without drama and hysterics) with which to restrain our children and keep their suggestible natures from being led further astray.

Taunting others and being taunted ourselves, hating others and being hated in return support a way of life, and we are often attracted to one another because of compatible quirks that form the matrix of our provocative-judgmental neurotic existences. People rarely notice their own corruption. Often they even enjoy being corrupted, equating it with the joy of growth. We fail to see the process of corruption for what it is because we like the amusement value of the temptation, the spirit of which seems to serve us. We get high and draw out the evil in others to serve our judgment and to support our failing existence.

This principle is operative anywhere you care to look. Rebels give power for hypocritical instituions to continue to exist, and the very existence of the establishment seems to provide the impetus for crime and rebellion. A mother secretly promotes her son's rebellion, thereby maintaining her much needed image of righteousness, just as society creates criminals for exactly the same reason. The child becomes corrupted by his rebellion against his mother to go on needing mother's nagging in order to maintain his existence as a rebel. The error evolving through the mother tempts the child to change through emotional reaction to her and through that reaction to feed the false values of the mother, who was herself treated in the same way when she was a child. The identity of the mother goes to the child, and the life of the child goes to the mother, supporting her in her error. If he is lucky, the child will then grow up to be a father who is attracted to a woman just like his mother, and the two of them will bring more children into the world. And it is in this manner that sin is passed from generation to generation.

You must understand, of course, that it is not really the mother herself who rants and raves at the child, making him do what he should not, but *something that has made a home in her* (and/or father) and that is preparing another home for itself in the child. This wickedness is an intelligence that knows exactly how to make us respond, and, in so doing, it shapes our lives according to its pattern of hell. It knows that once you are corrupted, you will appoint it as your kind, for it knows all about your weaknesses and whether you are a rebel fool or a conformist fool. If you are suggestible and favorably disposed toward some forbidden thing, it will entice you into that experience directly and make you dependent on it. If you are, perhaps, more stout in virtue, it uses the rebellious approach—"don't do this," it screams, until you are compelled to do it. It may even try to rescue you, a ploy calculated to harden you in your rebellion and itself in self-righteousness. This "not-you" lives in everyone. If you are a rebel, it came from the hypocritical square whom you detest, and it is the part of you that can't stand to stop rebellion—the part that leads you to taunt the squares for "kicks" (life-energy) so that it can continue to grow and project itself into others.

If you are ever to be free of the "not you," you must not be afraid to cease existing in the old way. It will not be the real you who ceases to exist; it will be the "not you" that you have identified with, and when it begins to die (as it will if you take away its "kicks"), you will feel as if *you* are the one who is dying and returning to Hell. This is one of its most effective subterfuges, since we all are afrcid to die. But pull back, separate: WATCH IT DIE! Only then can you come alive in a new way. Only then can you, the surviving observer, learn to live unto God.

Currently, you have two identities living inside

you: the you and the "not you." The "not you" feels like you because you have come to identify with it—you feel what it feels and, consequently, think what it thinks. The "not you" is interested in only one thing: survival—at your expense. It is defensive against the Light of Truth; it turns away from reality and toward illusion and the imagination. It never wants you to meditate properly; and it will attempt to prevent it by inclining you toward gurus, false religions, ineffectual forms of meditation such as those employing mantras, images or any excessive use of the imagination. Yours may be a seeking soul, but for some reason you are being kept from proper meditation. One part of you wants to come up to the Light, but the other doesn't. You are afraid; the negative side tells you "you are not ready," "you are not pure enough," "you don't need it—you're 'way beyond all that," "your motive is wrong"—anything that will work will do, because the "not you" is terrified of being exposed to the Light, for you will then see clearly that the "not you" does in fact exist within you, that *it* is not pure and that *it* has the wrong motive, etc. But since *you* feel what *it* feels, you also experience that terror, and such stark fear may even persuade you to stop meditating. Although the awful truth you must face concerns the "not you," the real you is bothered by the notion. As soon as you give up meditating, the "not you" may suddenly begin to behave itself for a season in order to lull you into a false sense of security by keeping its presence a secret from you. But you *must* separate the real you from the apparent you, or else you will die.

Fortunately, if you have read this far, the chances are very good that your motive is pure; otherwise you would not have been able to stomach the message in this book; and you would have thrown it down long ago, angrily. I believe, however, that the "not you" is now probably trying to make you believe that you are insincere. If it can thus confound your belief, then it can resume control of you, force you to think God is unjust for leading you on, and lead you to take final refuge in the comforting arms of sin as a hopeless case. DO NOT ALLOW THIS TO HAPPEN. No case is hopeless until death terminates the options. No burden of sin or error is so great that sincere regret, which is repentance, will not lead to its undoing. The mere fact that you are interested in this subject, that you are reading these words is evidence of the fact that there is hope for you.

But you must realize that only through meditation can the real you separate from the "not you," and only then can the Light stream in through the you and cauterize the "not you." You must learn to remain objective in all your experiences with feelings and thought. If you feel fear, don't add to it by fearing the fear. Simply observe the fear, and it will diminish. If you feel hate, watch that hate; don't fall into the trap of hating your own hate. Stand there and watch your wrong feelings unfold, in quiet disagreement with them. You will come to realize that there are actually two feelings involved in each one. For example, when you become upset, you get mad at yourself for being upset. If you can learn to watch the first level without invoking the second, if you can *see* resentment without resenting your own resentment, you will break the vicious cycle.

The problem is that you tend to want to deal with these feelings on your own, and you end up fearing fear and resenting resentment because that is the only way the ego knows how to deal with emotions. You must face the fact that you are simply outclassed in this area; *you have absolutely no means, of yourself, of resolving this problem.* The problem is bigger than you are, and so is the solution. But when we attempt to cope ourselves, the action of our egos prevents the Light from coming through the self to deal with the problem decisively. And in your frustration, the "not you" inside you persuades you to look at the greater evil outside you as a distraction from what is growing up within, and that makes you madder than hell.

Thus the evil in you keeps you tied to the evil of situations in your environment, and your inner conflict grows. You will remain helpless so long as you resent your own resentment and use resentment against the *enemy* as a means of conquering him, for that is nothing more than a distraction from your own guilt.

Meditation will not immediately eliminate all your reactions, but it will eliminate your reactions to the existing resentment or fear-anxiety reactions to pressure. You see, resentment produces a debilitating physical conditioning. We resent our inferiority, fear and helplessness, but this only *increases* the sensitivity of the flesh to stress. After you begin to meditate, you must be patient with your symptoms; learn to experience the humilation of fear without again resenting either the source *or yourself.* Once you have successfully resisted this temptation, you are free to observe your other anxieties out of existence. In this way, you will deal effectively with the underlying causes of any symptom. Once you have gone through a series of anxieties like this, you will eventually conquer your conditioned response to pressure completely and feel no response whatever.

The constitution of pride is a defense against truth. For example, if your zipper were undone, you might first feel embarrassed on having it pointed out to you, but then you would feel relieved at knowing so that the situation could be remedied. Although embarrassed, you would appreciate the correction. A foolish man, upon being told the same thing, would experience resentment in addition to the embarrassment. When conscience plays the role of the friend who bears embarrassing news it reaps resentment if its owner is a proud person, and resentment erects a barrier to correction. The honest man, although he may be uncomfortable, accepts correction gracefully.

This, then, is the crux of the matter. When your conscience pricks and makes you aware of something that you are feeling or doing wrong, how do you react? Are you grateful for being shown your error, or do you resent having to see your weakness? Does your attention become so focused upon the fancied insult of your friend instead of your own error that you fail to see that you are moving even deeper into error through your resentment of correction?

It is a paradox that the emotion you need in order to forget how wrong you are serves to fortify the memory of cruel people who like to remind you of your faults. Should it really make any difference whether friend or foe awakens you to a fault? If you resent the truth, regardless of whether it comes from friend or enemy, you ruin the modifying influence of awareness and forsake the discipline of understanding. And so resentment can bring you ultimately into agreement with your tormentor, because, through resentment, we actually become an extension of what he is.

BE STILL...AND KNOW the pain of anxiety—fears that need to be resolved. Wait to be fulfilled through the infilling of warmth that relieves and revives. Be aware of the tension and edginess caused by resentment. Observe body aches and needs; do not stifle your aching mind and body by reaching for outside comforts. Your needs will be met by the infilling, tingling warmth of God's grace.

When you are made aware of any fault, be careful not to resent seeing it come to light. For example, someone tells you that you should not smoke. Perhaps you already know that, but when someone else tells you, the resentment against being made aware could drive you to try to change whatever it is through the energy of resentment. If your child sucks his thumb and you nag him about it, the awareness of his shame humiliates him, and the nagging makes him angry. With the energy of anger, he tries to fight the impulse to suck his thumb, but it is that very resentment that creates additional frustration and adds impetus to the need he feels to blot out his problem by thumb-sucking. It is the same with any problem you care to mention.

So, *allow* yourself to be made aware of any error by the Light shining in your conscious mind. Be willing to be made aware of any error pointed out by a friend, or even an enemy who knows how to gain energy from the confusion he sows in you when he calls your attention to your faults. Don't resent the way, means or method by which exposure comes; just be aware of the error and bear the pain of shame without hating either the pain or the person who awakens you to it, regardless of his motives.

Be careful not to try to change your parents, the cause of your original dilemma, for this will only produce frustration and anger. Your change does not and should not depend on changes in your environment. Although your ego life was formed and your faults were supported as a result of your parents' failing to do right by you, and you are, therefore, the product of the environment they provided, your new life must have nothing to do with changing the past and the ground from which you sprang. Until now, your past was the determination of your future damnation, and unless you break with the past and live in the present, you will surely die. In your egotism, your only hope for a better life has been the prospect of changing your environment: altering your parents' attitudes or finding that special person through whom change would come. But you remain connected to their hell. You have always been manipulated by whomever could save you from your last trauma.

Your "loved ones" may also resist your desperate attempts to change them, and this, in turn, could threaten you so that your own resentment would compound your guilt. So learn this lesson well: Your new life must come from the Light inside you—that Light that now testifies to all that is being said here about the futility of striving to change the world outside you for the better. Repent of your part in this struggle; relax and let the Light do the work through you. Remember the causes of resentment:

1) fixing blame on others
2) reaction against being made aware of your faults
3) reaction against the problem itself (it could be a problem husband, wife, mother, child, sickness, or even a doctor who made you worse with his help)
4) reaction against injustice
5) reaction against a "friend" who had made you helpless and dependent
6) reaction against a dearly departed, dead or living, for depriving you of love (attention, support, approval, etc.)
7) reaction against a deformity or a disadvantage or an emotional block that prevented your success.

If you have an emotional block against learning, you can be sure that resentment underlies the cause.

Similarly, a block against loving or any other proper human activity indicates resentment, or else the object itself is wrong.

Any sort of conflict in your soul is the evidence that you have come into existence as the product of disobedience of some kind and that you are not as man was originally created. It is the sheer pain of your inherited existence that forces your awakening to the reality of your dilemma. It is the inclination of the individual soul that determines whether or not the mystery of salvation will be revealed and implemented.

You may start meditating in the belief that thunder and lightning will flash across the sky, or magic will occur, or you will experience a dramatic conversion like that of Saul on the road to Damascus. Perhaps all that you will see to begin with is that you hated your mother. But the first truth to see is the truth about error, and if it happens instead that we see the knowledge of our beauty and greatness (as is often the case with certain Eastern meditations), you will know that you have been deceived into meditating to the wrong god.

It is only the knowledge of our failings, experienced in humility and helplessness, that draws down the keys to the kingdom. It is only the pain and questioning of realizing that we are in the wrong place that inclines the soul to change. What you are seeking are the antishock and the antitrauma, which do not exist within the framework of will and striving. We attempt to force hell to serve us glory because what serves our illusions of glory feels good to us, and under these conditions, hell can appear to be the servant of God because you think God is you. Simultaneously, the wrath of Heaven feels like hell.

Shock seeds a change in us for good or evil, even as the first shock wave came through the soul's disbelief in God's command and became a belief in immortal life as a god through knowledge. Similarly, there will be a second shock wave to your system, which will come through the soul's seeking and, seeing the error of its ways, repenting. Finally, the soul must see that only death is achieved when Pride comes to knowledge.

It only remains now to thread our way back from the world of intellect, that Alice in Wonderland world of dreams without Light: We must allow the process of pride to be reversed.

The order of this reversal begins in the soul itself: One must desire to know God, rather than to know oneself as a god. At this point, the relativity of your soul changes, and, instead of being lost in the activity of the intellect, you begin to awaken from your nightmare existence. You are given objectivity as the first phase of the process as God responds to the yearning of your soul.

Thus, dear seeker, yearn for understanding, not knowledge, riches or power. Stand apart from all these things and from the confusion of your own mind and behold the first truth that you must see—your errors! You have become a slave to sin, which once appeared to serve you glory. Know that the wages of sin is eternal death and torture, glory unfulfilled, and abject servitude to a greater god of ugliness than you yourself. Behold how your backward soul has clung to the shocking lie on which the world's system of suffering, tragedy and death is founded and how it projects and spreads its infernal existence.

Seeking to know God qualifies you for the right kind of meditation practice, and the meditation will teach you how to become progressively objective. Until now you have not seen clearly the reason for your troubles. You did not will them into existence, but they are here nevertheless. What you will begin to realize in your new objectivity is that all tragedy, suffering and death come into this world through our subjective, prideful relationship with evil.

Our love of glory has to do with our love for the lie, which can only be experienced in the dream world of the imagination, fed by the intellect. And while we were busy dreaming dreams, our souls have been used to translate the world of the Devil into existence.

10 Believing, Loving, Hating

Everything you do is a result of what you believe. Because of what you believe to be true in the moment, you see your environment in a very special way, and you act in accordance with what you see. Rarely do you apply your will to endeavors motivated by such belief, because the function of the will is not to exercise force, but to believe.

Our troubles, then, stem from a series of faulty beliefs, each one growing out of the one preceding it, each subtly more outrageous than the last. You did not set out to make a mess of your life; you were confident and hopeful about the outcome of your marriage, your business, the cure of your illness. You did not will your sufferings into existence; they were the result of a chain of false beliefs built on your original belief in a lie. You did not will death and tragedy into existence either, unless, of course, you believe them to be the just deserts of a useless, guilty life. Perhaps you may view death as a well-earned rest!

So all of your troubles grow out of, and are based on, false beliefs: that is to say, beliefs in a system of ideas that promises that that it does not intend to deliver. In fact, we are dealing here with faith in a highly intelligent, malevolent spirit source that operates in our minds exactly as God would, only in reverse. Our souls are involved with a god of deception who provides for us—but he provides just the opposite of the gifts of God: He promises glory, but delivers humiliation; freedom, but delivers slavery; happiness, but delivers misery; he even promises eternal life, but gives us eternal death instead—and then it is too late to turn back, to believe differently.

And so your troubles continue to multiply and to grow as a direct result of your being misguided, deceived, misdirected or fooled: All of these are variations of the basic ego-glory-lie theme in which you follow the lie as gospel truth, simply because it appeals to your pride.

No one can will better conditions into existence, because it was not will that created tragedy in the first place. It all transpired through the more basic tragedy of belief: pursuing the wrong ideals and goals that lead you away from the ground of goodness and into "sickness unto death." And from this sickness sprang the belief in the cure, that cure that promised to erase the symptoms that stood between you and your goal, that seductive cure that offered relief and comfort without disturbing the faulty system of your beliefs.

A cure can be anticipated by one of two kinds of belief, but a valid belief that leads to a genuine, permanent cure can arise only as the result of repentance: that is, recognizing the original integrity of the Light in revealing error as error—seeing that the Truth (conscience) did not lie, but that the lie did. The lie, in its appeal to your pride, made the Truth *seem like* error, just as other people often try to make you look wrong for correcting them.

But if you cannot will yourself to believe the Truth, even though you see that you have fallen to error, what then? The answer is so simple that, in your pride, you may find it unacceptable: Regret that you are as you are.

Regret, which is repentance, has something to do with believing in a new way. Being sorry for what you have become leads you to question, doubt and, finally, to disbelieve that faulty system of beliefs that brought you to your present estate. It is not so necessary to believe the Truth directly as it is to recognize now and to learn to doubt the lie as it is revealed in the Light. For to disbelieve the lie in the Light is the same as to accept and believe the Truth about that lie and to shrink from any relationship with it. There is no other position; there is only true and false in which to believe, and human beings cannot function at all without belief. To accept the one is to reject the other, and to reject one is to accept the other. And this entire process pivots on the fulcrum of the soul's inclination.

THE SOUL HAS ONLY ONE POWER—THE INCLINATION TO BELIEVE—AND, DEPENDING ON THE DIRECTION OF THAT DELICATE LEANING, WE

EMBRACE EITHER A TRUE OR A FALSE BASIS FOR DISCERNING ALL THINGS AND FOR BRINGING A WORLD INTO EXISTENCE.

The most fragile inclination toward pride and ambition, and the Truth appears to be the grand lie; and from this point on, the Truth seems to be a wicked demon, whether it is perceived as conscience and guilt or as a person who discourages your ambitious efforts—a negative-thinking spoilsport. The lie and the liars, on the other hand, point to the "true" way, appearing attractive, if not downright godly and virtuous. After all, they are encouraging, exciting and exhorting you to greater achievement and excellence, aren't they?

So much for the lie. The truth is, you will never recover your health, your sanity, your happiness and sense of purpose unless Truth is gently and quietly revealed to you from within, through the stillness of your soul. You must not affirm a faith nor must you hope in any man-made system or concept, merely because you know that you can only be rescued from the false belief by faith. It is not simply faith that saves, but faith in the Truth.

Granted, things can become so hopeless that the only belief that seems tenable is that the worst is yet to come: You have been convinced by the overwhelming evidence of the present, which portends the future. Such a morbid belief, based on the horrible reality facing you, is founded on a series of more subtle beliefs, which are compounded by the belief of pride in false cures. The awful truth is this: Once you have accepted a false belief, you are compelled to go on believing in what is false, even if it kills you—and it does. Right at the core of pride's belief and the departure from reality is the pivot of belief that makes only false beliefs possible. All lead to disaster, more terrible tragedies and a more desperate need to believe in the assortment of false hopes and comforts offered by the lie masquerading in all its human agencies.

You cannot countermand all of the negative effects that have come into existence through your ego. You must go back further and further to the original Light standard so that you might know the error for what it is, for not only your life, but the entire world as you know it is based on an original lie. Your ego must observe how pride is rooted in ambition, locked into the ground of the spirit from whom comes the perverted *word* that is preached one to another among the deceived, the *anti-logos* that created the hellish world for you, his creatures, to live—and die—in.

You must also see how stubbornly your ego clings to the lie, which glorifies it and comforts it as it grows increasingly grotesque through glorification and how your devolved body adjusts to find pleasure in the stinking conditions it has projected, created through its own degenerate self.

See how you are magnetically attracted to all the wrong kind of friends. How right they look to you! They agree with and so reinforce the life of the lie that is growing up inside you. Your given identity attracts dishonest people because it is loath to be honest with anyone. It won't let you be honest, because honesty destroys the environment that the nature of the lie craves in order to exist. And so we drive away decent people and their world, and instead we draw near to liars, cheats and thieves who exploit our need and give us the misery we deserve in exchange for a few moments of ecstasy and renewed hope in ourselves and our ambitious, futile dreams.

After a while, you find yourself in a strange dilemma. You become so confused that you don't know what to believe any more. You finally become afraid to believe at all—and that fear paralyzes you. Hope turns out to be hopeless, and so you try harder to believe in the best; but it always turns out wrong. Then you try the opposite approach and believe in the worst to see if that works. It doesn't. Nothing in your life can turn out well until your life begins to revolve around the true principles of the Light (as opposed to the principality of darkness). Every belief or disbelief of pride introduces you and keeps you tied to the atmosphere of peculiar people and strange environmental conditions that are favorable to the growth of the animal, creature self.

But the Light admonishes you. And, if you will but permit It to do so, It will reduce your opinion of yourself to nothing, making repentance possible. It is from this turning point that new, true beliefs develop and new conditions grow up out of them, each one evolving from the one before it. Now when it is *given* to you to believe It, It comes to pass. Your disbeliefs derive from faith in the Light; therefore, you come to doubt the lie, not the Truth; and doubting anything on this basis is tantamount to believing in and cleaving to the integrity of the Light. Thus, doubt led by Truth leads you away from the abyss of temptation, and all of your beliefs and disbeliefs are fruitful.

Belief, in its original essence, is the soul's proclivity to accept or reject ideas that convey either good or evil. Idea does not become belief; belief generates idea: that is, the soul cannot originate thought; it can only incline to receive into itself thought essence to be. The soul permits ideas to enter and to germinate by means of the soul's cohabitation with them. Only through the gate of man's soul can the Kingdoms of Heaven or Hell enter into this world. As a man thinks in his heart (according to his inclination to believe), so is he.

Even as the first man believed a lie and, thus, allowed evil and its world to enter through him, so are men saved, raised up by faith to bring into being the promised Paradise.

An idea can carry terrible force. A false idea can reduce a man to a pathetic, whimpering shadow of his former self; or a counter idea, emanating from the opposite source, can be equally devastating to the lie and the world based on it. The inclination of the soul causes it to give its attention, to believe and accept as gospel either the lie or the Truth. From that moment, a chain of mystical cause and effect occurs, which results in the total transformation of a man, mentally, physically and, most important, spiritually, because this is where it all began—in the realm of belief—where one thing unfolds to become another, and where the invisible becomes the visible proof of the existence of Heaven or hell.

At this point of belief, the wrong idea, which separates the foolish ego from the ground of its true being, undergoes a transformation and becomes something else: obedience to the *source* of that idea, thereby interrupting the proper relationship between man and his Creator. Having focused his attention and given his allegiance to the source of the lie, he is no longer aware of the moment-by-moment direction from his Creator, and if he feels the touch of God at all, it is only through the pain of conscience. His continued obedience to the lie evolves to become dependence because of the need for reinforcement that the embryonic lie requires. This need we all stubbornly believe to be love for and love from something good. Our entire lives are then built on the crumbling rocks of misguided faith, which lead inexorably toward compulsive obedience to and dependence on false ideals, and the process of our dying will continue and all change will be for the worse until we are willing to see and to admit that we are moving in the wrong direction.

Once the conscious mind has been separated, through error, from the ground of its true being, it loses sight of the knowledge it must have in order to make the return trip. Without this road map, it cannot return to its original estate; it must remain a slave, devolving through all of the consequent slavish reactions, dependencies and beliefs that arose from the very first one.

Belief leads inexorably to response, and response is the heartbeat of change—for good or evil. Consider how evidence fortifies our false beliefs. We see death all around us; there can be no mistake: Everyone must die. "If that's the case," we think, "why not do as we please and grab all of the glory and pleasure we can for as long as we can?" See how our belief in death reinforces our belief in the kind of life we desire to lead? It is precisely this kind of thinking that causes us to die. See how frightening and threatening the thought is that *we are not supposed to die?* That is because we tend compulsively to justify our kind of ego life, based on a belief in the inevitability of death.

Even as the first man was forced to accept death as the climax of the life of pride, so must all egotistical persons regard the inevitability of the death they inherit as some sort of noble experience. Of course it isn't, but if we knew what death really meant in terms of pride and sin, we could not continue to live proudly. None of the proud sons of Adam has ever experienced the original choice of faith encountered by his forebear, nor have we faced the original-sin experience. Instead we have inherited the proud state of the mind and the fallen, death-oriented body of Adam, which seeks to maintain its life by wallowing in peculiar beliefs amid horrors on the one hand and sensual delight on the other.

The pain of conscience and the feelings of futility that come from being the product (victim) of environment are the evidence that something is wrong with the way in which we exist and that, somehow, the world as it is and the you that you have become are not meant to be that way. We have only known the mother who made us, unlike Adam, who knew his Father and stood once at the threshold of original Truth and that first misguided choice of faith that marked the original trauma of mankind.

The pain of seeing facts like these can set us on a path that, if we persist to the end, will bring us to the original state of paradise in being, which by its very nature can bring Eden into existence in this world. A belief in Truth leads to repentance, which in turn, guides us to profound changes mentally, emotionally and physically as well as spiritually. And it is in the realm of the spirit that these changes are most important, for that is where this cosmic tragedy of generations began.

A continued belief in pride and self-gratification, on the other hand, constitutes a continued dependence on whatever it is that knows how to appeal to our pride. Responding continually as slaves through emotion, we revel in a false life that is not life at all; and through the vision that pride has given us, aided by the source of deception, we look upon our revels and believe that this sham is the original and innocent life for which we were intended. And the truth we seek is only more lies and malignant experiences through which we may know ourselves more fully as the gods we are coming to suspect that we are. It is absolutely critical that you recognize the truth that man has descended through sin and pride, or else no Truth will be possible for you.

Unlike the animals we are, in part, man has two origins: the nature we inherit and the nature we have left behind. The progeny of Adam grows up to know its potential through conscience, which beckons us to follow and leave behind the ego-animal-male child born (through disbelief and disobedience) of woman.

The first stage of growth for man born of woman is the fulfillment of his animal-growth needs, which causes him to grow up to the point where he feels uncertain about his inherited male identity. Thus does man gravitate to his woman-based, death-oriented legacy of pride for reassurance.

The shock of the lie killed the first man. He was no longer as he was created, but instead came alive again with an altered state of awareness as a male animal around whose life revolved the female-oriented cause of his shock. This incident explains why men crave a woman's help to feel that their present existence as a male is really a man's existence. It isn't, of course, and that is why men slave their roguish, unprincipled hearts out for reinforcement of the lie and a better life that always turns out to be a worse one. When you try to prove that more monkey is really more man, then reassurance just makes a bigger monkey out of you. Assurance is really temptation in its second more subtle form, "curing" the problem it created in the first place.

It should be clear by now that man comes into being as a trauma-oriented being, and that the first trauma that men experience in their lives is in reality a second or third, simply because we are all born through the lineage of an original sin (trauma), the male ego having come into existence through an original wrong use of woman. Look carefully and you will see the Garden of Eden scene repeated endlessly—men still using their women in exactly the same way to *reinforce* the pride of ambition and a *sense* of manhood. This is not true love of a man for a woman, but a craving that compels the woman to play an unnatural[1] role for him. Nevertheless, the path of man born of woman keeps leading him back for more of the woman's consolation.

Provided that no serious traumas are encountered along the way, the stage is now set for the second phase of the original-sin trauma to begin; all that is necessary is that man and woman come together. By reinforcing the "he" and "she" aspects of existence, we eventually develop one another beyond the pattern of natural completion. Intrigue, cruelty, ugliness and perversion are the eventual fruits of this union. The reason for this tragedy should be obvious. This kind of love and respect for what is wrong in us makes the error grow worse. What is *wrong* with a man is what craves loves, and what is wrong with a woman is what thrives on that craving and encourages a man's error to continue to crave her.

I prefer not to dwell on the male-female relationship here, because I intend to deal with the subject in a book devoted to that theme. I think it is necessary, though, to provide a setting for what is to follow. The emphasis from this point on centers around the love-hate relationship. The "love" I mean is nothing more than an ego craving for reinforcement for the ground of its being—a quality of love that leads unfailingly to the

---

[1]Really, a natural role for the woman if you are sufficiently naive to believe that natural is normal.

hate or fear of what such love does.

Trauma is the result of shock, and shock is temptation, and temptation is evil; and it is Evil, in all of its forms, that we must learn to recognize and to deal with. We must learn to expose him in her and to see his methods of inducing trauma and realizing himself progressively through the shock experience.

Earlier I spoke of belief and disbelief. Look now and see how easy it is for the proud ego to *believe* that his craving for the female ground of his corrupted being is the true and original love. He will be most attracted to the female who agrees that this is indeed love, although the truth is that a man's compulsive craving for a woman, drugs, wine and song—anything at all—is actually a gradual falling away from what love is all about. So whenever a man is loved for what he is, it is really temptation working to make him more of what he should not be! And all of this leads to a greater need for love assurance and to the belief that this addition is the highest good that he can give to or receive from a woman.

Look carefully at your own love-hate relationship. See that there are two kinds. The godly man loves, is motivated by, and is dependent on a source of good. He takes his shape from the ground of good. He abhors evil, but that too revolves around a relationship with good, for a godly man shrinks from evil into the bosom of goodness. But the fallen man loves differently; he is attracted to what still corrupts by reassuring him: Evil supporting pride appears good in his eyes. It nourishes his pride, making him glow and grow. For the sake of this support he gives evil his first loyalty. If and when a man sees through the deception of what he has embraced, he then hates the evil he once loved, *and since hate is another response to temptation*, it is not long before that that was seeded by the trauma (corruption) of hate begins to need to be accepted for what it is.

Once you have been tempted to be a thief, you are obliged to seek reinforcement for your thieving nature, unless you are prepared to face the truth. Otherwise the thief identity—the only identity you now know—would disintegrate, and you could not function at all. Therefore to feel alive at all and to feel that a better thief is a better man, you are forced to return to your tempter for "love" that is the same as reinforcement and motivation.

Your tempter has a problem too, because his type of existence is now also supported by your existence as a thief. You will require him to be a little more dishonest in order to keep pace with your growing need for assurance—to provide more and more false beliefs to prop up the belief that falling is rising. And this is exactly what the proud man requires of his woman: to be a little more of a sexy female and a lot less of the woman she was meant to be.

There will also come a time in the life of this thief when he stands on the threshold of becoming a murderer as well as a thief, and as he approaches this threshold, the place where he has gone as far as he can to be the greatest possible thief, where there is boredom and no more pride and ambition to act as a growth factor, then he is ready for the next trauma, the temptation that will change him from a thief to a murderer; and as surely as you are reading this, he will find his helpmate to tempt and support him with the love he craves. And so a man eventually reaches the threshold of drugs, alcohol, homosexuality, suicide, *anything* as a result of the existing love-reinforcement relationship with a female. Once a man's corrupt behavior pattern is established, he craves the female to play the supporting role, to be his consort. His ego need tempts her to tempt him.

Let me make it clear that the female role in the temptation drama is not always played by a woman. There are female substitutes. For example, the bartender is such a surrogate for the drunk. Even as the craving of the pushover brings the drug pusher into existence, so does a wrong male tempt the female into a more miserable existence by his craving for her to serve his fallen male nature.

The pride of the female finds this demand impossible to resist. Her ego needs to be needed. His is a kind of worship for her. Her role as female center of man's existence depends on and is justified by his craving for her. That is to say, through his continual falling for her, he energizes the *she* of the proud female in return for the he-love that supports his existence. And beyond the boundary of femaleness is a witch. And beyond the boundary of maleness is a beast with all manner of perversions unfolding, created by the power he gives to the witch in the female.

The truth is that man gives up power to evil when he seeks security or comfort from it. Man and woman are locked in a death struggle. He cannot help craving her to be his wrong foundation, and she cannot stop encouraging his craving, which she needs for her own sense of well-being.

The proof of the pudding is in the eating, they say, and the evidence that man and woman love each other in a wrong way lies at the very core of their experience together. The love that makes the world go round is the cause of man's inhumanity to man and woman.

Men crave the love of woman to give validity to their being and purpose to their proud existences. When they get love, they are worse off, and so is the condition of their souls. Men never find real happiness in their love affairs, because, somehow, the advantage they seek always turns out to be a disadvantage. Here they discover slavery and deceit. Here, then, is the third stage or original trauma, which begins when men see for the first time just what is operating through the women they believe they love.

The shock of the ego's discovery of its fallibility and susceptibility to deceit is resentment, judgment and hatred, which are really one and the same thing. This hate becomes the pattern for the next change that requires loving. Hate changes the ordinary, mild-mannered male into a vicious animal or a pervert.

The insights of the male, having developed through the operation of his female's love, begin to glimpse what is lurking in the woman, dope pusher or friendly con artist. Whoever or whatever the female or female substitute is in his life makes no difference; it operates in the same way, and its purpose is the same. The ego of man begins to see that what loves him is no friend, as he first believed; it is an enemy, and a formidable one, lording it over him. He is shocked and angered at seeing what he couldn't see before he matured by the help of all that loving. This shock of hate introduces into him something of the nature of what has been perceived. Whatever it is has tempted him to be resentful and judgmental. Love and hate are merely pride's response to evil in different forms. Love and hate are *both* responses to evil.

When *it* gets inside him through hate, *it* craves support from the wicked female counterpart, who begins to seem beautiful again, and if she obliges, then that becomes love again, and this evil love nurtures what hate planted, and the cycle begins all over again, and the victim of all this spirals ever lower, believing all the while that he is rising. What is really ugly and evil looks more and more beautiful when it caters to a need it has created in us. The lower we fall, the better things that are even lower can look to us. The more hungry we become, the less particular we become about the food we eat, and the more rotten we are, the more rotten our helpmate must be in order to agree with our belief that rottenness is glorious.

At this point, *all of your problems now stem from the need to be loved and accepted just as your are,* and the frustration (hate) arising from being loved in a way that never satisfies the need to be loved.

Henceforth be warned! *Be it known that your craving to be accepted for what you are is always the lie in you seeking the ground that originated it!*

Observe this flaw in yourself and shrink only from the false belief that has lead you to think that by denying yourself love and consideration in the mundane sense you are denying yourself true love. All you are really giving up is that lying love that makes your ego feel divine. Be warned of all the cults and churches who play their skull-and-crossbones game with your mind and be particularly aware of the "Jesus loves you as you are" or "God loves you as you are" groups. Any messenger at all who tells you that "God loves you as you are" is another representative of Satan himself, in his most sophisticated form, singing into your feverish ears the kind of ultimate support you have always sought from the angels of Hell.[2] Doubt him, and be careful not to resent him; otherwise these demons will begin to look strangely attractive and draw you in. Once corrupted, we are drawn to what corrupted us. Cannibals need their cannibal kings to reinforce their cannibal identity, and the king will make his people worse with his lies, and soon the cannibals will need a more rotten king to love them.

Similarly, in the so-called civilized areas of the world, ambitious people elect dishonest presidents and dictators, who reinforce and reassure the kind of selfish people who go on electing them. As a democracy decays, its rulers become increasingly more decadent until a dictator arises and becomes the savior of a decadent people. He receives the swine who are the source of his power at the very bottom of their slide, and he accepts them as they are, even as Hitler did the German people in that era of infamy that preceded World War II.

America is a good example of a nation preparing for dictatorship,[3] because the people have come to interpret the word "freedom" to mean free to go to hell in any way they please. At the end of the slide, as they deteriorate mentally, emotionally and physically, they will need a leader who is the biggest liar of them all, one who is equipped with all of the substitute combinations of words—all the lies and the rhetoric that will make them feel glorious in their spiritual poverty—to make them feel that their descent into Hell is actually an ascent to Heaven and that he, their leader, is, after all, the angel at the door, ushering them in to glory.

All of this is equally true of the followers of the avatar, with his heavenly messages for unrepentant, glory-seeking, selfish people.

These observations could be multiplied endlessly, but it is the principle that we must fix in our minds if we are ever going to find our way out of the maze of error into which our egos have led us. Let us, therefore, return to the heart of the matter.

There are two kinds of belief available to man, a creature who cannot function without belief. And there are two kinds of love and hate that revolve around these respective beliefs. Although people tend to believe that love is the opposite of hate, such is not the case: They are the same when they both revolve about error. You hate, and that leads you to seek love—to be loved as you are—and that leads back to hate again. It is an endless cycle because its reference point is wrong. This is the love and hate that revolves around pride and ambition.

But there is a true love and a proper hate that revolves around the opposite principle: humility, which results from recognizing your errors, regretting them and thus abandoning pride. Whichever system of belief you doubt brings the other into being, and you will be living—or dying—right in the middle of the world you believe in.

"Now faith is the substance of things hoped for, the evidence of things not seen." Hebrews 11:1 AV

"Through faith we understand that the worlds were framed by the word of God, so that things which are seen were not made of things which do appear." Hebrews 11:3 AV.

11 Ambition, Pressure, Suffering

Every problem in your life stems directly from ambition: your need to be, do or have something. It is this process of setting up goals and attempting to achieve them that is the cause of all your fears, suffering and—ultimately—your death.

Because we are not aware of the availability of proper guidance from within ourselves, we react to the pressures of our environment ambitiously. Sensing a need, we attempt to identify it by means of outside reference points and then plan a course of action that we believe will satisfy it. Not only do we fail, but somehow things are worse because of the trying. We resent our wasted effort and our failure; and this wrong emotional reaction adds yet another layer of ills and confusion.

Because of pride that blocks us from our proper source of guidance, we err, and one error seems to attract another to it, each less subtle, more serious, more grotesque than its predecessor. The movement of prideful ambition is downward: away from the spiritual and toward the natural, led by that that operates in a realm just beyond the border of the material world. When we fall away from grace by way of the temptation of pride, a bond of flesh is created between ourselves and the thing or person that tempts us. And both the tempted and the bond become subject not only to time, but also to that that operating in space beyond the material it holds up as the tempting goal.

A goal that is exciting, then, one that can motivate us to take action, has to do with failing and dying, for dying is a movement of our consciousness through the material realm down through the evolutionary strata toward the spiritual cause of our temptation at the end of the journey. To reach out for prideful goals, then, is to fulfill the purpose of evil, which is to draw us away from our proper source of guidance from within. As this process develops, there is a growing sense of futility—an intuitive awareness that we are dying.

Distressing as this sense of futility may be, it is, nevertheless, a kind of blessing because it is a result of the Light wanting to make us aware of the subtle evil that is leading us to both physical and eternal death. To admit that there is futility is also to admit to a wrong path in contrast to a right one. If there were neither wrong nor purpose, then one could never experience futility. Some people seem to escape this awareness, but that is because they won't stop long enough in their headlong plunge toward death to let the reality of it overtake them. To be still within is to realize that the spiritual counterpart to escape from the reality of awareness in the present moment is eternal oblivion. Temptation always gives you more than you bargained for. And so we move faster and faster toward unawareness, lured by a false sense of achievement, and we expire before our time.

Ambition, then, stems from ego and is linked to goals. This stick-and-carrot philosophy of goal-reaching is in turn connected to suffering, tragedy and eternal death—beyond which the author of our egos' downfall waits like a hovering buzzard. A goal always represents a pressure: The moment you set a goal, it introduces a time factor that is a kind of pressure that becomes your impetus to move.

In our ambitious state, we recognize the limitations imposed by time: We have only so much allotted to accomplish "our thing." We use this time either in "doing our own thing," or in escaping unwisely from the futility of doing it, in the vain hope of evading the inevitability of death.

This, then, is the dilemma: The ego, limited by time through goals and, later, by death, experiences a new type of impatience. As the seconds, days and weeks tick by, we have less and less time to find ego satisfaction from our goals. Either we are confused about what those goals should be, or else we are overconfident about accomplishing them. Whatever we accomplish, however, is unfulfilling and, often, downright frustrating, so that we are left with less and less time for our egos to find fulfillment.

As long as this ego fulfillment is our goal, we become locked in to failure even more deeply, prisoners of aging, deteriorating flesh, either excited or menaced by time. The more ambitious we are, the more painful the time element becomes. We strive, we move faster to compensate, to make up the lost distance by greater speed—another facet of impatience.

Impatience and pride cannot be separated. We are impatient with ourselves and the achievement of our goals under the pressure of time, which is a factor introduced into the equation by establishing goals. In this manner we are fashioned into time-oriented animals with an evil, indwelling identity, who comes to share this new creation with us and remains to rule.

For those who are fortunate enough to see the futility of goal seeking, there is yet another pitfall. Since we must work to live, and we do not know how to work without pride, even our labor produces futility. We may then come to hate work, and our resentment simply quickens the process of our deterioration.

If we cannot run away and we cannot enjoy even the illusory release of anger and resentment toward our enslavement, then what?

In space, time slows down when the speed of light is approached. Time, motion and distance are all relative to each other. I mention this principle of relativity as it pertains to the physical world in order to make a point about our egos. As the ego moves ambitiously faster and faster away from its true self as well as to escape the pain of seeing its own failings, it moves toward unreality, and like a navigator, it has reference points, but in this case these points are goals, each more unreal than the last, pointing the way to ultimate oblivion. Instead we must learn to be still in order to see the reference points to reality so that the Truth, not our ambitions, determines our heading. For out of the eye of that stillness will come not only our true direction but a hurricane of power to move us along the course.

But in our ambition we cannot sit still for the Truth to move us. We keep moving faster and faster, the energy of our motion driving us away from consciousness of reality and toward a goal motivated by impatience. The soul can move cyclically in the mind at such high velocities that time literally slows down. In that movement at the speed of light, time ceases to exist. To the insane mind, this can become a way of cheating death.

Ambition, then, has to do with losing spiritual altitude and coming into existence as a more gross, finite being always in a hurry, limited by time, to reach the particular goals of pride. It is also related to moving nervously, hurriedly toward a prize or goal with the energy derived by the pressure of time, nervously because of the conflict behind the movement away from self. The goal object gives birth to the time-pressure factors (the goal that leads us away from our center of reason and also excites the mind and bodily functions). What moves the tempter to tempt moves us to be like him.

Impatience is a wrong motivating force that blinds our reason. When it is injected into the course of our lives, direction is then imparted to our minds in a manner dictated by the intelligence that holds up a goal. The goal is rod and staff to the sheep of evil. It is the goal that excites us and blinds us to the truth that we are growing as well as going in the wrong direction. The level of our consciousness and the quality of our flesh are lowered— lured down into the time/space existence by a fiendish intelligence operating from beyond time and space through the material objective of the goal. This, then, is the sequence: pride, ambition, impatience, excitement, frustration (resentment-guilt), sickness, tragedy and death.

Temptation kills—but as long as we are glory bound, our egos tend to accept the inevitability of death as part of that kind of life. In the early stages we can, perhaps, brush death lightly aside; but later on we may find it harder to do. Possibly the reason we can think of death in such a cavalier fashion is that pride instills the illusion that as we grow in greatness we are coming into our own as gods—and gods, of course, are immortal—or else we suppose that beyond death there is eternal life for us as gods.

The serpent said to the first candidate of pride just before he fell for the lie: "For God doth know that in the day ye eat thereof, your eyes shall be opened, and ye shall be as gods, knowing good and evil." (Genesis 3:5 AV) But God told Adam that to have another goal before His Will would produce death. It was true then, and it still is.

The wages of sin are death, and so we all inherit death as a part of this life of pride. We become aware of the truth concerning this ancient curse as we edge closer to doomsday through goals that are still held up by many as the holy way.

Evil, then, is the god of the concept of pride and the author of all the illusions of pride that lead to death. Evil, operating from behind the scenes of materialism (the throne of ego), becomes our "truth," the gospel for our climb to glory.

Truth is axiomatic, that is to say it is self-evident; therefore, it cannot be denied by a true seeker.

Evil is also self-evident, for the identity that springs up inside of us as the result of ambition matches that spirit that originally tempted us and now leads the ego animal. Therefore, the closer we edge to Hell through ambitious, death-oriented people (the angels of Hell), the more we see or sense the father of our corrupted nature. And we see also how our nature matches his and how impossible it is for us to deny what we are becoming so that eventually we must yield ourselves up to him who is the author of our failing and death.

Our level of consciousness is locked into the way flesh has sprung up in response to various temptations. It has bred the kind of body that matches the evil of Hell's emissaries, but it creates conflict with latent good beyond our souls. Guilt or conflict is actually the knowledge of God we have left behind, reaching for goals.

So the lesson, then, is this:

Recognize that all of your symptoms (fear, guilt, anxiety, frustration, procrastination, indecision, etc.) trace back to ego goals that OTHER MISGUIDED

PEOPLE HAVE SET FOR YOU. Goals have something to do with SOMEONE ELSE giving you ideas—which they got from other misguided people before them, back to the point at which the world was founded on a lie.

Your labor, then, is not a labor of love. Love's labor carries its own reward, the infilling of God's love. But your labor is one of futility through a pattern of behavior set by your tempter or corrupter, and one that you act out for his approval—mother, teacher, or dope pusher; it makes no difference who.

You strive ambitiously, you are comforted—perhaps approval is withheld if you don't strive enough. If you falter or hesitate, your tempter may reinforce the original temptation with exhortations like, "Just think of all the good things you can have, or the important man you can be!" With newer glittering, glorifying goals, you forget your doubts (and conscience) again.

The way back is simply through seeing and recognizing what has been described to you and then fitting your own particular circumstances to the principles outlined.

You must understand that there are thousands, even millions of combinations of guilt, fear, frustration and original circumstances, but they all have the same thing in common: appeal to pride and ambition.

As your inclination brings you closer to the Light, you can begin to identify your personal goals and pinpoint the author of your confusion: your need to be loved because your mother hated you, for example, or your desire to be rich because you hated poverty, or even to be poor because you hated your rich, ambitious father.

The point is, YOU must give up YOUR goal, and it makes little difference what that goal might be: "love," money, fame, power, profit or glory. Wanting and having the kind of home you never had as a child can also be a goal, so can seeking a peaceful place of bliss in the woods under a banyan tree. There are two main flaws in all of these goals because they involve 1) your ego attempting to find its own innocent peace after it has been corrupted and 2) your attempt to run from the ugliness produced within you toward anything that helps you to avoid or deny that indwelling error.

I say again, it need not be a goal of money or fame that perfects your ego. The effect is the same regardless of what your goal or dream may be. Whatever you have lost to your environment through your wrong reaction to circumstances cannot be recovered in this world. You cannot make up your loss to yourself. Any attempt to do so only makes you sink deeper in the quicksand of pride. What you have lost, in reality, is your own true identity—and you have lost it through being separated from the timeless ground that would have nourished it. To seek for yourself outside yourself is madness; it is to be hopelessly lost in time, space and eternal death.

You cannot, through your own efforts, regain what you have lost. It is God's wish to give you all things proper to your estate, including a true identity. But, as a creature of free will, it is within your power to reject that that you cannot create. If your will is so inclined, you remain separated from God through the striving and writhing of your own pride, your own pitiful attempts to give yourself a paradise, to restore what you have lost, to force the world to give you back your purloined dignity.

You are separated from God through temptation to pride. It is as if the energy of your own striving toward a goal, the electricity of your impatience with your problems, has created a force field through which the saving grace of God will not pass. Unlike the tempter, the Creator does not violate the integrity of our freedom of choice; therefore, until the polarity of your soul changes, until you DESIRE to incline your will toward the Truth, you will continue to repel the only force on earth or in heaven that can save you.

Realize the futility of striving toward any goal. Wait, poised with a clear, inquiring mind and you will be given understanding. Recognize your impatience as a deterrent to your salvation. Relax and cease all of your efforts. Let go; let God. Slowly, by degrees and without effort give up the comforts that have helped your ego forget the error of its striving, for all of this has lead to the grossness of the flesh: too much music, too many hobbies, that strategic drink, or cigarette. Yes, as you have been striving (falling), physical changes have been taking place, possibly unnoticed, in your body. You are now more susceptible to disease and untimely death.

As you deny yourself goals and comforts by degrees, your soul will be released and awakened from its sleep, which has been induced by the increasing grossness of the flesh to which it is connected.

Comfort is a subtle form of temptation that rewards us for our errors and helps us to remain ambitious. Our faulty natures come into existence because of striving after goals. Our troubles and woes are the projections of our faulty existence. So if you will but trace your life back to the original pressure to succeed, your "pusher" and your resentment toward her, you will discover an understanding that allows the saving grace of God to repair the damage done to you and make you whole again.

This is not a simple-minded placebo. Make no mistake about it, seeing your life as it really is, your choices as they really are, yourself as the grotesque creature that you have become, is one of the most painful experiences you will ever undergo. But consider with care the alternative!

So deny yourself ego comforts, free your soul to discover what else you must deny. Remember, if you are "loved" as a thief, you will only become a bigger thief. Comfort *unfailingly* lowers your level of consciousness and inspires you to live more ambitiously and animalistically.

One of the most subtle temptations to ambition is what I term the "Kleptomaniac Syndrome." The tempter merely waits for the right moment when his victim innocently picks up an object, then the tempter becomes hysterical, accusing, forbidding and insinuating. The victim gets upset and rebels; and from that moment on he desires the forbidden thing in a compulsive manner.

Once we have been tempted to desire anything, the

object itself keeps exciting us to possess it. A challenge or a dare has a similar effect. Someone says, "You can't!"—so you do it to prove you can. Often, instead of being dismayed, your tempter will applaud you for your "courage."

Just as the alcoholic must keep on drinking to forget the guilt of drinking, so we respond and become addicted to all things that challenge us. It's a simple matter of conditioning from that moment on. When challenged, we feel big—but in reality we are actually diminished in stature and grace, guilty for falling for the ruse.

Now the problem is one of conditioned response: Everything that says you shouldn't, mustn't or can't challenges your ego to prove itself—to rise above the failing of the last experiences. The moment of challenge or rebellion presents an excitement that pulls the ego away from the awareness of guilt and anxiety and offers it another splendid moment of *temporary* glory. Then the moment passes and we find ourselves once again with an inexplicable anxiety that nothing can relieve—except the exciting thought of another challenge to "prove ourselves" once again.

Once the syndrome starts, it is impossible to stop without a full understanding of what has taken place. The growing sense of anxiety and guilt seems to find relief in the challenge, but the challenge (the "cure") is really the cause of the next anxiety. What we are not supposed to have we then want. Having it (apparently defeating another's will or authority) is an *ego* achievement that we have been *tricked* into experiencing.

Once we have tasted this kind of false victory, we suffer the guilt and dissatisfaction that demands yet another *denial* and an apparent victory over it. Something sitting there (from a female tease to merchandise in a store) becomes exciting to us. Remember the motivator's trick: Once your pride has been stimulated to experience anything at all in order to find an illusory satisfaction, the forbidden object itself thereafter can assume the role of tempter.

Women who motivate their ambitious husbands often lose their man to money. Money becomes (sexually) exciting. Once we achieve a goal, the goal itself becomes exciting as a motivator and can assume the job of motivating agent entirely. Religious symbols associated with the excitement of "religious conversion" can reproduce the same effect as the original experience created by the motivator/priest. All this acts like posthypnotic suggestion, which can be duplicated under laboratory conditions.

So once we are tempted to reach for anything—even out of rebellion—we find an ego gratification followed by a conflict that seems to whisper to us: "Do! Take, earn, make, achieve more and more. Be something bigger to get an even bigger reward for yourself." That moment will often find us conscious of the wrong we are poised to commit. We may sense and resent our weakness, and in that instant there is often a flashback to the mocking tempter's (hypnotist's) suggestion. We are made aware of the original scenario that set us upon our present path to greater glory, a script that will lead to even greater futility that must be conquered by an even greater response to the challenge of the forbidden.

So we feel the conditioned and conditioning pull upon our senses. We feel the lure of the challenge already beginning to give us relief from the anxiety of the last challenge. The renewed thought tantalizes our mind. We know the outcome, though. We know we shall be sorry later and we shall hurt more than ever.

And that is why we feel resentment, and it's at this point that we repeat the big mistake—because resentment is the sustaining force of *every* error.

It was mostly through resentment that a tempter originally got to your pride. It was resentment toward a tormentor that originally made us fall from the bounds of reason, and it was resentment that helped plant forbidden desires in our mind. Resentment, you remember, is hypnotic by nature.

So if you even resent the memory of your tormentor, if you resent the object that tantalizes as a means of dealing with it, you will give your problem unbearable power over you.

If you will but resist that twinge of resentment toward your own feelings, the compulsion will be conquered, the cycle broken.

Naturally this won't be possible if your ego enjoys challenges to justify its existence. Some people love the rottenness of society and enjoy being cheated a little bit because it gives them the excuse and motivation their ego needs to go on cheating and getting the better of others.

Willing willfulness and unwilling willfulness both depend on two temptation-produced factors, namely:

1) challenge (involving resentment) and later,
2) reinforcement.

The only way out of this morass is through a change of heart, a realization that you are not really leading your own life. You must realize that your problems and resentment stem from the humiliation of your ego, arising out of an original challenge that, like a fool, you rose to accept. In reality, however, you fell at that moment. That is a fact that you neither wanted nor knew how to face. So in order to avoid seeing that you fell, your ego felt compelled to continue resenting and proving itself: for example, by drinking to forget the guilt of drinking.

All this is just an attempt to get above or even merely to forget the memory of the tempter, which seems to mock you more in your frustration. When you are challenged by the gang to smoke, it is this principle that is operative. You feel you must keep smoking to get out of it what it seemed to promise originally. We end up smoking to forget the underlying failing that the smoking actually represents.

So you can see, then, that you must watch this resentment against your own compulsion. Don't become disgusted with yourself because you haven't the will power to break a habit. Instead, simply observe your weakness, be sorry for it, and yearn to be free of your compulsions. Be mindful that a compulsion is supported by the energy that first enticed you into doing whatever the compulsion involves. This same principle holds true for *everything* you wish to be free from: DO NOT RE-SENT IT. The power that keeps you enslaved derives from the resentment.

For example, let's consider your job. You may find yourself in a situation that you hate; yet it is that hatred (resentment) that is the very motivation that makes you function on that job. And although resentment provides drive, it also causes guilt and a growing sense of futility, which comes from moving in the wrong direction, propelled by the wrong motivation.

This same resentment can even drive you to further goal-setting: You want to quit and get a better job just to show "them" what you're really worth. Even if you are looking for a job, don't decide, for example, that today is THE day you are going to get one; this attitude is ambitious, and it breeds nervousness and fear. The trouble is that in this success-oriented world most employers want only people who are eager and ambitious, the type who will give up their principles in order to serve and gratify the hellish egos of their bosses. Don't force yourself. You are better off not going through that door. Persist gently, and you will eventually find your place with the right kind of people. Setting an ambitious goal, however, you become pushy and nervous; if you get the job, you will not be able to cope. It will make you sick so that you will wish you hadn't found it, and then you won't want to work at all. You can even develop a fear of work because of the futility.

Even though you may not be working, the idea of work will remain as a pressure because you still have the ego need to succeed, and that requires a goal. The goal beckons and excites, but the fear of being unable to cope frightens. And of course there is a generous portion of resentment and frustration mixed into this recipe for failure.

What I wish to stress here is that hating anything is a motivating force, and it is always used to overcome or accomplish in an ego sense. If you continue to resent your work, you may find that you become compulsive about it. And if challenge is what motivates you, resenting your work will compel you to do it "better" and loathe yourself for it at the same time.

Realize, then, the complete folly of resentment against whatever it is that is making you unhappy: your vice, your work, your long list of tempters, motivators and comforters. Eventually, you will be able to repent of your resentment against whomever or whatever trapped you originally. You must face your last and most immediate problem first, then, as the Light leads you, the others, one by one, all the way back to the original trauma.

Another thing: You may find that when you give up resentment against, for example, your work, the driving force that motivated you will disappear, leaving you without energy. You will nearly always feel guilty for not continuing to drive yourself, but this feeling is really the discovery of a guilt that was there all along—a guilt you lost sight of through resentment and striving to make something of yourself. For that accomplishment, you may have received you usual round of applause (from the tempter—who else?), and you may have also resented the applause. But you never actually lost your guilt; you only lost sight of it by the distractive process of striving to be a bigger or better something-or-other. Frustration at the end of each sequence of striving became the new driving force, and it drove you on to "success"' or the bottle. You always became more guilty as a result, but so long as you kept resenting and moving "forward," you stayed ahead of the mocking memory of your tormentor and your conscience. So when you finally grind to a halt, you will discover the additional guilt that you have been adding through your labors, challenges and compensations.

Often a man breaks down under the strain, becomes sick or even bedridden. His guilt catches up with him, but still he can't take his mind off his work. The very thought of work upsets him, but the challenge of not being able to work upsets him even more and makes him depressed.

When he works he is frustrated—but when he stops he discovers it is even more painful. Labor that is a source of pride acts like an opiate on the mind. The first thing that comes to the alcoholic mind when conscience catches up is the thought of another drink to distract him from his guilt. Thoughts of drink and the drink itself provide "salvation" from the knowledge of failing. Even work can be used as a distraction. We can labor to forget the futility of labor. We must stay busy achieving and being rewarded and applauded. The moment we stop, we become terrified.

We are prone to believe that our guilt stems from

not striving enough and being as good as striving can make us if we try harder; but the truth of the matter is that *we are guilty for not living our own lives,* for failing to look at the origins of our compulsions and labors. Somewhere in our past a temptress lurks who has set us upon a wrong path through some form of subtle trickery.

It is strange, but the ego mind refuses to admit that ideas and behavior can originate from anywhere except itself; hence, the chatter of excuses and noise that arise in the mind after each mistake. Finally, when we are forced to face the facts because our excuses break down, we can't stop doing the thing that terrifies or revolts us because resentment keeps the top spinning. For example: Resent your drink, and resentment starts to play tricks with your mind. Resentment, you see, increases the very anxiety that drives you to drink; so if you resent *anyone,* you can be driven to the bottle. Then, if you resent the distraction itself for enslaving you and making you more miserable, drink becomes more attractive than ever.

In addition, there is a quirk of the mind that can make us feel guilty for the resentment we feel toward anything. So, just as we can make up to people whom we have resented, we can also "make up" to our drink, our work or our boss—all of whom reward our (false) repentance with false comfort, which keeps us addicted.

So the basic lesson, again, is: Watch out for resentment and blame (disguised resentment). Resist the temptation to rise above your weakness with resentment; resist the impulse to conquer what has defeated you in memory and imagination or what, in reality, is trying to conquer you, what mocks and dares you to prevail (egotistically). Don't give in to it. *There is discipline in just understanding.*

The moment your pride is motivated by challenge, you forsake principles; you also leave behind the ground from which you could resist. (The tempter often does this by making us aware of our inadequacies, which we resent.) But the ancient rule set by Christ was: Seek the Kingdom *first*, and all other things will be added in due course.

The motivators, appealing to pride, reverse this principle. They say: Seek the things to be added first; never mind your principles; you can't eat principles; who needs principles when you are great and powerful? It is to their advantage to make you believe this. Not only do you leave behind the ground from which you could have resisted, but in doing so, you also leave behind the criteria for argument against the deceiver.

So begins the slow but sure process of dissipation and dehumanization. Once you have been had, it is impossible to stop moving after the things you *grow* to need. The motivator rides herd, making you desire the things that frustrate and tempting your mortal (materialized) heart to strive harder.

A motivator is born (or spawned) when a person turns his disadvantage into an advantage. That is, he learns he can get rich by tempting the life out of others: doing unto others what was done unto him. He finds this an easy matter because, being born subject to sin, no one knows how to resist the sin within himself.

Every motivator is a tempter, a devil incarnate, and is responsible in part for the futility, meaninglessness, and suffering of today's world. The dope addict, the wino, the suicides, mental cripples, the sick, criminals and all the corruption that is rampant everywhere are the result of *motivation* to the pride of ambition. There is just so much motivation a person can take before he can't take any more; then his whole system revolts against the concept of existence. It dies, or it goes on and on and, finally, dies anyway. Up to that time, the motivator of our stupid, aspiring pride waxes fat and rich; as long as there is prey, those vultures feel content. In the animal kingdom, it's harvest time for the buzzard and the jackal when there is drought or famine. In the same fashion, the motivator lives at the expense of his failing brothers.

As long as men live separated from Reality, they have no resistance to the pressure of the motivator's presence or his rhetoric and charm, which lures them to new forms of "gain and glory." Observe him, and he will flee from you. He is a coward at heart. The moment you show signs of understanding and life, he cringes away like the vulture he really is. As you start to become whole and well, these people become sick and begin to falter. They literally starve to death, for you are no longer feeding them their spiritual carrion. Remember, the tempter has no life of his (or her) own; he has only the life he can obtain by tricking you out of yours.

But wait! Don't go rushing to the aid of these people, or else they will help themselves to you again. They can appear so pathetic as they start to wither away that the appeal of helplessness is flattering to your pride. Steady there! Don't fall for it; *you cannot help them!* To think that you can is another challenge, another high (playing god-savior), and this results in your falling again and their getting "well" again on the strength you give them. Their withering away is due to your holding up the Light that prevents them from feeding on and taking advantage of you. You *are* helping them then, you see. They *must* suffer through this experience or else they cannot know that anything is wrong with their way of life. As long as they succeed in draining you and planting their guilty identities in you, there is no shame; and, therefore, no repentance is possible.

So be aware that by not rushing to their "aid" you are not hurting them; it only seems that way. The hell in them is dying, and it feels to them as if they are dying—and you are held somehow responsible. So if you feel guilty for what you see happening to the fallen tempter, don't believe it. These guilt feelings arise in a very special way.

Your motivator has always commended you for what he made you do. If he taught you to drink, he would compliment you for your effort so that you didn't have time to see the guilt; then he would fill your glass again. This same procedure holds true for any temptation you care to cull from your own experience.

And so your guilts have grown; but the corrupter

has always accepted your striving or else goaded you for not succeeding or trying hard enough. Now that you have slowed down and the tempter can't get his way, you are minus this "respect" (the compliments in which your own ego once found refuge). Remember that you also *discover* guilt when you give up resentment.

If you have always looked up to your tempter for support, you have self-respect only to the degree that your tempter agreed with what you did. You have labored for his approval; you craved that approval, and you got it as long as you didn't shame the tempter, but pleased him in some way.

Pleasing him required you to respond to him, to obey his will that you enjoy things in a lowly way so that he could enjoy you. He loved you as a lion loves his prey. You were really being devoured, but you thought you were being loved. You looked up at him for looking "up" at you (he was really just putting you on).

The tyrant gets his power from the people to tell the people what the people want to hear from the tyrant. The lie frees them from their consciences and makes beasts out of them and again gives power back to the lie in the tyrant. So it is with your own private dictator—you have given power to your tempter to lead you and build your ego into greater and greater conflict with self.

So don't worry if you see your dictator reduced in rank. He has only lost the power you gave him to lie to you—and you are free to feel your own real guilt. You can see through his game, you don't need him any more, and he can't make a living out of your dying. So, like the Wicked Witch of the North in *The Wizard of Oz*, he melts into steam under the Light of Truth. What is really dying with him is your false salvation, and good riddance to it!

Don't think that your guilt stems from what you have done to your "poor" victim; don't feel it is any of your doing, or you will *fall to the rescue* and once again become entangled.

It is through understanding and compassion that you can allow your tempter to *suffer* like this. Meanwhile, you will suffer the loss of his approval and the pain of conscience reappearing; for after all, you are a part of his dilemma even as he is part of yours. There is some responsibility for his plight because for years you have been letting him get away with murder (yours). You are guilty for yielding to his temptation as he is guilty for tempting you. So suffer this pang (which is your guilt) you *cannot* help, and the pain you suffer for not helping in the old way will bring you the strength you need to let him suffer for the strength he needs.

That is love.

Who never *lets* us suffer never lets us recover. In one form or another, there is a tempter to console you in your suffering. Remember, the tempter will try to capitalize on your guilt. He knows that as he suffers, you also suffer; he will accuse, moan and groan and put on a big show to make you think that you are totally responsible for the pain he feels, while the pain *you* feel is due to your failing to do what is "right" by him. DON'T FALL

FOR IT! Instead, let him feel the addiitonal guilt that he would cast upon you reflected back upon himself. Then he will have two guilts to suffer: (1) the guilt of what he is, and (2) the guilt of trying to make you guilty. If he succeeds with you, he experiences relief. Your ego may also believe that it has some sort of mystical healing power because once you start to feel sorry for him, he begins to recover miraculously.

But you have to become sick to provide for his "well-being."

Here is where he comes to your rescue by comforting your ego to be his support and so take away what's left of your miserable life. When you know what you are dealing with, you will see that *what is dying needs to die.* As long as he stays strong and lives, he will destroy you and find other victims to tempt and drain, to lead to futility and death, providing "comfort" all the way! *So don't give of yourself to other people!*

Remember—you are not really denying your brother love; you will actually be *giving him love!* You arc only denying yourself to the evil that holds your brother captive. As he dies, the Evil One lets go of him. Your children, your wife, your husband and friends, even your enemies are looking for delivcrancc in a person such as you must become. When you have the fortitude and determination to give up the "love" of the world and not worry about what people will think of you, you will be renewed in spirit and come to know what real love for people is.

Again, I warn you: Don't feel sorry for people. In a

roundabout way you are only being sorry for yourself. If you yield and give them the sympathy they seem to need, it appears to take your suffering away. But does it really?

Just before you feel sorry for someone, there is that twinge of resentment for calling on you to save him, for challenging you to assume a burden of responsibility you really don't want or know how to assume. (The appeal can also act like a challenge to your pride in that it temporarily makes you feel very inadequate indeed.) Instinctively, you resent what makes you aware of your fallibility. Resentment turns into guilt, which drives you to help relieve your resentment and fear.

Let me show you one more way that resentment works against your better interest. A certain young woman doesn't want to smoke, but she is pressured into smoking in school by her "friends." Using resentment, she resists successfully. She goes home, and her Bible-thumping, pressure-mongering mother is suspicious about her away-from-home behavior and starts sniffing at her to see if she has been smoking. The daughter resents this deeply; then, lo and behold! The resentment leaves two alternatives: to conform or to do just the opposite from the pressure that screams, "Obey!" She finds herself in the peculiar dilemma of doing something she never intended.

Now the crowd accepts her and comforts her in her failing, which only increases her confusion. She finds herself smoking more and more to soothe the tension. In an attempt to reassert herself, she again finds herself resenting the crowd. But resentment increases her tension and guilt, which she relieves by agreeing with the crowd again—which of course means she is smoking to gain their acceptance as well as to relieve the anxiety of resentment.

Remember the rule: If you don't know how to overcome resentment (which produces unbearable guilt), you are forced to conform to or agree with the pressure that has caused it.

Agreement in this case means to accept the *idea* of smoking; but now, in addition, we have a *real need* to smoke to soothe the anxiety of this psychic dilemma. It then becomes a combination of factors—but underneath it are resentment and pride suspended between conformity and rebellion, trying to free themselves. Smoking was only the beginning of trouble for this young woman, because once this kind of condition begins, it sets the stage for other forms of corruption based on the same principle.

So be careful! Don't be trapped into rebelling against suggestions people make to you. It can well be that such is just the opposite from what is intended for you. If mama pressures you to be a good boy, she may unconsciously want you to be a bad one. So when you rebel, *you are actually conforming* to her hidden motive.

We won't go into all the reasons for and variations of such cruelty. They would fill several volumes. It is sufficient for you to understand the principle behind the wicked game being played. The emotional key is resentment. Repent of it, be patient, and you have won.

Your ambitious motivators and tormentors are people who have themselves fallen victim to temptation in one form or another. They have little tolerance for innocence. Your innocence threatens their vampirish existence and makes them aware of their own guilt. In order to use you to relieve themselves, they are obliged to destroy your awareness and purity. They may not fully realize the games they play, what they do, or why. They only know that if you conform to the sin of ambition and fall for them, they feel relief when you yield. They feel as if something of value has been accomplished. They feel good if you fail because at that time they receive a false sense of well-being and self-respect, and before you know it you find yourself turning around, doing unto others what was done unto you.

So the curse is handed down from generation to generation through the medium of our falling, and it comes to pass through this and many other tricks that hell has its way on earth; and in your prideful struggle to be free you sink deeper into despair. Through your own attempts to offset pressure or to go your own way you always go to extremes. If you conform, you are doing what the tempter wants; or if you rebel, you are falling to just another variation of "its" foul purpose.

Give up resentment, and you will discover a new factor, a choice that was blocked by resentment. Give up resentment, and your tormentor will be faced with two choices: to repent and come over to the will of Heaven operating through your patience or to rebel against the goodness in you—and "self-destruct."

So, to repeat the basic lesson:

Repent of ambition (that's how you give it up). But for goodness's sake, don't repress or deny ambition by an effort of will, for that would be an act of will-ego-pride. *Trying* to give up ambition is just another form of ambition, as is trying to be religious to atone for a worldly selfish life, because the purpose of your behavior is to appear humble and, thus, great.

Also, give up (repent of) resentment against the frustrations and disappointments resulting from your goals, against those who foiled your plans for an ideal life and those who lied and led you to despair.

If it doesn't drive you into your shell, resentment can have the effect of making you redouble your efforts to achieve. You set your sights a little higher, only to become more impatient and excited trying to reach an even more difficult goal, one that only frustrates again and again.

Frustration is really a by-product of resentment and impatience, and it can produce a compulsive, maddening drive to achieve. Recognize this danger and understand that if you do not set goals, there can be no impatience, no frustration or resentment of any kind. The moment you are tempted to set a goal, that is the moment when you experience excitement and impatience, and it is impatience that leads to fear: an impending sense of disaster and death.

Material things we are driven to possess constitute the frontiers of hell. Walk around any grubby downtown area in the inner city, with its cheap stores and glittering lights, full of cheap and glib fast-talking con artists standing inside their lairs waiting to pounce upon the unwary eager beavers passing by, suckers who are looking to swell their pride with shoddy trinkets—here you find the pornographic sex traps, the honky-tonk beer joints behind which hell lurks, ever ready to gratify the nature that springs up within the victim.

There are different social levels of this, some more obvious and others more sophisticated and subtle—but all appeal to your pride's desire to have, to own and to be something—and the antidote to frustration and failure is booze and pleasures of all kinds.

Repent (that's how you give up) of your resentment against the harm and mischief your goals have brought upon you, as if it were all their fault and not your own. The compulsion to smash things to smithereens stems from a hatred (blame) against the frustrating object. This attitude can have the most unpleasant side effect of locking you into the object.

Say that the goal when it is finally achieved makes you feel anxiety, even guilt. Okay. Now suppose you hate it, in an attempt to make yourself blameless (a typical ego trick). What happens is that your resentment will also make you guilty, adding guilt to guilt. Now this apparently leaves only one way out—materialism as a means of escape from that particular guilt. So then the fixation on a goal can suddenly become more intense and appealing.

The alcoholic or drug addict can experience something of this effect; he resents his drink for making him feel worse, and not better as it promised to do—the resentment makes him feel more misery, more guilt, and that makes the drink look more attractive.

It seems almost as though he had done the alcohol a disservice by hating it, and so all it takes is to be loyal to the alcohol, and everything will be all right again—only it doesn't work out that way!

People you hate for having misled you can have exactly the same effect—you are fooled by them and think that they are your friends, but only because they cater to your ambition, which makes you blind to what they are doing. They take you for all you're worth, and your hatred of them makes you feel guilty. Your guilt makes them look right, and from the depths of your despair their promises and approval appear even more glittering. You see, the more hopeless, lost and guilty you are, the more your ego *needs* direction, hope and comfort from the deceiver (who else?). As the truth becomes more painful, the lie becomes more attractive and exciting to our egos, which are desperately trying to escape in order to avoid seeing their miserable selves.

Awareness of our failing makes us *more* desperate for glory, because in that hoped-for glory is also the escape from the knowledge of failing. So our hunger for material gain and fame may begin as a desire for that elusive state, but we end up achieving them as a means to an end, hoping to escape the realization of our failing.

The preceding description of what takes place in our souls is sufficiently encompassing to include the entire human race. Perhaps you now have a better insight through which the web you have been caught in may be untangled by the action of understanding.

Your level of consciousness is locked into (1) your ambition and (2) your means of escape from the guilt of ambition through pleasure and comfort of various kinds.

Resentment and blame also lock in your attention to the tempter, and the temptation itself pulls your awareness down still further through self-incrimination. Whenever your conscious attention is fixed in any way at all, it will appear that you have not come down at all, but are standing on the threshold of taking a step forward and up. You feel stronger, better, superior and more hopeful when you are tempted or angry. This excitement to pride prevents us from seeing that "step up" to glory is really to come down (in consciousness) to receive it, and it is the reason why we don't see clearly at that moment, only later (if we don't get high again on someone or something too quickly)!

Temptation can also seem to free you. It produces a temporary sense of freedom because it releases you from the awareness of your conscience. But whatever is free from conscience is really a slave to that that freed it; and so we repeatedly become dependent on temptation to maintain this false sense of freedom in which we are released to experience whatever fulfills our ego aspiration. It seems as if we are coming closer to perfection, but we are only staying ahead of our conscience, fleeing from reality, and avoiding the guilt of conscience, which makes us feel again as if we are progressing toward ultimate perfection. We experience no need to face our failing. How else could we feel proud?

Again, escaping from guilt (the action of conscience) can be construed by the blind ego as coming into its own as a god: that is, we are guilty only because we have not been persistent enough to reach the goal. In reality, we are guilty for working toward our own glory, but from the perspective of our egotism we don't view it in this way. We usually interpret guilt to mean that we are not achieving, loving or drinking hard enough!

Watch out for this trap. Turn and hold it up to the Light and bear the anxiety that catches up to you when you cease striving and resenting. It may seem that you are being cheated of something very vital. Vital, yes! but only for the life of pride, which is living death in the truest sense. "For whosoever will save (preserve) his (ego) life shall lose it: And whosoever will lose his (ego) life for my sake (Christ's) shall find it." (Matt. 16:25)

When you find yourself in an ambitious environment of deadlines and goal-setting bosses and associates, you will know it by the drab futility and pressure you feel. As an ambitious person yourself, you will require the motivation provided by the time pressure of goals the motivators set for you to make you slaves in their private hells.

Once you have become a goal-oriented person, you find yourself goal sensitive *even against your will:* that is to say, you will answer to pressure whether you like it or not simply because it is there. You must learn to cope with pressure by following these basic rules: Recognize that any present response grows out of the slavishness of your pride; and if you will trace your response back to your original goal and give it up, all that remains for you to do is to watch your responses to time pressure objectively, without resentment, until your reaction subsides. Be careful not to resent the pressure or try to deal with it in any other way. Remember that resentment is always a failing, whatever the provocation. It is a response to temptation, requiring your own ego efforts to rise above the problem.

The solution to all of your problems comes when you give up goals and striving! Trying desperately to clean up your mess or sickness produces panic because it is by its very nature also a goal, one that produces a time pressure to overcome, and that is the very condition that makes matters worse. The true and permanent solution is a by-product of your doing less, relaxing, being still and eventually coming to know what to aim for and then waiting for the proper motivation to achieve it.

Timing is an essential part of our existence, but ambition always produces the wrong timing and the wrong impulse to move. Ambition pulls us out of our timeless center of grace, away from the presence of God and the impulse to do His Will and Purpose. Away from Him we do everything by the tempter's schedule, and everything we do serves Hell's purpose. Whether we realize it or not, all ambitious people are beast men and Devil's pawns!

True timing is a profound element of correction, for it emanates from the Lord of time, from a different, timeless dimension in contrast to the ambitious and impatient realm of time pressure. This is why you must give up all ambition before you can be truly patient. To the degree that you recognize your impatience with another (even to correct him), you will be able to hold still and wait for the right moment, which will be determined by your need to know.

You want to correct your loved ones, I know, and you would like to help bring your friends back onto the path, but beware of your impatience in this matter. Impatience is a symbol of your ambition. You are playing god again: You think that if you don't help them, who will? Because helping them has become your goal, and you believe your total responsibility, you think you are given only so much time in which to accomplish this aid. But the idea of only so much time has to do with your setting the goal: Pride is involved again. You have been tempted to take too much on yourself, and the *pressure* comes from *time* because of that *goal.*

Now, because you fail to operate from the dimension of grace, your compulsion to help your loved ones will cause them to rebel—and even if they did conform to your wishes their plight would be compounded. They would not be helped because they would only be, like you, a product of ambition, even more ambitious than they were before, being tempted by your ambition. This, in turn, makes you feel guilty for failing and hurting them.

As they become worse (they are dying, actually), they edge closer to their limits in time, which you, in your impatience, have set for them. Watching their deterioration, you are again motivated by impatience to help them without the proper knowledge of timing: and so things get worse again, and you panic! But, if only you will give up your ego and the goal of helping them, you will feel the relief of release from pressure.

NOW—

You yearn to help them but *know* that you do not have the power or the means or the authority to change another person for good. Then one day—it just happens! Your opportunity arises and the words seem to pop out all by themselves. *It simply happens*, and *you* didn't do it; you are only the instrument.

When you wait patiently, without anxiety, you will lose your guilt and fear. Yes, even though someone dear to you may suffer, you intuitively know that it is now God's responsibility, *not yours*.

You trust in His judgment rather than your own. And through that faith comes patience, and patience does its perfect work through you so that you become whole, lacking nothing. "Now faith is the substance of things hoped for, the evidence of things not seen." (Hebrews 11:1)

". . . we glory in tribulation also, knowing that tribulation worketh patience; and patience, experience; and experience, hope . . ." (Romans 5:3ff.)

12 Restoring the Soul

A little girl went into her father's room late one night and said, "Daddy, I see a big spider in my room. I don't think it's a real spider; it seems more in my mind— but it scares me just the same."

"In that case," said the father, "you must just watch that spider until it disappears."

The child returned to her room and quietly watched the spider from her dream world, and she soon fell into a peaceful sleep.

This simple little story illustrates one of the most vital lessons that we must all learn: Observe problems in a detached manner, and they will finally melt away. Evil, operating through the medium of imagination, cannot function when it is consciously observed by the aware mind, because once it has been exposed, little more is needed to counter its effect. Simply continuing to watch, without becoming involved, is enough. You must not allow yourself to be tempted to resent any of the feelings and thoughts you observe as they rise into the Light. To react to them in any way, and, particularly, to resist them, causes you to become impatiently entangled in the stuff that thoughts, feelings and remembered experiences are made of. And so you perpetuate the problem by providing it further substance.

The soul that stands still knows that, of itself, it can do nothing at all; therefore, it has the faith to attempt nothing except to watch and allow the Light to shine on the fantasy, the guilt and demons of the darkness until they cease to exist in the Light. *All* problems must be resolved through the decreasing motion of the consciousness—a discipline of stillness we receive through meditation.

Let me emphasize that meditation is not an elaborate procedure; on the contrary, it is the very essence of simplicity. In fact, the only real problem in learning how to do it properly is realizing just how simple it is. Your role is entirely that of an observer; you must resist the impulse to make things happen, especially in those moments of impatience (doubt, really) when nothing new seems to be occurring.

Some people commence meditation expecting fiery revelations, colored lights and angels singing; yet the only kind of thing they may discover in the beginning is that they hated their parents. The first truth is always the truth about your own faults. In the beginning, you must not expect to become much more than an ordinary person; don't expect to become a saint. The way back from where you are now to a normal, natural self involves a seemingly endless series of discoveries and a mental sorting-out process that can become quite painful at times.

Do not try to make your mind blank. It is proper to

think while you are observing your thoughts passing by. Only the improper thoughts will attempt to attract the observing self to follow them; however, you will be made aware that you have been caught up in your own mental activity, and that very awareness restores your objectivity. This process of becoming involved with wrong thoughts, being made aware of your involvement and being returned to the objectivity of the moment will happen often and for a long time to come.

Through your meditation, you must grasp the principle of remaining aware and staying in the moment. This is the key to the Kingdom. Do not project by looking forward or anticipating future events. Looking to the future or dwelling in the past causes you to remain in the world of your imagination. Because of this fact, you fail to apprehend reality and to appreciate the true beauty of the Ever Present Presence, filled with vital meaning in the true present moment.

You can enjoy every moment properly only if you remain objective. If you seem to find joy in nature, hobbies, new clothes and other material objects acquired through ambition, you are really in a trance. These pleasures constitute a counterfeit mode of living in the moment; in reality, you are emotionally involved, escaping into a manipulated relationship with present time, away from the Presence. This type of false pleasure is nothing more than relief from the knowledge of anxiety, and it is due in part to your awareness being caught up in the ecstasy of escape.

Although all things exist in time present, only man

can live in the Presence (the Original Cause of time present) also. When the soul is still, in the timeless way, and not caught up ambitiously in the web of time, there will come from the Presence, through the stillness, a new world, containing a host of new spiritual values and joys.

Observe, then, the two ways to relate to everything in the present moment. The lower way requires you to be emotionally caught up with the glorifying object in a type of trance, and the joy you think you experience exists solely in the illusion that all is well with you. You have momentarily forgotten your misery as it is revealed in the Light of the Ever Present.

You can even become involved with this book in a similarly unwholesome way. Excited by my thoughts, you lose yourself in these words and appear to discover your own wisdom and goodness flowing up in you, as if all were coming from an original source of purity that you have just uncovered. Do not let this occur! These words are only intended to awaken you to the Light of the Ever Present, Which will bring you to repentance. But lofty words *can* be used hypnotically to excite your mind away from the knowledge that you need repentance. In such a case, your mind becomes alive with religious words and phrases, and the joy is reduced to an egotistical reveling in what then appears to be the discovery of your original innocence.

But, sooner or later, the Presence overtakes you and reveals your hypocrisy; and, in that moment, if you do not run away or become involved with study and beautiful words again, you could find joy welling up into the absolute present from the Presence as your soul is held still and apart from the stream of time. Don't you see that if you can observe time, you cannot at that moment be a part of time? Instead, you are an extension of the Stillness out of which the first moment of time came.

You must yearn to be in this objective stillness at every moment; therefore, you should read these words calmly and unemotionally. Observe your tendency to be carried away by words or imagination. Do not be too eager to learn or to grow. STOP READING WHENEVER YOU ARE AWAKENED TO THE LIGHT, and by that Light reflect calmly upon the errors you will see about yourself. The Light, shining through the still, objective conscious self, will then incline your soul to the attitude of repentance. Change for the better in your life can never come through an effort of your will; rather, it follows an attitude of repentance, which is preceded by the willingness to see your faults. Salvation is the fruit of a soul's recognition of its own shame in the Light of the freely given grace of God.

Do not attempt to hasten this process by using these words or the knowledge they impart to bring about change on your own. Words should never teach you; they should awaken you and make you more aware of what words really mean. They should deepen your understanding, so that if you are truly seeking, the first truth you come to know is the truth about your own failings.

What I am saying about the words in this book applies with equal force to all words of wisdom or admonishment: They must originate when they are needed from the right dimension. When you see what these words mean, you will notice the futility of attempting to communicate with people who are not ready or who do not want to hear. If there is any eagerness in them to receive your words of admonishment, then they are surely sensitive to your timing and to whether your words come from rote memory or originate in an understanding, spirit-led heart. The right word at the right time is really a message from God. Such words awaken the soul to the *meaning* of the word—they do not teach. The right word at the wrong time (your time) arises from ambition and compounds the very problem you are trying to correct. By such words psychological barriers against learning are erected, or else these messages, if they are accepted, sow confusion, because the believer will have absorbed knowledge he really does not understand. Not only does such a process not work toward correcting error, it also swells one's pride and causes terrible guilt. Only the love of God can lead a believer to guide another to the threshold of discovery for himself.

When it is welcome, the Living Truth in you will find the time and place to express Itself and awaken others. When you sense resistance, when you feel your words bouncing back to you like an echo from a wall—hanging in space and becoming hollow and meaningless—you are untimely; perhaps your hearers are not ready, or else they are *learning* you—using your knowledge as a form of entertainment and ego inspiration. Be aware that waiting for the right moment to act or speak is another form of timeless patience. Simply take note of error. Do not react. Wait for the right moment. Do not force awareness upon others on an intellectual basis. Observing patiently may be all that is necessary, and being watched may be all that others need.

If you buy, sell, or say anything with resentment or ambition (that is, with imperfect timing and knowledge), you will feel anxiety (impatience) and apprehension. Guilt arising from such resentment or ambition can also cause you to believe that what you said was wrong, even when it is technically correct, and this can lead to yet another complication of prideful ambition—complete with faulty timing and false knowledge. Suppose, for example, that by chance, but from ambition, you land in the right job in the right place at the right time. You will still experience futility. Suppose further that you then quit your job to find another. Now, out there in the wrong place, you feel even more futile. In such a case all that is necessary is a new motive for what you are doing and new motivation with which to do it. Remember this rule: Whenever you feel guilt about anything, that feeling relates to an underlying motive or a motivation. When both your motive and your motivation are pure, you cannot possibly say or do anything out of place. All will be in order. There are not enough books in the world to contain all of the examples and variations that could be written on this theme.

It is vitally important that you distinguish between motive and motivation. You can do the right thing in a wrong way when you are motivated by resentment, greed or ambition. Suppose, for example, you feel guilty regarding a criticism you made of someone. Let us say that what you said and did was correct, but the way you felt (your motivation, which gave you the energy to act) at the time was not; you were simply hostile. In such a case you need be sorry only for the twinge of resentment (motivation) you felt and make this quite clear to the offended party.

Variation: You could be guilty for the factor of ambition in your work, but not for the kind of work you do. You could also be guilty of resenting (blaming) your work, as if it were the cause of your futility and pressure you feel, instead of recognizing that it was your ambition and greed that led you to your present condition. You must consider not only what you do but also what you feel and think about what you do, your attitude and the basis of the urge that causes you to act.

Should you find yourself in a work situation where you know intuitively that you do not belong, or in one that is morally wrong, you will not have the power to stay in your center, and, consequently, you won't be able to cope with the pressure. Similarly, the pressure will also become unbearable if you take too much pride in your work. In the latter case, you need only change the way in which you relate to your work and not the work itself.

In like manner, these same principles apply to all areas of your life. Regarding sex, for example: You are only guilty for lust, never for an honest sexual expression within the setting of marriage. Your motive could be wrong, however, and you could use sex for an ego trip, as a means of getting your own way, or to relieve the various pressures of guilt; and then the act would no longer be honest, even if it were not motivated by lust. Food, music, learning can all produce guilt if your motive for being involved with them is not proper or if the force of energy that motivates your actions in relation to them is wrong. The list is endless.

It is necessary, then, that you look more closely at the root of your problems: Change the motive and keep the job, or change your motive and change the job also, or change your motive and your motivation and do the menial tasks gratefully, graciously. Almost any honest work will do until you find yourself. Even if it is not exactly what you had in mind, you may learn humility and patience if you relate to it properly without resentment. Things must forever change. Through patience you will find hope in better times to come. Remember, work, food and sex have basic values, so that by learning to relate to them properly you will grow to find greater meaning and joy in your present existence. If you will only look within, yearning to understand, the Light in you will show and how to ease your burden and then provide you with the grace to do chores that were once drab and humiliating in a cheerful and effortless manner. Once you are properly oriented through meditation, you will never feel as though you are working. Time ceases to drag. You recognize a proper measure of joy in everything you do, no matter how simple or ordinary. But whatever you do with a wrong motive will breed only futility and guilt, even though it may appear to offer all your heart's desires. "Judge not according to the appearance . . ." (Jn. 7:24 AV) ". . . for whatsoever is not of faith is sin." (Rom: 14:23).

As you slow down because you are no longer compatible with the old motivations you once needed to support your ambitious activity, you may feel guilty again. Careful! Do not construe this lethargy and the guilt that may accompany it as being caused by laziness. You have always been guilty, and you became even more so by thinking that you could cure guilt by sheer hard work or by slaving your heart out for people approval. When you slow down, past guilts, which you have been eluding by keeping so busy, tend to catch up, that's all. Here the lie that led you is laid bare. You have been listening as the lie has been whispering such things as:

> "You are guilty for not doing enough for your children. Do more. (In *trying* to help, you have really made them worse.)

> "You feel guilty because you do not give (or receive) enough sex.

> "You feel guilty for not giving your family a better way of life (more material things, clubs, vacations, etc.).

> "You feel guilty for not studying harder."

Such guilt has nothing to do with what you have done in the past. You have compounded guilt by attempting to escape from guilt through work, sex, or some other pursuit. When you slacken your pace, you simply discover that guilt. Be still, do not run or panic. *Let anxiety and guilt grow,* and do not resent it. Resist the temptation to misuse sex, friends, work or anything else, and soon you will begin to interpret more clearly what your conscience has been and is now trying to say. You will then experience the hidden knowledge of conscience operating, in the beginning, as a painful hindsight. You will find yourself in agreement with the inherent will and purpose of your conscience, and you will be motivated (receive the impetus to act) by it. You will suddenly have an intuitive knowledge of what to do, which way to go, as well as the motivation to follow through with what you now see as your proper course. The action of conscience in the unrepentant person is felt as the discomfort of guilt, which, in reality, is resistance to being guided by the Light—the true life of all men. When one accepts that guidance willingly, there is no longer any discomfort or guilt. In fact there is very little feeling at all, except, perhaps, a quiet sense of well-being and confidence.

True awareness is a healthy, observing attitude that protects from all dangers. But in your subjective state of preoccupation with worry and ambition, you have fallen into ridiculous predicaments. You have had accidents and become involved with the wrong people. Frightened and realizing your need for greater awareness, you may have even tried to force awareness. You began by making sure you did not repeat the same mistakes. Unfortunately, this procedure leads to a limited, subjective state of mind. You become so suspiciously aware, so preoccupied with each incident that you tend to make even more mistakes than you otherwise would—and you are even more mystified by them in view of the fact that you are trying so hard.

For example, while at the beach you cut your foot on a piece of glass. The next time you are there, you are more cautious, ever conscious of the potential danger of glass lying half-hidden in the sand. You are so preoccupied with the fear of that possible danger that you fail to see a volleyball coming straight at you. The next time at the beach you are so worried about glass and volleyballs that you do not even see the dog that bites you after you have tripped over him.

This type of forced awareness, which results from concentration and self-effort, is really a diminishing awareness, increasingly preoccupied with more and more things and circumstances. You are taking in too much knowledge unbuffered by understanding.

Being suspicious of people falls into this category of forced awareness. There is just so much deceit that you can cope with. At some point, preoccupation with it blinds you to your next mistake, the next trap, the next con artist with his bag of new tricks. Despite the obviously unsatisfactory results, and even though you can ruin close relationships through suspicion, you are unable to give it up because it seems to be a sort of total defense against error. If you mistrust everything and everybody, how can you possibly be taken advantage of?

The security you really need arises from the poise

of objective, true awareness that can be achieved through meditation. Worrying over problems is an ego trip—a distraction. The less you think with thoughts, the more aware you become and the more you understand. In other words, the less you are involved with your thinking as a way of solving problems, the more aware you tend to be and the fewer mistakes you make. The more protected you are, the less there is to be worried about.

What I am attempting to point out is that human beings do not learn from experience as animals do. You can only learn by rising above the experience itself, as well as the need to experience. The ego that "learns" from experience is guilty and never really learns at all. Observation alerts you to all dangers as they approach your field of vision. With less to worry about, your awareness advances a notch upward and inward. You are then more alert to perceive what temptation is up to because you are closer to the Light. This awareness is effortless and all-encompassing. When the tempter senses how aware you are to his intentions, he is obliged to keep on changing his plans, to the point that he is more often than not disabled from perpetrating any of them on you. If he trics to pull a fast one, you are still ahead, because to be truly objective is to be a step beyond time itself.

When you fail to reach true awareness because of ambition, improper pursuits and preoccupation with problem solving, you become defensive, suspicious, worried and geared to intellectual answers that not only cannot protect you from the unforeseen and the hidden, but, themselves, always contribute to your downfall. The fear of having another accident is relevant here. You sense that your last one was caused by not being aware; but your worry, instead of helping, makes you even less aware than you were the last time. Sensing this, you become fearful that the same thing will happen again or that something unforeseen—and much worse—will befall you. And under these circumstances, it usually does.

Unfortunately, there is little use in praying for guidance in the customary manner, because rehearsed words keep you locked in a subjective state so that you are unlikely to receive any meaningful answer. Besides, the "not you" lurking in your subconscious may take charge of your wordy prayer. For this reason, it is possible to become afraid to pray to God, because you always receive wrong answers—those that please your ego. Stop fingering your beads, mumbling unfelt formula words, or chanting mantras. Be still, and you will know.

Meditation is the proper form of prayer, for it leads to objectivity, and objectivity is stillness and emptiness, and emptiness is need, and need is a wordless prayer to God—receptive to the answer of that very need. Meditation is everything. It is reality: the sum of your awareness. If you will only be still and separate your conscious mind from the chatter of the subconscious, then it will not be you who prays, but the Holy Spirit interceding on your behalf; and then, if the words are of any value, they will come together in your mind through the action of the Light.

There may be a strong temptation presented to you to cry to the familiar "Christ" or "God" of your early religious training. Do not accede to that temptation, for you are being led to embrace a puppet, a "front man," controlled by the unholy spirit of evil. If you make this mistake, you will revive old conditioning by the way of false symbols and images that you were taught to cling to as a child (e.g.: a statue or image of Christ, Whose behavior characteristics are defined by your church). By such means, you are really controlled by the spirit of the men behind the scenes who pulled the strings of the false Christ image and made you serve their ends rather than the purpose of the true Lord Christ, Who is within you. It is a vile trick perpetrated in His name, and you must see what has happened so that you will not lose faith in the real Christ, Who quietly testifies to these words.

"Beware of wolves in sheep's clothing!" said the Lamb of God. *God cannot operate where there is an image or preconceived concept.* Cry when you experience the pain of affliction in your soul! Cry that you might know how to believe the true belief in the true Christ. Cry out in a wordless desire to God, Whom you have only known as conscience, or words in a book, and He will reply in His time and make Himself known to you— ever so gently and gradually.

"Before they speak, I shall hear; and before they ask, I shall answer," thus saith the Lord. The Father knows what you need before you ask Him. He does not need to hear you speak the words in vain and endless repetition. The cry of the sincere soul is, to God, like the cry of the baby to its mother. There is no need for formality, for the Father knows the mean of His child's cry. And He answers.

You must also realize that you cannot willfully gratify your own needs without becoming gluttonous and sensual. You must make a practice of stopping slightly short of satisfying any natural desire. Less is the rule, not more. A man is rich in what he can afford to do without. There is a very fine line of difference between filling the normal needs of the body and gratifying the ego need for escape. As your awareness develops, you will see which habits need modifying, especially in relation to food and sex. You will also discover those practices you must abandon entirely.

At that tickle-point where you once employed pleasure to dull your mind to the awareness of your problem, you can now become conscious of your need for escape and the reason behind it. Observation is always a sufficient power to bring about change.

Remember, it has been through self-indulgence that you have gloried in every need that has grown out of your continuous falling. In the excitement and pleasure of gratifying those needs, you have forgotten that those growing desires are a sign of failing. Cakes (unnecessarily sweetened bread) and other delicacies seem more desirable the more you satisfy your appetites, and gradually you come to be addicted to more and more unnatural and bizarre stimulants to your growing sensual desires. You can use food as an escape from the knowledge of what is wrong with you, including, but not limited to, your craving for food. It becomes boring to eat simple, unstimulating basic foods without embellishment, because we tend to discover anxiety and indignity connected with an awareness of the way we exist. And so we spice up the basic bread of life and make exotic sweetmeats to induce a stronger measure of forgetfulness. Food must be made more and more entertaining and stimulating to our senses. We equate our sensitivity to and our desire for variety and the "finer things" of life with progress of some kind instead of the incontrovertible evidence of failing that it really is. It is amazing how we can take something so gross and make a glorious ritual of it!

Let us say that you have just had a particularly stimulating meal, either because of the gourmet nature of it or simply because you overate. As soon as the stimulation begins to wear off (assuming you are not trying to escape via a nice cigar and brandy), you will feel terribly guilty or anxious as you become conscious of your error. But if you continue to concentrate long enough on the memory of what you have done, it can start to appeal to you all over again, and you will forget the guilt as you are stimulated by the recollection. You must not, therefore, use memory as a form of entertainment that will whisk you away from the knowledge of what memories are. Stand back from the entertainment (worry) value of your failings. Observe them in the new way I have taught you, and then they will be understood and either eliminated or modified by the Light. There is absolutely no need to use will power to break any habit pattern; infact, any attempt to do so will simply tie you to the source of error. Instead, you will discover a new factor of choice arising from objectivity: No longer do you find that you *must* light that cigarette or take that drink. You will be distinctly aware that the compulsion is broken and only your true desire will determine your course of action. On the other hand, if you remain pridefully subjective, the only "choice" you will have will be among the forms of indulgence and escape. If you do not accept a means of escape, you will be forced to face the truth about yourself, to see the stark truth about your miserable, futile existence—your ego will experience shame, inadequacy, guilt, anxiety, pain, fear and terrible depression. You will face reality.

In order to maintain pride, its images and illusions, you were forced to come down to a place where your feelings wallowed in one piggish pleasure after another, even after they reach the point of diminishing return and gave you more pain and guilt than relief. You had no other choice than to indulge, even though you hated it for what it did to you, even when your whole body revolted against the harmful side effects and even though you wanted to vomit at the thought of it. You had no other choice except to escape into habits that became even more revolting. And so you clung to "pleasure" because it was the only way you could find to forget the horrible reality of what your life was really like—a crazy quilt of sin.

Since meditation is an exercise in objectivity, it will help you to approach the sensual experience in a way that diminishes illicit desire. You will discover a new factor of choice, for even though the conditioning of your body's craving leans toward temptation, your soul does not. What has made sensual delight so irresistible in the past is your *agreement* with the concept and the means of escape. Thus your soul became even more guilty for that attitude, and your need for escape increased. This agreement, this attempt to take comfort in feeling, added sin to the sin you were trying to escape and made the soul burn as if in Hell for more deliverance from reality and the recognition of evil it provides, through sensuality. You had no choice but to use this means.

It is sufficient to disagree consciously with the temptation, to realize that it is no longer you who craves, but the "not you" dwelling in your body. Realizing this fact, you know you are not really denying yourself life when you elect not to accept a given temptation. It is only your pride, your ego life, that feels cheated of its pleasures and the rewards it believes it deserves. When this pride is devitalized by denying to it the stimulation that keeps it alive, your soul revives in the realm of Light. "For whosoever will save his (ego) life shall lose it: and whosoever will lose his (ego) life for my sake shall find it (true life)." (Matt. 16:25)

So stand still and begin to take careful note of your food habits and your sexual practices. I do not mean for you to starve yourself or to stop your moral sexual activities by an effort of your own will. The natural functions of your body need to be understood, not condemned or

319

condoned; therefore, if each moment finds you aware but neutral, neither condemning nor condoning, no longer carried away by the emotions available from your environment, you will not only learn, but you will also relate properly, automatically, knowing just at what point the body needs end and the ego needs begin. And you will effortlessly reject the ego needs.

Do not follow so-called experts on sex and diet, or you will remain a cripple, depending on others for their knowledge and guidance in living your life. Follow a diet or a sex plan at great peril to your own identity. If an outside authority becomes the source of your guidance, the result will be greater guilt and then a greater dependency on the teacher and his plan of salvation via pill or diet. When that plan fails, as inevitably it must, you then have a worse problem than you had before, because there will be added to your condition hate and resentment toward your doctor, teacher or guru because he misled you. As much as these leaders torment you, that much more do you come to need their kind and their plans to save you. So if you have already been misled and are on your way back to the Light, repent of resentment toward authority figures, because it has not been all their fault. A part of your trouble has been caused by your own gullibility.

The soul that is separated from God through its pride is locked in to the fleshly, base self, which is the evidence of its own failing. Notice how you respond to people who awaken and cater to your wrong desires. They offer a special kind of value to you, which is based on judgment. See also how you become involved with judgment in connection with things that stimulate pleasurable feelings. You even derive stimulation from judging the feelings themselves. ("I felt really great after that concert, sermon, lecture, etc.") Your feelings toward people, places and things are really based on judging how they make you feel in response to them; and your craving for sensation is linked to the subtle ego pleasure of passing judgment—e.g.: that was a good cigarette, a sensational meal, a fine brandy, etc. And when you are not "loving" these "good" feelings, you are hating your rejection, depression or fear.

Through humility, which comes with awareness of reality, the appetites of your soul are altered, and temptation finds no basis for appeal, no opening through which death can enter. You can easily deal with any bodily craving, provided that you, the observer, no longer have an ego use for body needs. A temptation is only irresistible when your pride is in agreement with sensation and uses its own body as a means of staying high. For an ego that is dead wrong, pleasure and excitement equal LIFE and feelings of rightness. Your ego *must* escape from the awareness that it is dying into a temporal feeling of life and animal breath, for the agony of knowing what it has become without being willing to change is, quite literally, unbearable. And since you have identified your soul's life with your animal life, which grows to displace your true self as you fail, then you too experience the agony of pride as if it were your own, and you become its willing consort in a headlong flight from the

Truth. And as you come down from your latest emotional high, you wonder, fleetingly, why it is that you failed again.

What the ego has lost spiritually it trys to compensate for in a material-emotional way. We are slowly dying as spiritual beings. After each high, each escape from the moment, we "awaken" to a life on a lower and lower plane of existence. With each step down that you take, your ego tries desperately to believe that it is closer to the top of the staircase, because, enthroned on the dais of pride and ambition, it cannot believe that it is moving from life to death.

The excitement that supports this life style is distraction. You are trying your best to remember how alive you are and to forget how dead you are becoming. If your soul is true, it is already in disagreement with, and somewhat dissociated from, bodily sensations. If such is the case, all you need do is watch the body calling to you, and at certain points, quietly refuse to answer. Meditate and watch patiently until your body's claim over your former use of your body diminishes in intensity. If you do not, you will become even more guilty at that point.

The body is like a spoiled child before it is converted and becomes responsive and respectful to its parent. You, as the parent, must wait patiently until the tantrum (an obstinate craving for animal life or breath) is over. The soul that gleefully goes along with its body cannot receive sound instruction. New life comes only from the Light as we die to the world.

The vain soul, lost in pleasure, falsely believes that it has already found the true answer to its own needs. Unlike the seeking, objective soul, which can hear reproof and benefit from sound instruction because it is no longer lost in feeling and sensation, it does not yearn for correction—the key to freedom.

The principle behind the meditation outline in this text is the one and only way to learn the mystical knowledge of how to control the body in such a way that you actually hold sway over feeling and desire from your own center. Through this technique of meditation, your objective, understanding mind becomes connected to your knowing, intellectual mind, and lines of communication and authority are established in such a way that, instead of being impinged upon by outside feelings from your environment, the true life feeling flows outward from your center within and alters your environment. Learn the technique of accepting or rejecting ideas quietly. It really is not necessary to build up a head of emotional steam before deciding to say "yes" or "no"; you only think it is. Observe *without responding* to what is true or false, and if something does not sit well with you, simply stay in your center—do not forcibly evict an idea or a person from your mind. Just watch, listen without emotionally agreeing or disagreeing.

Learn well the lesson of meditation. Become consciously, progressively free from your involvement with self-images. Observe, but do not yourself decide what to remember. Neither should you try to reject anything or struggle to determine the meaning of what you see. If you don't know, simply wonder and wait to be shown. Suddenly, when you least expect it, you will understand, and true understanding will favorably alter both your behavior and the very essence of your life itself. You will find yourself reviewing old teachings that you can accept in a new way. The block to learning and growth will vanish. Useless knowledge will seem simply to fall out of your mind.

The emphasis in the progress of meditation is always on more objectivity. The more objective you become, the more you will see how much more objective you can be. This is the key. Practice standing back and watching your thoughts and feelings without becoming involved with them, not only during meditation, but throughout the day. You must meditate without ceasing. The less you do, the more happens.The objective state is passive and inactive. Light streams through your conscious mind as if through the clear lens of a projector, impressing your mind with a new identity and energizing it to think and be in a new way. When you are objective, you can look at the error and feel remorse at what you have never been able to see before. And after that initial sadness, you are glad, because the sadness is really repentance in the Light; and from that act of contrition arises a need for correction that is answered by the Light.

This need for correction is a development from your first nonverbal cry to know God. It is a yearning for Truth, which lifts you above the clouds of emotion and fantasy into the presence of the Light, and in that moment you begin to know yourself. Seeing your faults, being grateful, not resentful, for being shown, you evolve a need to be corrected of that fault.

"Blessed are they which do hunger and thirst after righteousness: for they shall be filled."

The same Light also shows you that you are helpless against the problem, and that very helplessness becomes a cry to the Light, and it is answered with real and meaningful change.

"Blessed are they that mourn: for they shall be comforted."

BE STILL, AND KNOW THAT I AM GOD . . . Ps. 46

For a complete catalog of our books and materials or a list of radio stations that air Roy Master's program nationwide.

Please write to:

The Foundation of Human Understanding
P.O. Box 1009
Grants Pass OR 97526

or call toll-free

1-800-877-3227